Per

The Yale

Re_
Trar
Cap

Edited by:
Kanu Agrawal
Melanie Domino
Edward Richardson
Brad M. Walters

The MIT Press
Cambr
Londo

Perspecta, The Yale Architectural Journal
is published in the United States of America by
the Yale School of Architecture and distributed
by The MIT Press.

Massachusetts Institute of Technology
Cambridge, Massachusetts 02142
http://mitpress.mit.edu

Printing: Phoenix Press, Inc.
New Haven, Connecticut

MIT Press books may be purchased at
special quantity discounts for business or sales
promotional use. For information, please email
special_sales@mitpress.mit.edu or write to:

Special Sales Department
The MIT Press
55 Hayward Street
Cambridge, MA 02142

ISBN–10: 0-262-51199-5
ISBN–13: 978-0-262-51199-5
ISSN: 0079-0958

Send editorial correspondence to:

Perspecta, Yale School of Architecture
180 York Street, New Haven, CT 06520

perspecta.reurbanism@gmail.com

Perspecta 39 Re_Urbanism: Transforming Capitals investigates capital cities across the globe currently undergoing major redevelopment of their architecture, infrastructure, and urban fabric. This edition examines the forces driving the reconstruction of national capitals as well as the new forms these cities take.

Capital cities are evolving to cater to the influx of global capital via efficient service centers—hence, the emergence of specialized enclaves attached to existing cities. At the same time, capital cities are reasserting their traditional function as symbols of national sovereignty in an era of globalization. What is startlingly common among these cities is the recasting of their political, economic, and social roles, manifested most perceptibly through architecture, infrastructure, and urbanism. We term this reconstruction of the capital city driven by globalization as **Re_Urbanism.**

The capital cities examined here have been chosen for their sustained activity and continuing relevance to debates over architecture and urban design. Some, like Abu Dhabi and New Delhi, are competing domestically with more globally focused enclaves. Others, like Belgrade and Kinshasa, are rebounding after years of internal strife or political turmoil. Scarcity of housing and natural resources also drives many of these transformations, as does the legacy of colonialism. The essays presented should not be understood as comprehensive case studies but rather as an index of past experiences and current conditions.

Capital cities have complex architectural histories sedimented through periods of varying political importance and bound to narratives of national identity. Modernization—epitomized by architectural and infrastructural interventions such as standardized housing, transportation systems, and public works—restructured the city to meet the demands of new political and economic organizations. This pursuit of unity and cohesion as a reflection of national sovereignty required keeping city limits under control. But the development of the global market forces many capital cities to face transnational competition. As the borders of a nation become permeable, so too do the boundaries between capital city and country.

Capitals are fast adapting to these changing conditions by altering their architecture, infrastructure, and urban design strategies in radical ways, often merging hard statistics with fantasy. As capitals expand from contained cities into their neighboring regions, vast hinterlands are transformed by speculation. Political capital becomes financial capital and vice versa. This development can be considered as dynamic and as transformative to capital cities as previous phases of modernization. As the world's population becomes increasingly urban and globalized, what remains of the resistance to the unimpeded flow of money, goods, services, and people emerges from capital cities as the regulation and legislation of the state. As the political center, the capital city remains the ideal site to voice dissent, float manifestos and build an architecture of subversion.

Kanu Agrawal
Melanie Domino
Edward Richardson
Brad M. Walters

Extrasta

Keller Easterling

The nation-state often portrays itself and its network of capital cities as an ultimate form. Yet as power amasses and disperses in recurring patterns as it has throughout the ages, the world's capitals preside over empires and regions as well as nations. Some are city-states unto themselves.

ecraft

Emirates Palace Hotel, Abu Dhabi.

In the fabled pairing of, for instance, Beijing and Shanghai, Washington, D.C., and New York, Ankara and Istanbul, the national capital is the more sober inland location that stands in contrast to its market partner, often a maritime city with a long record of promiscuous trading and cosmopolitan intelligence. The mercantile city is sometimes cast as the sister city or the shadow entity, seemingly ceding power and official jurisdiction so that it can grow extranational power outside of the cumbersome regulations of government. Yet contemporary versions of this sister city are not merely alter egos of the national capital but often something more like independent city-states—the descendants of Venice or Genoa when they were the trading centers of the planet. Recombining urban power genetics into yet another species of urbanism, they exceed the interests of global financial centers such as London, New York, Frankfurt, or São Paulo.[1] They also exceed the requirements of the fabled "region state"— the financial and transshipment nexus of late twentieth-century globalization theory.[2] Some contemporary world cities like Hong Kong and Singapore are not only the crossroads and destinations of national expedition and franchise but also the centers of global franchises that have property nested in holding companies and national territories all around the world. Their franchise agents may be global trade conglomerates (e.g., Singapore's PSA or Hong Kong's Hutchison Port Holdings) which are the modern descendants of organizations like the Dutch or the British East India companies. Merging the techniques of free-port traders, pirates, and mercenaries, the free zones of the new world city create legal habitats for contemporary trade that naturalize the insertion of extranational territory within national boundaries.

While Western superpowers have perhaps grown accustomed to the idea that world cities like Singapore or Hong Kong are much more than the product of their own colonial ventriloquism, an emergent world city like Dubai presents an unusual political foundation and an abrupt conflation of ancient and contemporary worlds. The usual pairing of Abu Dhabi and Dubai as capital city and mercantile city, respectively, would appear at first to follow familiar models. The two play their roles well until it becomes clear they are both capital city and world city in another time and dimension. The UAE is a federation of some of the world's last functioning kingdoms, seemingly asleep during the most bombastic chapters in the grand history of national sovereignty. During the very centuries that nations have emerged as a dominant framework, so too have substantial networks of transnational business exchange and infrastructure-building. The UAE is reawakened by oil at a moment when nations bluster patriotic while also developing more relationships in this transnational milieu. Already an "anational society," the UAE is evolving, within the legal climates of free trade, a form of governance for which national/democratic structures are mimicked for use in organizing dynasties.[3] Mixtures of bargains and monarchical decrees are designed to handle global dealings with businesses that have managed to shed some of the most cumbersome national regulations that the UAE never possessed. In these dealings, ancient kingdoms and contemporary empires recognize and merge with each other to form a world capital of sorts.

The presence of world capitals like Dubai does not support the assumption that transnational sovereignty is waxing as national sovereignty wanes. It may be more accurate to see a historical continuity of global activity within which state and nonstate forces, acting together, craft the most advantageous political and economic climates by alternately sheltering, releasing, and laundering their power. Business may, for instance, seek out relaxed, extrajurisdictional spaces (SEZs, FTZs, EPZs, etc.) while also massaging legislation in the various states they occupy (NAFTA, GATT). The stances of any one nation or business are therefore often duplicitous or discrepant reflections of divided loyalties between national and international concerns or citizens and shareholders.

The customary portfolios of political indicators will not always reliably return information about these complex state-nonstate partnerships. They often create political events that exceed epistemes of war, nation, citizen, and capital. In a contemplation of world capitals, the UAE exposes the limits of the national capital as a self-styled unit of grand historical continuities. With the insulated caprice of petro dollars and free zones, the UAE leads with the increasingly common duplicitous handshake. The triggers and levers of this power may not be easily moralized and analyzed by the left or the right; they may be more venal and evasive as well as more shrewd and innovative. The UAE embodies a transnational *extrastatecraft* filled with both the dangers and opportunities that rule the world today.

1 Credit might naturally go to Peter Hall and his book *The World Cities* (1971) or to Saskia Sassen's *The Global City: New York, London, Tokyo*. This train of thought is however closer to an analysis offered by Roland Marchal, "Dubai: Global City and Transnational Hub," in Madawi Al-Rasheed, ed., *Transnational Connections and the Arab Gulf* (London: Routledge, 2003), 93–110. Marchal uses the term *world cities* in reference to Fernand Braudel's work on city-states and trading capitals from Fernand Braudel, *The Structures of Everyday Life: Civilization and Capitalism 15th –18th Century* (Berkeley: University of California Press, 1992), reprinted from 1979 Librairie Armand Colin, Paris.

2 Kenichi Ohmae, "The Rise of the Region State" in Patrick O'Meara, Howard Mehlinger, and Matthew Krain, eds., *Globalization and the Challenges of a New Century* (Bloomington: Indiana University Press, 2000).

3 Frederick F. Anscombe, "An Anational Society: Eastern Arabia in the Ottoman Period," quoted in Marchal, 21–35.

Dubai by Robin Moore, cover.

Dubai. The hot spot...Where adventurers play the world's most dangerous games...Gold, sex, oil—and war.

Dubai. A wild, seething place in the sunbaked sands of Arabia, where billion-dollar carpet-baggers mix explosive passions with oil. And exotic pleasures pay fabulous dividends.

Whores, assassins, spies, fortune hunters, diplomats, princes and pimps—all gambling for their lives in a dazzling, billion-dollar game that only the most ruthless and beautiful dare to play.[4]

—Jacket copy from *Dubai,* by Robin Moore

In 1976, after *The Green Berets, The French Connection,* and several other global intrigues, Robin Moore published a novel titled *Dubai.* The novel opens in 1967. Fitz, the monosyllabic hero and American intelligence officer, is fired over his pro-Palestinian/anti-Semitic remarks that appear in the press just as the Six Day War is launched. Dubai, like the not-yet-middle-aged protagonist, is still fluid and unsettled. It is still a place where adventures and deals are flipped and leveraged against each other to propel small syndicates to fame and fortune. Fitz quickly scales a succession of events in the UAE's history during the 1970s. He arrives when a handful of hotels and the new Maktoum Bridge across Dubai Creek are among the few structures that appear in an otherwise ancient landscape, one that has changed very little in the centuries that Dubai has been an entrepôt of gold trade and a site for pearl diving. Just on the edge of Sheikh Rashid's plans for an electrical grid, the air-conditioning in Fitz's Jumeirah beach house must struggle against the 120 degrees and 100 percent humidity by means of an independent generator. The story proceeds by moving in and out of air-conditioning, syndicate meetings, and sex scenes in the palaces of the sheikh or in hotel cocktail lounges between Tehran, Dubai, and Washington. The tawdry glamour of tinkling ice and Range Rovers is frequently interrupted for a number of rough-and-tumble adventures that are evenly distributed throughout the book. The discovery of oil has already propelled the development of the Trucial States (states that have made maritime truces with the original oilmen, the British).

Fitz's first escapade uses the old gold economy to capitalize on the new oil and real estate economy. The syndicate's *dhow* (the traditional vessel on the creek) is souped up with munitions and technology that Fitz has illegally stolen from the American military. Dubai is an old hand at smuggling, or what it likes to call "re-export," during embargoes or wars that are always available in the Gulf. Shipping gold to India usually involves armed encounters in international waters. The *dhow*'s U.S. military equipment vaporizes the Indian ships, thus trouncing piracy and resistance to the free market. Fitz plunders enough money to bargain with the sheikh for shares of an oil enterprise in Abu Musa, an island in the Gulf halfway between Dubai and Iran. He has enough money left over to finance a saloon, equipped with old CIA bugging devices, and an upstairs office with a one-way viewing window. From this perch Fitz entertains the growing number of foreign businessmen who are laying over in Dubai and the growing number of Arab businessmen who want to see and approach Western women. He continues in his plot to become a diplomat to the new independent federation of Trucial territories, the United Arab Emirates, to be established in 1971.

Fitz (like Dubai) gets things done. With a wink and a nod sheikhs and diplomats reward him. He even manages to single-handedly crush a communist insurgency in the desert (most Robin Moore novels fight the old Cold War fight, although his most recent forays take on the new devil: terrorism). In the novel, America's heroic Cold War deeds in the Gulf have made us simple lovable heroes with both naughtiness and vulnerability. Fitz wisely realizes that most political activities are not vetted through recognized political channels. In *Dubai,*

4 Robin Moore, *Dubai* (New York: Doubleday, 1976), frontispiece.

the naughty hero formula even goes one dyspeptic step further in engineering sympathy for the character and happily signal the end of the novel: Fitz hurts his leg fighting the insurgency. Despite his wounds and even though he has contributed a suitcase full of money in campaign contributions, he doesn't get the ambassadorship. He is unfairly tainted with the centuries of regional piracy and the only too recent hotel-bar intrigues. Nevertheless, Fitz gets the girl in the end, the daughter of a diplomat living on the Main Line in Philadelphia, and they begin to plan their middle-aged life "on the creek" in Dubai.

The novel's oblivious mix of Cold War piety and soft porn is, however fictional, appropriate evidence. Indeed, the novel is strangely more informative than most of what is currently written about the United Arab Emirates in its own self-produced coffee-table books and marketing copy. The country is currently producing a dazzling story of real estate development for the consumption of an obedient press that reproduces its sound bytes. Even snide and brainy bloggers of architectural critique have assembled willingly in the trap, printing enthusiastic remarks about hyperbolic development projects. Most accounts are looking for yet another big opener to top the last story about new offshore islands, theme parks or shopping festivals—another prefix meaning superlative to "mega." The Emirates get things done in a fast-forward time lapse of oil wealth. The coffee-table books do not present the complicated history of foreign paternalizing, meddling, and arming that has matured into something very different from what either the U.S. or the UK thought they have wrought. For some time, the U.S. and the UK have perhaps behaved as if the UAE was simply an outcropping of Western real estate techniques, occasionally offering condescending praise that the Emirates have been an exceptionally good pupil. The UAE is happy to nod as if in gratitude and perfectly happy if the global press bites on that line. It may even be good for the real estate market.

Robin Moore's *Dubai* ends in 1970, just before federation in 1971. Abu Dhabi and Dubai were sibling territories, offshoots of the Ban Yas tribe that migrated between pearl diving and the interior desert oasis of Al Ain. Abu Dhabi, a coastal archipelago with some fresh water, became the headquarters of the Al Nahyan family. In 1833, Sheikh Maktoum bin Butti led a group that seceded from Abu Dhabi to settle farther east along the coast in Dubai, a small fishing village, and the Maktoum family has ruled in

Dubai ever since.[5] Since 1820, the British had entered into agreements with these coastal sheikhdoms to regulate piracy and other maritime concerns. In 1892, the so-called Trucial states signed a joint agreement establishing an exclusive relationship with Britain in exchange for its protection. American and British companies negotiated their first oil concessions in the late 1920s to mid-1930s. Still, Abu Dhabi did not begin to drill for oil until after World War II and did not discover commercial quantities of oil until 1958.[6] Soon it would become clear that Abu Dhabi was dominant in not only land area but also oil production. Dubai, endowed with far fewer oil resources, did not export oil until 1969. Even early on, Dubai planned to pursue tourism, finance, and trade as its chief sources of revenue.[7] When the British pulled out of the territories east of the Suez in 1968, the UAE was flooded with foreign businessmen from all over the world, and the Range Rovers gave way to Japanese cars.[8] Yet, well into the 1960s, the Trucial states were barefoot, with no roads or health care, few clothes, and brackish water.

> We lived in the eighteenth century while the rest of the world, even the rest of our neighbors, had advance into the twentieth.
>
> We had nothing to offer visitors, we had nothing to export, we had no importance to the outside world whatsoever. Poverty, illiteracy, poor health, a high rate of mortality all plagued us well into the 1960s.[9]
>
> The business of government is manufacturing opportunity.
>
> —General Sheikh Mohammad bin Rashid Al Maktoum[10]

As a kingdom-nation, the UAE produces partial reflections and tinctures of Western governmental institutions, yet it operates with

a different set of civil and legal assumptions. Moreover, these significant structural differences often allow the country to thrive off of many of the very complications that trouble Western democracies: the contradiction between citizenship and the need for cheap labor; the curious position of public space within urbanism conceived as a privately themed spatial product; the naturalized state of exemption from law in corporate paradigms, and the influence of special interest in official political representation. As if in a state of amnesia for these perennial problems of contemporary participatory democracies, the UAE seems not to perceive them.

UAE nationals are not only a constituency to the representative body but a beneficiary, conduit, and pivot of much of the country's business; they are at once the wealthy elite and the welfare state. While Dubai is currently pursuing an urbanism that is measured in the *Guinness Book of World* records (e.g., the world's tallest building, the world's largest man-made islands, the world's largest shopping mall, and the world's largest underwater hotel), Abu Dhabi also lays claim to a *Guinness* record made by one of its most legendary leaders: Sheikh Zayed was once offered the largest bribe in history. The Saudis offered him $42 million to relinquish Abu Dhabi's claim to Al Ain. Sheikh Zayed's refusal during a time when even he himself had only a few hundred rupees was consistent with his commitment to manage Abu Dhabi's ensuing wealth in a way that made its citizens beneficiaries. After becoming the ruler in 1966, Sheikh Zayed also issued land grants for each national, to ensure that development would benefit the population, and, by 1976, he had also offered 5,000 units of "people's housing."[12] The land grants are similar in principle to the many other laws that stipulate partnerships or enterprises in which UAE nationals are either associates or beneficiaries. "Offsets" are among these structuring devices. Defense contracts with the UAE must first negotiate with the UAE offsets group. The contracts must be profitable, and a UAE national must own 51 percent. Moreover, the contract must seed an offset venture in a non-oil industry. So far, these offset projects have funded a variety of industries including fish farms, air-conditioning, medical services, shipbuilding, and even leisure activities like polo grounds.[13] Since the number of nationals is small, the UAE has managed to convert the typically corrupt relationship between government and private-interest lobbies into a form

5 Frauke Heard-Bey, *From Trucial States to United Arab Emirates: A Society in Transition* (Dubai and Abu Dhabi: Motivate Publishing, 2004, first published by Longman, 1982), 174, 238.

6 Mohammed Al-Fahim, *From Rags to Riches: A Story of Abu Dhabi* (London: The London Center of Arab Studies, 1995), 73–74.

7 Heard-Bey, 238.

8 Al-Fahim, 147.

9 Al-Fahim, 88.

10 Essam Al Tamimi, *Setting up in Dubai* (Dubai: Cross Border Legal Publishing, 2003), 3.

11 Moving west to northeast, Abu Dhabi, Dubai, and Sharjah are the first three emirates, and they each have a chief city of the same name. Continuing further north, toward the Straits of Hormuz, are the smaller emirates of Umm al Qaiwain, Ajman, and Ras al Khaimah. Finally, on the eastern coast of this rocky peninsula is the seventh emirate, Fujairah.

12 Al-Fahim, 405.

of hyper-representation.[14] In Dubai, this direct benefit to a manageable handful of constituents is regarded as government welfare and beneficent leadership.

The UAE has found an advantage in the notion of the temporary citizen as laborer, expat, or tourist. As a temporary citizen, the tourist arrives to deposit vacation money at shopping festivals, golf tournaments, and theme parks. Having paid their taxes in tourist revenues, they then leave without further demands on government. The UAE has also institutionalized migratory labor arrangements, in some cases even using it as a source of fees and other revenue. UAE nationals were themselves the guest workers for oil companies before they essentially became partners in the oil wealth.[15] Rules are established for managing and housing the labor in groups, and problems are the responsibility of the agent who has contracted for the labor. Laborers and contractors must agree to and abide by certain rules or be deported. Thus, Dubai can then boast that it is one of the most diverse places on earth as its curates its inhabitants from Africa, India, Pakistan, and elsewhere in the world. All of the arrangements are perhaps more transparent than in those countries where citizenship is the impossible option and the guest worker exists in a zone of denial and secrecy. Yet the arrangements have also yielded a situation devoid of responsibility and consequence, except for the outside contractors. Enforcement applies to the infraction of rules but not to procedures or events that exist outside of them. Human-rights concerns continue to center around the trafficking of human beings within a large volume of migratory workers as well as around the networks of domestic workers for whom there is no record keeping or oversight.

The UAE epitomizes the shadow jurisdictions that reside in transnational exchanges, out-maneuvering some official acts of state, and serving as de facto forms of global governance. Indeed if that shadow government is loosely defined by the scatter of headquarters and zones around the world, the UAE is something like a parliament of this global headquartering. The "park" or free trade zone is naturalized as the ideal urban growth unit. In recent decades, the free trade zone, export processing zone, special economic zone or other similar incarnations have evolved to allow businesses immunity from taxes, labor regulation and environmental restrictions or to streamline the logistics for transshipment, materials handling or duty-free retail.

Like any nation, the UAE publicizes its ennobling dispositions, often embodied by the partnership of Sheikh Zayed and Sheikh Rashid. Deploying a familiar modernist script, the two used technology for nation-building. Both Sheikh Zayed and Sheikh Rashid capitalized experimental projects that demonstrated their eagerness to diversify. Dubai sponsored a project that paired aluminum production and desalination. Sheikh Zayed sponsored the planting of millions of palm trees, planning to manage water and wildlife with the help of remote-sensing satellites. Since the modernist script usually comes with equal parts traditionalism, the UAE associated this technological expertise with a native wisdom about environment and natural resources. Accessorized with the perfect mix of modern signals and traditional customs such as falconry, horses, and camel racing, Sheikh Zayed's leadership solicited general adoration, almost deification, until his death in 2004. His face appears everywhere, on billboards and talismans. To traditional music with a new-age beat, the official Web site celebrating his life follows the silhouette of a falcon across the sands from a silhouetted skyline of *barasti* mud huts to the silhouetted skyline of Dubai. Moreover, part of the UAE's beguiling formula for government, involves generousity to the neediest countries in the world. By the mid-1970s the UAE and Sheikh Zayed had developed a reputation for philanthropy that was to become a permanent ingredient of the country's mystique.[16]

As if in suspended animation or taking a break from the twentieth century, Abu Dhabi and Dubai might have seemed, in the 1990s, like sleepy holiday locations offering a growing number of modern developments, air-conditioned hotels, and office buildings. Both perhaps maintained the peculiar relaxation and freedom of a place where one does not stay long, but after the 1990s the difference between the two emirates and the two cities accelerated. In 1997, Dubai's fabled development boom began when it allowed for freehold property for all nations in special development areas. In 2006, the emirate legalized foreign property ownership. Somewhat more sober, Abu Dhabi recently clarified its 2005 freehold laws by allowing only GCC nationals to own freehold property, while non-GCC members are required to have a contract for 99 years.[17] Traveling between the emi-rates is a jolting journey forward and backward through time— between ancient landscapes, national capitals, and new world capitals.

The earth has a new center.

—Billboard advertisement for Dubai Mall on Sheikh Zayed Road

"Dubai is like someone who owns many horses," he said. "He doesn't just put one horse in the race, he puts many with many chances of success."

—Sultan Ahmed bin Sulayem, adviser to Dubai's Maktoum family[18]

In 1979, Sheikh Rashid completed two projects in Dubai that established it as a regional capital of the Gulf and the Middle East: The World Trade Center and the Jebel Ali port.[19] As Robin Moore's novel spins around a corridor between Dubai and Tehran, it accurately reflects alignments of power, influence, and relationships that have caused Dubai to be called "the economic capital of Iran."[20] The World Trade Center signaled a willingness to foster regional partners and reinforced the image of Dubai as a Gulf nexus. Situated at the border between Abu Dhabi and Dubai, the Jebel Ali port was the largest man-made port in the world. The free-trade zone permitted complete foreign ownership of land and no taxes. The stretch of development between the World Trade Center and Jebel Ali port, comparable to the length of Manhattan, has since been rapidly filling with a corridor of skyscrapers since 1990. This highway, called Sheikh Zayed Road on the Dubai side and Sheikh Rashid Road on the Abu Dhabi side, is a deferential handshake that is perhaps more unevenly extended as development in Dubai outpaces that of any other emirate.

Business practices that have long been familiar to the Gulf entrepôts but which have also emerged as contemporary global business models are the perfect accompaniment to Dubai's overarching approach to trade. A city of warehousing, smuggling, and gold trading, Dubai was on the circuit of the Gulf's Qawasim pirates, brought under control at approximately the same time that the Barbary pirates were defeated in the Mediterranean.[21] More important than product stability has been the movement of volumes of goods. Products are best when they are capable of behaving like

13 See http://www.state.gov/e/eb/ifd/2005/42194.htm; http://www.abudhabichamber.ae/user/SectionView.aspx?PNodeId=802.

14 Only 18 percent of the population are UAE nationals. The majority of the population (65 percent) are Asians. http://www.datadubai.com/population.htm.

15 Heard-Bey, 107.

16 Al-Fahim, 163.

17 See http://realestate.theemiratesnetwork.com/articles/freehold_property.php; http://www.ameinfo.com/110401.html.

18 *New York Times*, February 17. 2006, C1.

19 See http://www.emporis.com/en/wm/bu/?id=107779; http://www.jafza.ae/jafza/; http://www.dnrd.gov.ae/dnrd/Profile/JabalAliPort+.htm; http://www.dpworld.ae/jafz/jafz.htm.

20 http://www.datadubai.com/population.htm; and Marchal, 96. The population of the UAE is over 3 million and at least 70,000 UAE nationals have Iranian background. Marchal quotes Fariba Adelkhah's "Dubaï, capitale économique de l'Iran," in Roland Marchal, et al., eds., *Dubai, Cité Globale*, 39-55.

fluctuating currency. With more choices, more merchandise, and more labor from around the world, the odds are better for playing currency and wage differentials.

General Sheikh Mohammed bin Rashid Al Maktoum, recently succeeded his brother Sheikh Maktoum bin Rashid Al Maktoum, who ruled from 1990 until his death in January 2006. Sheikh Mohammed has been for some time the mastermind behind the most recent chapters of hyperbolic development going on in Dubai. Underlining the important of duplicity to power, his Web site features four portraits of him at the top of the page: in traditional dress, in a business suit with glasses, in military uniform, and in casual sporting attire with sunglasses and a baseball cap. On his watch, Dubai has developed seven-star hotels and has pursued projects for which megaprojects are the subset. Dubailand, an enormous, 2 billion-square-foot tourist installation, will include 45 megaprojects and 200 subprojects. Traditional Nabati poetry is Sheikh Mohammed's competing passion. One of his most famous, written is 2003, was referred to as the Sixth Riddle and became the subject of a contest. No one was able to solve the riddle. The answer, as finally revealed by Sheikh Mohammed and after prizes were delivered for "several thousand" close answers, was "Dubai."[22]

Dubai has rehearsed the "park" with almost every imaginable program, beginning with Dubai Internet City in 2000, the first IT campus as free-trade zone. Calling each new enclave a "city," it has either planned or built Dubai Health Care City, Dubai Maritime City, Dubai Silicon Oasis, Dubai Knowledge Village, Dubai Techno Park, Dubai Media City, Dubai Outsourcing Zone, Dubai Humanitarian City, Dubai Industrial City, Dubai International Financial Centre free zone, and Dubai Textile City. [23] Dubai is becoming one of the world's free zones, keeping everyone's secrets, researching everyone's forbidden products and procedures, and laundering global identities.

Dubai has also shared its real estate expertise with regional partners. On December 20, 2005, with Abu Dhabi as the host of the GCC summit, Sheikh Mohammed announced the commencement of work on King Abdullah Economic City, a man-made island formation to be built on the Red Sea coast just north of both Jeddah and Mecca.[24] The Dubai-based developer, Emaar, which claims to be the largest development company in the world, is sharing expertise they have gained building large, engineered islands along the coastline between Dubai and Abu Dhabi. The first of Dubai's largest man-made islands, Palm Island, was started in 2001 and is now to be joined by two more palm-frond–shaped formations, the Palm Jebel Ali and the Palm Deira. In the interim, The World, another archipelago of islands, this time in the shape of the world's continents, created a global media sensation. Island properties associated with their position on the globe were sold as private compounds to celebrities like Rod Stewart and Elton John. The World anticipated its own critique. Since governments legally engineer their own status as islands of immunity and exemption in free-trade zone loopholes, or archipelagoes, The World, as an archipelago of archipelagoes, is an extravagant global witticism that is advertised by its own potential critics. Similarly, mutations of Portman/Hines/Jerde malls and atrium hotels like Burj Al Arab, Dubai Mall (the largest mall in the world), or Ski Dubai, an indoor ski resort in a 120-degrees desert, appear so quickly that they seem to exceed all expressed ambitions and critiques of the experience economy.

Dubai's recent acquisition of the UK's largest port conglomerate, Peninsular and Orient (P&O), reinforced the profile of Dubai as a world capital. The $6.6 billion loan needed to acquire the company was the largest in Middle East history. Perhaps more importantly, the move reaches back through hundreds of years to Dubai's own history. Dubai World Port, or DubaiWP, and its intermediate acquisitions organ, Thunder, are still a possession of the Maktoum family. The story then becomes even more extreme as it once again returns the power of these large global franchises, vestiges of the old franchises and mercantile companies, to dynasty. When the deal encountered political obstacles in America, Dubai simply and quickly avoided these quaint negotiations of democracy.

"Many journalists have booked rooms in prestigious hotels here, but instead of covering the summit they have gone to Dubai to shop."

—A journalist from the Saudi delegation headquartered in Abu Dhabi for the GCC conference, 2005.[25]

21 Heard-Bey, 68-72, 284-86.

22 See http://www.sheikhmohammed.co.ae/english/index.asp.

23 See http://www.dubaiinternetcity.com; http://www.arabsat.com/Default/About/OurHistory.aspx; http://www.dubaiholding.com/english/index.html.

24 See http://www.kingabdullahcity.com/en/.

25 *Gulf News* (December 19, 2005).

Our long-term goal is to establish Abu Dhabi as a centre for development of new technology in energy. . . . We are looking forward to seeing Abu Dhabi as world capital of energy.[26]

Passing across the border on Sheikh Zayed Road to Sheikh Rashid Road, the difference in political disposition is visually clear. The forest of skyscrapers gives way to cultivated palm trees and somewhat dated and earnest public-works buildings. Abu Dhabi's urbanism is more conservative. Tall buildings conform to a grid and regularly offer a very similar retail podium. The emirate invokes gravitas and tradition, playing the role of the more responsible sister, closer to the ecological and philanthropic ethos established by Sheikh Zayed. Sitting on a giant spout of oil, Abu Dhabi has no intention of competing with Dubai's world-capital ambitions. Still, it too must deliberately acquire components of culture that craft the correct global profile and provide more lasting sustenance than petro dollars. While Abu Dhabi borrows from Dubai some world-capital techniques for power-building, it will also work to strengthen its position as a regional/national capital. If the UAE is to become more than a source of oil, a temporary warehouse for goods, or a stopover for labor and tourists, it must send a variety of special signals to the rest of the world.

Sheikha Lubna Al Qasimi, as the first female government minister of the UAE and a protégé of Sheikh Mohammed bin Rashid Al Maktoum, is one of these signals. Previously at the Dubai Port Authority and CEO of Tejari, an e-commerce company, she is now Minister of Economy and Planning for the nation. Among the present concerns is the need for jobs and leadership positions for the nationals who either immigrate to jobs elsewhere or have less expertise than foreign candidates. [27] Ailing economies in the larger region threaten stability and present some mutually beneficial opportunities for investment and philanthropy. The UAE must also partner with both national and corporate powers to sponsor innovation and simultaneously appropriate technological expertise. The raft of initiatives is designed to engage economies and power centers around the world.

While tourism is one avenue of growth, Abu Dhabi plans to distinguish itself from Dubai by being a center of culture and education. One new initiative, Saadiyat Island, will serve as demonstration of some of these new initiatives. Saadiyat Island, promoted as "half the size of Bermuda," will be home to one of the most contagious global spatial products for architourism and culture: the Guggenheim organization. Frank Gehry has agreed to provide a departure from the Bilbao franchise that is to be a reverie on sky and water.[28] With typical UAE hyperbole, GAD (Guggenheim Abu Dhabi) will be 25 percent larger than Bilbao and will be completed in 2012. A performing arts center by Zaha Hadid, a national museum by Jean Nouvel, and a maritime museum by Tadao Ando have also been commissioned. With these signature buildings in place, Saadiyat Island is to become an "international cultural hub for the Middle East on par with the best in the world."[29] The island will also include residential, business, education, and resort districts. There will be residential areas for 150,000 inhabitants, two golf courses, twenty-nine hotels, ecological preserves, and a marina for a thousand boats. All three phases and six districts of Saadiyat Island are to be completed by 2018. Perhaps as important as the museum franchise is the university franchise now becoming increasingly popular around the world as a tool of nation- and region-building. Not only museums but also educational institutions are being shaped as spatial products and inhabitants of zone enclaves. Saadiyat Island, like Education City in Qatar, King Abdullah Economic City, or any of the university incubators in IT campuses or medical complexes around the world, will house outposts of major universities, including the Sorbonne.[30]

Kingdoms and brands have a mutual understanding about mythmaking. Both deploy ambitious and comprehensive use of traditional imagery, capitalizing, tabulating, and constantly refreshing the effects of irrational desire and value. Fetish and symbolic capital, no longer merely ineffable enhancements of capital, are themselves fully capitalized as commodities. In Dubai's versions of experience economies, the collapse between architectural language and logistical envelope becomes complete, and it becomes even easier to float more fantastic fictions over a revenue stream. Without introspection, experience economies instantly blend with the

26 "Energy 2030 To Get Under Way Next Wednesday," Emirates News Agency (October 27, 2006).

27 Marchal, 107.

28 *The Independent* (July 10, 2006): 24.

29 Emirates News Agency (September 7, 2006).

30 *Gulf Construction* (June 26, 2006).

Emirates Palace Hotel and Conference Center, Abu Dhabi.

New construction, Abu Dhabi.

natural urges and talents of a dynasty. Like the Burj Al Arab's imagery of sabers, turbans and billowing *dhow* sails, sheikhs, more than Jon Jerde or postmodern architects, come by it honestly. But in this sense, Dubai only makes a broad cartoon, a vivid indicator, of the ageless mutually sustaining partnership between power and fiction. There can be no hand-wringing over the potential power of a totemic marketplace to wipe away meaning. Indeed, Dubai may well demonstrate that there never was the possibility for such consternation. The supposedly tragic, meaningless sign of the spectacle is, in Dubai, a subtextual indicator of a willingness to be in the game. It may therefore also indicate a willingness to make bargains of all sorts, within which efflorescence and meaninglessness are instrumental political lubricants.

In many countries, innovation can occur only when there is no risk of financial instability from changes to transportation, energy policy, and public health care. Perhaps because it has chosen to sustain itself on the movement rather than retention of business, the UAE often perceives no problem in selected innovations. For instance, even though located at the epicenter of oil, the country is pursuing some of the world's most sophisticated experiments with rail. The UAE plans to join the Arabian Railway network connecting Abu Dhabi and Dubai with a larger Gulf circuit, making it possible to travel from Dubai to Damascus and Beirut to Cairo by rail.[31] The Emirates also has its own internal plans for a railway that would link the coast ports While this UAE railway would begin as a freight network, it would eventually service passenger travel. Dubai is also building an automated metro system, and Abu Dhabi plans to follow suit.[32] The UAE also pursues alternative energy technologies. In November 2006, Abu Dhabi sponsored a global energy conference to discuss alternative energy. Hosted by the Petroleum Institute and sponsored by the Abu Dhabi National Oil Company, the conference took up the issues raised by the Kyoto Protocol, citing the need to plan for energy usage after the exhaustion of current fuel sources by considering solar, hydrogen, and thermal energy.

The UAE is also partnering with African nations, and it might first seem that these partnerships could yield economic adjustments to alleviate some of the extreme suffering exacerbated by oil on that continent. Yet the UAE does not advocate the same techniques by which it shared oil wealth with its own nationals. For instance, in Khartoum, the capital of Sudan, the UAE is reaching out to offer Dubai-style real estate development instead. Almogran, 1660 acres of skyscrapers and residential properties, only underlines the extreme discrepancies between oil wealth and the exploitation of oil resources in mostly black southern Sudan. The overt, even hyperbolic expressions of oil money have been among the chief tools for instigating war and violence within non-Arab populations in the south. Most chilling is the sense that outside the UAE an ethos of using oil for nation-building and social welfare need not be deployed for non-Arab populations like those in the Sudan. Indeed, this episode would suggest that oil-related violence is somehow appropriate in a compatible form of oppression rather than war. The Middle East real estate casino has yet more material, but will it leverage assets for a diverse nation or for a kindred culture?[33]

The United Arab Emirates has earned the dubious distinction of having some of the worst labor conditions in the world. Human Rights Watch has cited the country for discrimination, exploitation, and abuse. Many foreign workers, especially women, face intimidation and violence, including sexual assault, at the hands of employers, supervisors, and police and security forces, the rights group said.[34]

It's a funny thing about Dubai, the minute people get here they try to figure out how fast they can get out.

—Robin Moore, *Dubai*

[Through Alameen]. . . . the public can assist and communicate any information related to security matters to law enforcement personnel. The service is considered unique in employing the latest technologies and in not requiring the presence of the caller. The information is dealt with in complete confidence, without focusing on the caller's identity or motives; the focus is on the subject and the authenticity of the information. The service runs 24/7 in complete confidence.

As an indication of its success, Alameen in its first year received 1,178 calls, of which 107 were traffic information, 87 prostitution reports, 30 fraud, 28 illegal immigrants and workers, 20 drug, 15 begging, 12 harassments, and 7 witchcraft, 5 money laundering, in addition to various suggestions.[35]

In September 2005, workers marched down a highway to focus attention on their mistreatment. The UAE's Ministry of Labor estimated that 10,000 workers had organized in eighteen strikes during 2005.[36] In Dubai, labor problems such as nonpayment are brought before the Ministry, which in turn insists on compliance with the rules, exacting fines and administering cures at least in those situations about which it is made aware. The volume of corruption has increased with the volume of labor. Laborers, primarily from Asia, are organized in crowded labor camps, with fifty to sixty immigrants per house and six to ten workers per room.[37] Workers develop various coping mechanisms to achieve ten or twelve times their normal

31 Global Newswire, MENA business reports (December 13, 2005).

32 *Construction Week* (December 17-23, 2005): 1.

33 See http://www.alsunut.com; "Glittering Towers in a War Zone," *The Economist* (December 7, 2006). Alsunut Development Company Ltd. is a venture of the Khartoum State, National Social Insurance the DAL Group Company Ltd.

34 *Herald Tribune* (September 26, 2005).

35 See http://www.dubai.ae/portal/en.portal?dae_citizen,Article_000214,1,&_nfpb=true&_pageLabel=view.

36 Associated Press (November 2, 2005).

37 Sulayman Khalaf and Saad Alkobaisi, "Migrants Strategies of Coping and Patterns of accommodation in the Oil-Rich Gulf Societies: Evidence from the UAE," *British Journal of Middle Eastern Studies* (1999) vol. 26 no. 2: 292.

wages at home. The labor camps that are legal and partially transparent are largely for men in jobs ranging from taxi drivers to road workers, but the domestic workers are largely women, isolated in individual homes. The volume of projects has also drawn a volume of workers that has overwhelmed the regulating agencies.[38]

The UAE merges traditional, commercial, and civil practices to address a variety of political issues, including the labor issue. For instance, in the absence of familiar forms of citizenship or representation, workers may communicate grievances through a hotline. The country has also long relied on sheikhs or *majlis* to settle commercial or personal grievances. The majlis, or council, that one seeks from others in making decisions is an instrument that can be scaled from the home to the federation. In one sense, these practices establish a "civil process" for negotiating acknowledgement rather than simply excluding from citizenship. It may even be unanticipated reflection of the very sort of intermediate organ for which Étienne Balibar argues when he argues against evangelical assumptions about national citizenship.[39]

The practices nevertheless establish extreme ghettoes or camps, only some of which can be safely regulated. Moreover, the sense of entitlement to racial religious purity by the UAE nationals may be more extreme than that found in *entrepôts* of the fifteenth century, like Venice, where "communities of fate" were thrown together for an urbanism that did not confer citizenship except after long durations of time or as a result of selected marriage unions. Indeed, the UAE operates with something similar to the caste systems of Venice's *nobili* and *cittadini*, except that there is no popular culture shared in urban situations.[40] The segregated camps that be sites of labor's own entrepreneurialism, in the sense that workers are also playing currency and wage differentials. But they prevent the mixtures, masks, and camouflages that allow citizens to achieve their own *popular* sovereignty based on wits and machinations. Just as there is a hotline to report labor abuses, there is also a hotline to report suspicious activity or people for deportation. Dubai is then at once rehearsing new techniques that acknowledge labor contradictions and evading responsibility for labor's alienation from culture.

Take wisdom from the wise—not everyone who rides a horse is a jockey.

—*A verse of poetry by Sheikh Mohammed bin Rashid Al Maktoum written in island masses and visible from the air in the proposed Palm Jebel Ali[41]*

Oh Cloud above all others!

Oh sea of generosity let nothing bring you harm

Nourishing rain that brings life to kith and kin

But denies to your adversaries

Is pure for your neighbors but not for your foes

To whom it offers but a bitter draught of woe

Fearless hand of generosity

No sacrifice we make for you can be too great

You war off all misfortunes

All dangers banished with no efforts spared

In your inscriptions in the book of glory

Every letter betokens honour.

—*Poem by Sheikh Mohammed bin Rashid Al Maktoum in memory of Sheikh Zayed*

In some sense the UAE is an example of "new/old" or "the new oldness and the old newness," to borrow from the activist group Retort.[42] For Retort, the phrase describes a dyspeptic mixture of primitive power urges accessorized with sophisticated techniques of spectacle. Yet the UAE is free to be largely oblivious to modernism's various decrees and boundaries in the twentieth century and equally unaffected by the supposed supremacy of the institutions of national stability. The country has dropped some customary cultural constants in favor of more fluid policies, allowing the country to float its financial sustenance over an even more obdurate ancient script. The UAE maintains these and other contradictions, because if they are the right ones and if there are enough of them, they become the means of sustaining their own purity. The bargain and the settlement, a larger, more diverse population of players, and the connections to rest of the world: these are the ingredients that increase the odds of success. Entrenchment and zealotry may be the very things that threaten the right to maintain an internal supremacy in family and religious tradition. The UAE has found the agility of the bargain to be ultimately more sustaining than publicly resolute entrenchment. The new/ancient is at once more resilient and stable than the Western spectacle that it absorbs.

Tutored by its world capital, the UAE will, like the pirate, engage in many different deals but always stop short of war. Its wars are fought by others. The Emirates have found a number of lubricated techniques for pirating the world that are both primitive and sophisticated. Some of those techniques override the entrenched corruption of national stances to initiate mechanisms of intergovernmental cooperation, while others intensify that corruption in outlaw environments designed to avoid global compacts. The UAE recognizes that aggression, but never violence, and keeps the money flowing. In the same way that American opposition to the Dubai port deal was more subtextual than forthright, so most politics operate through subterfuge and contradiction rather than in environments of conceptual or ethical purity. If the Emirates can maintain enough contradictions and the secrets of enough foreign powers, no one can call the bluff.

The UAE's embrace of duplicity has rendered a global model for development that the entire world wishes to emulate. Now ma-

38 *Construction Week* (December 17-23, 2005): 32.

39 Étienne Balibar, *We the People of Europe: Reflections on Transnational Citizenship* (Princeton: Princeton University Press, 2004), 132.

40 Braudel, 518.

41 See http://www.thepalm.ae/index.html.

42 Iain Boal, T. J. Clark, Joseph Matthews, Michael Watts, Retort, *Afflicted Powers: Capital and Spectacle in a New Age of War* (New York: Verso, 2005), 18; and *"An Exchange on Afflicted Powers: Capital and Spectacle in a New Age of War,"* interview with Hal Foster and Retort, *October* 115 (Winter 2006): 5.

Construction site, Dubai.

jor cities and national capitals that did not have a sister city are engineering their own world city Döppelgangers on the Singapore or Dubai model. Navi Mumbai or New Songdo City outside of Seoul are perfectly designed to legally legitimize nonstate transactions. The world capital and national capital can shadow each other, alternately exhibiting a regional cultural ethos and a global ambition.

As various types of zones continue to breed, recessive or unlikely traits begin to appear. Dubai Humanitarian City or Saadiyat Island, demonstrate that the free zone can be an intentional community filled with prestigious cultural institutions, universities, or NGOs. For instance, within the bounds of Dubai Media City, there are no restrictions on free speech or free press. In these cases, the zone shifts from an organ of outlaw dealings to one

of delicate cultural sea changes — internal negotiations that may even be attempting to answer critiques about gender inequality or representation in the country at large.

All of the UAE's apparent beneficence and innovation need not be merely tools of their own public relations machine; rather, these changes demonstrate how penetrable some supposedly apolitical constructions may be and how susceptible they may be to indirect moves and ricochets that may have a political instrumentality counter to the initial stated political climate.

Social critic Mike Davis loads, aims, and fires his bracing message from the left, saying that the future of Dubai "looks like nothing so much as a nightmare of the past: Walt Disney meets Albert Speer on the shores of Araby."[43] Does that sentiment seem at

once constitutionally at a distance and yet strangely too close to the right's decision to label the region as a harbor of fascism? Neither left nor right politics nor the politics of resistance from within are complex enough to navigate these political waters.

Yet some backstage knowledge of the bagatelle in exchange, the players in the game, and the cards being dealt perhaps returns information to spatio-political activism. Outside of the purity of cultural scripts that we might regard to be politically authentic are rapidly mutating political scripts that may be the most immediate tools in the world's urgent situations, despite their lack of national pedigree and reference to political theology. These are the dirty tools and techniques of an extrastatecraft that might be tilted toward many different political aims.

43 Mike Davis, "Dubai: Sinister Paradise," Mother Jones (July 14, 2005). See http://www.motherjones.com/commentary/columns/2005/07/sinister_paradise.html.

Bangkok: The Architecture of Three Ecologies

Brian McGrath

The main doors of the *ubosot* of Wat Pathumwanaram, like the shutters in the colonnades, frame scenes of wet-rice cultivation and the water-lotus gardens that once surrounded the temple.

Framing scenes of rice-paddy farming, carved gold-leaf wooden shutters depict grazing water buffalo and lotus gardens floating within an encrusted background of miniature, diamond-shaped mirrors. These reflective surfaces evoking a bucolic, water-based life animate the raised colonnaded ambulatory of the *ubosot* (a structure containing a Buddha image), which houses temple Wat Pathumwanaram's main Buddha image in the heart of Bangkok. When saffron-robed mendicants circle the temple, the glimmering surfaces mirror the sky, trees, lotus gardens, and worshippers in a kaleidoscopic mosaic of shifting reflections. Recently, the mirrored shutters also reflect a new urban panorama: the cranes and scaffolding of two vast construction sites surrounding the temple just outside the new Siam Central Station, the main junction point between Bangkok Transit System's first two Skytrain lines, which converge just outside the monastery walls.

The temple was constructed within a water lotus garden during the early nineteenth century by King Rama IV; it was part of a royal enclave of villas, accessible by the San Saeb Canal. With the expansion of the kingdom of Siam and its growing commercial contacts with Europe, the Grand Palace at the center of Bangkok grew overcrowded, and the Thai elite began to experiment with the architecture, landscapes, dress codes, and decorum of colonial Europe, while simultaneously rediscovering rituals and pleasures from the rediscovered historical capitals of Sukhothai and Ayutthaya. Today, this kilometer-long stretch of Rama 1 Road, parallel with the canal, is the setting for new, mass-consumer desires marketed through a potpourri of historical and contemporary references. The monastery now shares this long block with four major shopping mall/mixed-use commercial complexes that make up the Central Shopping District of Bangkok. Surprisingly, the recent profusion of reflective and transparent architectural skins and surfaces more and more come to resemble the aesthetic dematerialization, if not spiritual dimensions, of Wat Pathumwanaram's glimmering, illusionary shutters. Digital-screen printing as well as new glass and LED technologies can create luminescent images that send cultural reflections back to city inhabitants wandering through the malls or gliding above the city on the elevated Skytrain.

The spatial and temporal compression—a collapse of histories, geographies, and

The three principal structures of Wat Pathumwanaram are, from back to front, the *vihran, the stupa,* and the *ubosot.* A sculpture of the mythical Naga water serpent is in the foreground; the construction site of Siam Paragon shopping mall appears in the background.

cultures—within this corner of contemporary Bangkok is a vivid example of Felix Guattari's critical collapse of three ecologies: the environment, the socious, and the psyche.[1] Unlike Reyner Banham's remarkable analysis of Los Angeles, here ecologies are not understood as topographically defined separate zones in the city but as nested circuits of relationships between urban ecosystem processes and human consciousness.[2] Furthermore, the embedded scales of Guattari's ecologies parallel Bangkok's originary Hindu-Buddhist cosmologies. The *Traiphumikata*, Thailand's Theravada Buddhist canon, describes three worlds: one formless, one comprising form but no sensation, and the world of form and sensation, which is divided into thirty-four levels of existence.[3] For eight centuries, Siam has constructed symbolic urban realms embodying modes of behavior that interpret this cosmological model in architectural details and ritual space, as well as in city planning and design.

Radical contemporary Buddhism now interprets the *Traiphumikata*'s supermundane realms as psychological states in the here and now.[4] The repeating cycles of human existence based on suffering, death, karma, merit making, and rebirth can be understood best through meditation practices that still the body and mind in order to bring attention to reality as constant flux and change. Contemporary ecological thinking has also been radicalized through new, open, non-equilibrium disturbance models. Rather than seeing ecologies as closed systems in balance, ecosystem science today conceives of the world as an open, impermanent system of patches in flux.[5] The global context in which both contemporary Buddhism and disturbance ecology are imagined has radically shifted as well: for the first time in human history, the majority of people are urbanites. Nature can no longer be conceived as the wild "other" of the city, isolated from human disturbance, and cities can no longer be conceived as closed, human systems outside nature.

The following three sections intersect these new vectors of thinking by considering contemporary Bangkok's three embedded ecologies. *Liquid Perception* presents the Chao Phraya River Basin as the regional environment within which the historical, geological, topographic, and climatic condi-

Wat Pathumwanaram is sandwiched between Siam Paragon and the Central World office and shopping complex. The water gardens of the palace and temple have been replaced by underground parking, with a reflecting pool above.

Photograph of construction fence around the Central World Plaza construction site. A glass arcade is planned to resurface the mall so shoppers can walk through giant LED-lit advertisement billboards.

tions of Siamese urbanism can be understood within a watershed framework reconceived in an era of global tourist and media flows. *Transpolitanism* describes the Lower Chao Phraya Delta as a dynamic social patchwork, continuously transformed by a distributed network of human agents operating within fluctuating political, cultural, hydrological, and market conditions. Third, *Simultopia* revisits the mediated human ecosystem that comprises the commercial blocks surrounding Wat Pathumwanaram as an architectural expression of Bangkok's current collective psyche. While the scale of inquiry is expansive, it is my intention to portray architecture as the primary agent for situating the nested space of Guattari's three

ecologies within a framework of sensate human perception, social experience, and material existence. This chapter's spatio-temporal collapse seeks to understand ecosystem processes and connective logics across scale and time, rather than defining historically discrete or topographic limits to urban ecologies or architecture. Contemporary ecological frameworks—watersheds, human ecosystem, and patch dynamics—are employed here to understand contemporary Bangkok as part of an emergent human ecosystem, while its three ecologies are presented as new design models for confronting the primary environmental, social, and psychic dilemmas present in twenty-first-century architecture and urbanism.

1 Felix Guattari, *The Three Ecologies* (London: The Athlone Press, 2000).

2 Reyner Banham, *Los Angeles: The Architecture of Four Ecologies* (London, Allen Lane, 1971).

3 Pinraj Khanjanusthiti, *Buddhist Architecture: Meaning and Conservation in the Context of Thailand*, Dissertation (York: University of York Institute of Advanced Architectural Studies, 1996).

4 S. Sivaraksa, *A Socially Engaged Buddhism* (Bangkok: Thai Inter-Religious Commission for Development, 1988).

5 S.T.A. Pickett and White P.S., *The Ecology of Natural Disturbance and Patch Dynamics* (New York, Academic Press, 1985).

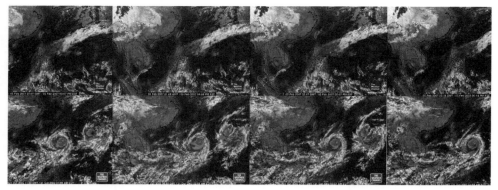

Weather maps from dry March (top row) and rainy October (bottom row) show Thailand situated downstream from the snow-encrusted Tibetan plain and above the equatorial tropical storm belt.

Liquid Perception

Along the 14th parallel, day and night oscillate neatly between predictable, twelve-hour divisions, and months pass with little change in temperature, barely affected by the Earth's axial tilt. However, between May and October, a slight shift in atmospheric currents brings monsoon rains from the Indonesian archipelago to the mountain ranges ringing northern Thailand. The runoff feeds the Mae Nam Chao Phraya River Basin and Bangkok, sprawling across its flat, silted tidal delta. Seasonal cycles of precipitation rather than temperature extremes of winter and summer bring rhythm to life just above the equator, putting into motion human cycles of planting, harvest, and migration, as well as shaping Siamese beliefs and rituals. The mountain rainforests release a sacred mixture of rain and nutrients that follows the geography of the kingdom of Siam's capital cities through the alluvial valleys at Sukhothai (thirteenth century); terraced floodplains converging at Ayutthaya (fourteenth to eighteenth centuries) before ultimately depositing in deltaic Bangkok (eighteenth century to the present). Siamese urbanity and domesticity evolved from an intimate association with climatic, topographic, and hydraulic conditions. River-, canal-, and lagoon-based garden cities retained six months of rainwater for the following six dry ones, staging ceremonies and rituals in synch with attentive observation of hydrological cycles and variations.

The Siamese fluvial geography was overcoded by a feudal tributary power system. Upstream vassals and lesser kings sent annual gifts to the royal houses in the successive downstream capitals, from which auratic power was reflected back to village hinterlands.[6] Honorific space materialized a layered Buddhist cosmology of distant kings and river-valley kingdoms with distinct watersheds. Power was primarily symbolic, as villages made decisions about land and water management locally. Contemporary life in a newly industrialized country follows the less predictable flows and fluctuations of global capital. Thailand's strategic Cold War alliance with America catapulted the kingdom's economy to a world stage. New ideas and fantasies from abroad now freely mix with ancient myths and rites. When rice prices fall and word of jobs in Bangkok reaches small subsistence agricultural settlements,

6 Thongchai Winichakul, *Siam Mapped* (Chiang Mai: Silkworm Books, 1994).

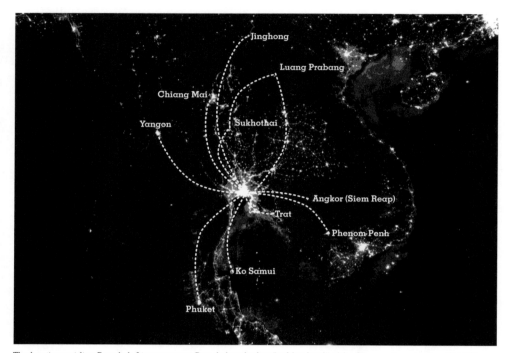

The boutique airline Bangkok Air reconnects Bangkok to the lost "golden land" of the Siamese imagination. Cold War-era boundaries dissolve as borders open between Thailand, China, Vietnam, Laos, Cambodia, and Burma.

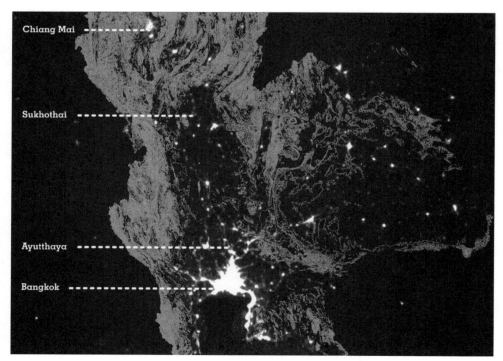

The geography of Thailand consists of three distinct urban regions, in addition to the southern peninsula not shown here: northern cities in the intermountain valleys, northeastern cities on the Korat plateau, and cities of the central plain.

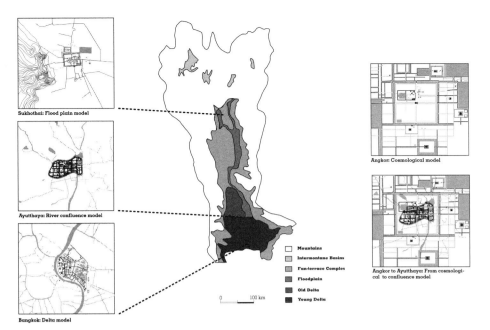

Sukhothai: Flood plain model

Ayutthaya: River confluence model

Bangkok: Delta model

Angkor: Cosmological model

Angkor to Ayutthaya: From cosmological to confluence model

☐ Mountains
☐ Intermontane Basins
☐ Fan-terrace Complex
☐ Floodplain
☐ Old Delta
■ Young Delta

0   100 km

The Chao Phraya watershed, with the successive capitals of Siam: Sukhothai located in the flood plain of the Yom River, Ayutthaya at the confluence of three rivers, and Bangkok, located in the river delta.

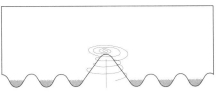

Cosmological Model

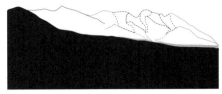

Small Watershed Model

The Indic cosmological model that dictated the strict hierarchical order of Angkor (above) is localized in palace and monastery complexes in Siamese cites. The Hubbard Brook Experimental Forest atop impervious New Hampshire granite allows ecosystem scientists to develop and test models based on monitoring water chemistry in small catchments.

economic migrations trickle and then flood the capital city. Now, media flows in a reverse direction of the watershed, and television broadcasts from Bangkok infiltrate nearly every household in the kingdom. Modern Bangkok disseminates images and messages much more rapidly and viscerally to the rural majority's T.V. screens than news and laws from the distant kings of the past, producing more impulsive and less predictable human responses.

A short flight between deltaic Bangkok and the mountain-ringed river-valley northern capitals spatially and temporally compresses the tributary geographies and complex histories of the Tai language group, Siamese urbanism, and Thai nationhood. Bangkok Air has marketed boutique travel routes through the ancient capital of Sukhothai, with connections to other Southeast Asian heritage sites such as Luang Prabang in Laos and Angkok Wat in Cambodia. These transnational tourist circuits allow those in search of narratives of pre-nation-state origins to visit the precursers and the origins of the kingdom of Siam. A huge new airport at the eastern fringe of Bangkok has been named for the pre-modern and pre-colonial golden land of Suvanabhumi that encompassed most of continental Southeast Asia. Media, capital flows, tourism, and consumption give context to new liquid perceptions from within and from without, recreating a mythical land through international package tours.

Sukhothai, the first capital of Siam, emerged from under Angkor's vassalage

and diverged from imperial Hindu Khmer planning precedents and technologies to create a unique urban model based on indigenous Tai animist and transnational Theravada Buddhist beliefs. In the building complexes of Khmer, like Angkor Wat, every urban element was created in relation to an ideal Indic cosmological layout and the supreme hierarchy of the god-king Rama. Khmer cities are monumental materializations of an ideal cosmos, divided into concentric rings of continents and oceans, with the sacred Mount Meru at the center. Angkor's hierarchical political structure commanded a huge infrastructure of palaces, religious buildings, walls, canals, and giant artificial reservoirs called *baray*. Ceremonial space brings attention to the macrocosm through concentric circumambulations around successively higher ambulatories. Stone bas reliefs in the colonnades of Angkor Wat depict epic battle scenes and the immense peace-time human effort of "churning the sea of milk," or maintaining the liquid life force of the empire. The ruins of this city are located in the Kolen Hills a safe distance from the natural reservoir of Tonle Sap and the unpredictable Mekong River, necessitating the huge and exhaustively maintained *barays* to ensure a water supply and food production for a centralized imperial city.

In contrast, Sukhothai's urban cosmologies are multiple and amalgamated within a reconception of the Khmer kingship based on Theravada Buddhism and animist respect for local spirits, and it constructs a capital city with a new relation to water. In Siam,

the king assumed the status of *Mahadhammaraja*, a guardian of the way of Buddha, the Lord of Life, protector of mountain forests and life-giving water. While the orientation of the original Khmer colonial city just north of Sukhothai is in the cardinal direction of East, facing an artificial *baray*, the Thai city is re-oriented twenty degrees south of East, perpendicular to the line of the low mountain watershed to the west and oriented to the Yom River catchment to the east.[7] During dry season, the city's temples, palaces, moats, and water gardens are part of a water-retention and rice-paddy-field irrigation system. However, once monsoon rains have filled the river to its limits, there is a backflow from the Yom River into the paddy-filled floodplain, the basis of the seasonal rhythms of wet-rice production. In northern Thailand, water is distributed and retained at the village level through a system called *Muang Fai*. Locally managed and maintained weirs divert river flows to rice paddies. During the rains, the monks retreat to the forest monasteries, where the highest form of Buddhist meditation is practiced and taught. Floods are annual reminders of an unseen power beyond observable and controllable local water flows—the entire upstream river-basin floodwaters descend from an unseen source.

From 1351 to 1767, the Siamese kingdom grew to regional prominence with the rise of Ayutthaya over Angkor. The new Siamese capital was "the greatest amphibious city in history."[8] In a radical departure from Angkor's location at a safe distance from the Mekong, Ayutthaya is located at the

7 Betty Gossling, *A Chronology of Religious Architecture at Sukhothai* (Chiang Mai: Silkworm Books, 1996).

8 Sumet Jumsai, *Naga: Cultural Origins in Siam and the West Pacific* (Bangkok: Chalermnit Press & D.D. Books, 1997).

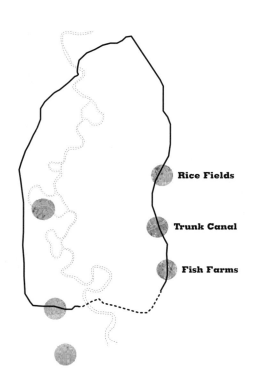

Rice Fields

Trunk Canal

Fish Farms

Bangkok's eastern periphery is dominated by rice fields irrigated and connected by trunk canals, some built during the Ayutthaya kingdom. Cornell social scientists examined a rice-growing community in Minburi along the San Saeb canal from its origins. Following construction of new highways, many rice fields are being replaced by housing subdivisions and factories. Fish farms dominate the southeastern fringe.

Old Meander

Fruit Orchards

Shrimp Farms

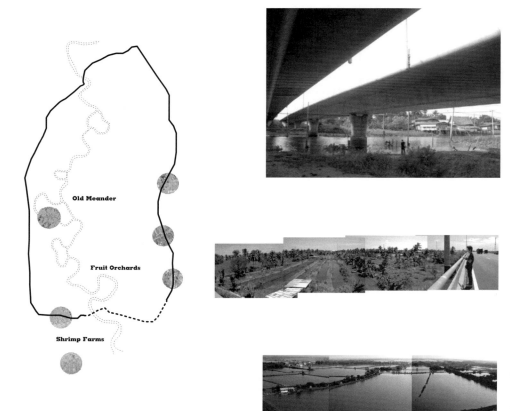

Bangkok's west bank consists of canals that follow the old meanderings of the Chao Phraya, before shortcuts were dug by Ayutthaya's kings. Fruit orchards dominate this part of the city, making it very attractive for new home buyers. Shrimp farms dominate the southeastern coastline, replacing mangrove forests.

confluence of three rivers. A major canal was cut as a regional water diversion measure, creating an island city surrounded by flowing rivers at the southern edge of the prehistorical Chao Phraya River Delta. In addition to the rivers that engulf the city, it is crisscrossed internally by canals. Ayutthaya plays a pivotal role in Siamese urbanism: it is not only the historical confluence of Siamese environmental and social *tributary* systems of urbanization, but it also initiated the development of the modern *distributary* network city occupying the multiple river and canal systems of the lower delta. Ayutthayan kings excavated long trunk canals, interconnecting the four rivers of the lower delta, where the canals served as new homesteads for people, military outposts, and market nodes in a productive distribution system.[9] Ayutthaya thus initiated the process of agri-urbanization in the lower delta, creating a dispersed, multinodal network city over a vast region below its royal and religious island enclave. Outward-looking, capitalist, productive, and sustainable in its watery and vegetated milieu, the water body of Siam was supplemented by a networked market structure and a river port connected to global trade. After Ayutthaya was destroyed by a Burmese invasion in 1767, a small settlement in this region became the next capital of Siam: the Royal Rattanakosin Island citadel of eighteenth-century Bangkok.

"Liquid perception," according to the cinema theories of Gilles Deleuze, is the promise or implication of another state of perception, "a more-than-human perception, a perception which no longer has the solid as object, condition, or milieu. It is a more delicate and vaster perception, a molecular perception, peculiar to a 'cine-eye.'" For Deleuze, there are two poles of perception: one is determined by the common-sense single point of view, a fixed center of human indetermination; the second is a universal perception in things, an eye in matter that defies assimilation within a common-sense framework. In between is liquid perception, comprehensible from a floating, flowing perspective no longer constrained by bodies.[10]

Contemporary ecology is conceived around the measuring of ecosystem performance through a watershed framework. In the Hubbard Brook Experimental Forest, ecologists developed a working ecosystem

9 Terdsak Tachakitkachorn, *A Comparative Study on the Transformation Process of Settlement Developed from Orchards in the Chaophraya Detla*, Dissertation, (Kobe: Graduate School of Science and Technology, Kobe University, 2005).

10 Gilles Deleuze, *Cinema 1: The Movement Image*, (Minneapolis, University of Minnesota Press, 1986).

model by measuring the inputs and outputs in a hydrologically defined, small experimental watershed in the White Mountains of New Hampshire.[11] In the Baltimore Ecosystem Study, experimental models derived from Hubbard Brook Experimental Forest are being tested for the first time in urban, suburban, and exurban sites.[12] The social-science model for this study, the Human Ecosystem Framework, links critical biophysical resources to social systems through the flows of individuals, energy, nutrients, materials, information, and capital. In urban ecosystem science, both urban and rural patterns are recognized as recombinations of vegetative and built sections that are structured by watersheds identified as patches. Urban ecological structure and performance are understood by measuring the inputs and outputs of flows through relatively small, bounded patches over time.

The discipline of urban design is now being added to this framework to create new, dynamic design models of urban ecosystems. Much of the work points to a reassessment of the way rivers and waterflows have been engineered to pass around and under cities rather than through them. A pre-modern, locally controlled ecosystem watershed model structured and sustained Siamese cities for centuries. An animist tradition combined with an inherited Hindu-Buddhist cosmology created a tributary culture for a locally managed forest and agricultural production society with a Dhamma king as the symbolic Lord of Life. Today, the Chao Phraya River Basin is managed by ministries in Bangkok by a vast network of hydro-electrical and draught-control dams and reservoirs. With World Bank and American assistance during the Cold War, modern dams and huge reservoirs replaced cities as locally controlled and maintained water-retention systems modeled on the Tennessee Valley Authority. Water and floods were thought to be technologically controllable and manageable in a system that is more ideologically aligned with the Khmer empire than with the complexities of indigenous Thai socio-hydrology and urbanism. Contemporary urban ecosystem science and Siamese urbanism both point to the development of cities as water-retention systems, not dams, for socio-cultural and environmental reasons.

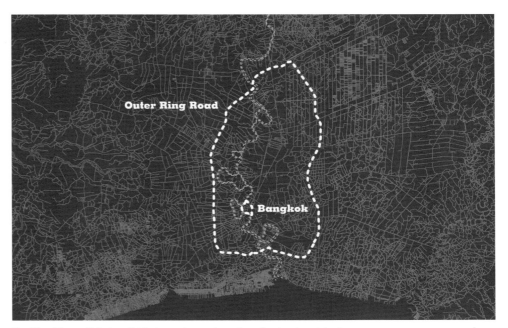

The Chao Phraya Delta is a distributary urban system where the river inundates the area every monsoon season. A highway and expressway system has been superimposed on an intricate network of waterways. The fruit-orchard and floating-market networks are now accompanied by just-in-time industrial production and delivery.

Transpolitanism

The Bung Tong Fishing Hut is a long, covered wooden deck built over an expansive grid of fish ponds twenty kilometers west of Bangkok. The ponds fill excavated rice fields, the top soil sold to pay off debts and taxes. Now Bangkok's Outer Ring Road—a giant ellipse stretching ninety kilometers north to south and thirty kilometers east to west—provides high visibility and easy accessibility for the fish farm, restaurant, and recreational fishing huts, as well as the transportation of the one million fish grown here every year. The Outer Ring Road passes over and through a dynamic patchwork of urban, agricultural, industrial, residential, commercial, and leisure spaces encompassing the entire Lower Chao Phraya Delta. Danai Thaitakoo, from Chulalongkorn University's Department of Landscape Architecture, employs remote sensing to measure regional land cover change and conducts van excursions around the Outer Ring Road to survey changing land-use practices. Thaitakoo interviews rice, fruit, fish, and shrimp farmers as they respond to falling prices and increased costs. The new economy of the Outer Ring Road now consists mostly of land speculation for new house subdivisions and commercial complexes. Labor-intensive rice transplanting and orchard farming has disappeared in greater Bangkok in recent decades as labor costs have outweighed the greater productivity of this type of rice farming. Some farmers grow turf instead of rice or sell topsoil for the lawns and golf courses of the housing developments. Hollowed land with no topsoil is converted to fish farms, easily flooded in the subsiding delta.

Thaitakoo's work follows decades of research by social scientists from the Thailand Cornell Project, which studied the transformation of the rice-growing community of Ban Chang to the east of Bangkok, from the mid-nineteenth century to their vantage point in the middle of the twentieth century. Social scientists Lucien Hanks and Lauriston Sharp were thrilled to see the invisible hand of Adam Smith at work in indigenous Thai urbanism long before the Americans arrived.[13] In *Rice and Man*, Hanks documents the socio-ecological change through participant observation in Ban Chan over long time periods and traces historical change by interviewing villagers and examining archival records.[14] Hanks identified the fear of abandonment and isolation as the imminent threats to this frontier rice-growing village along Khlong San Saeb, but what continually fascinated the group most was the *transformative* capacity of Thai agri-urbanism, as evidenced by one farming village that changed from shifting to broadcasting and finally to transplanting cultivation and slowly became incorporated into the extended networked market economy of greater Bangkok.

Terdsak Tachakitkachorn from Chulalongkorn's Department of Architecture maneuvers his pontoon boat through the watery labyrinth of canals

11 F. H. Bormann, and G. E. Likens, *Pattern and Process in a Forested Ecosystem*, (New York: Springer-Verlag, 1981).
12 See http://www.beslter.org.

13 Lauriston Sharp, and Lucien Hanks, *Ban Chan: Social History of a Rural Community in Thailand*, (Ithaca: Cornell University Press, 1978).
14 Lucien M. Hanks, *Rice and Man*, (Chicago: Aldine Publishing, 1972).

This early-twentieth century map shows the culmination of the royal palace district at Pathumwan. The princes lived within income-generating irrigated rice fields in villas surrounded by water gardens that retained the monsoon rain for use in the dry season.

along the Mae Khlong River, one hour west of Bangkok. From his floating research lab, he documents urbanization patterns and interviews orchard farmers. Their stories, together with historical documents and maps, convey the difficulties of transforming a swampy delta jungle into a network of individual household farms, markets, and villages. Small irrigation canals feed raised-bed orchards, while houses line natural levees along rivers and larger navigable canals. Where these house-lined waterways intersect, informal markets formed, first floating retailers, then formalized into waterside market districts. Market cities grew at major intersections between canals and rivers. Amphur Wa is such a market city, positioned along a canal immediately off the Mae Khlong, which became a regional node in this enormous, centuries-old fruit production and distribution network. The muddy jungle marsh of the lower, new delta of the Chao Phraya was transformed into an extension of the island capital city of Ayutthaya beginning in the seventeenth century.[15] By the mid-nineteenth century, this agri-urban settlement pattern stretched for hundreds of miles along the water distribution channels of the lower delta. The transformed landscape became the setting for the relocation of Bangkok as the capital of Siam in the late eighteenth century.

Clarence Aasen has referred to an essential Tai—the linguistic rather than the Thai national group—transnational ethnic architecture, which between 500 A.D. and 1500 A.D., traversed an area from southwestern China to northeastern India to the Malay Peninsula.[16] The intricate, furrowed river valley and mountainous geography is one of the most ethnically complex regions in the world. The migrant Tai linguistic-group urban system was initially stateless and polynucleated, with little urban and rural differentiation and multiple and overlapping allegiances and sovereignties. Tai syncretism was based in animism, primarily honoring spirits that inhabit a place. Contacts with India, China, Ceylon, the Mon, and the Khmer created an admixture of practices and beliefs: Mahayana and Theravada Buddhism as well as Brahmanism. This ease of assimilating and adapting foreign influences continued in modern Siam during the colonial era. Situated between the French and British empires, modernizing kings deepened contacts with Europe and America and sought expertise in a great range of modern disciplines from multiple sources, rather than a single colonial ruling power. King Rama IV traveled the entire country as a monk, learning English and Western thinking from missionaries and European traders. King Rama V circuited first colonial Southeast Asia and then Europe seeking knowledge in political, military, economic, scientific, and legal affairs; he established the foundations of a modern nation-state and metropolis in the early years of the twentieth century.

Twenty-first-century *Transpolitanism* replaces the late-twentieth-century prefixes *de-*, *dis-* and *ex-* with *trans-* for contemporary urban theory.[17] *Transpolitan* theory is a call for an in-betweenism beyond Eurocentric concepts of modern global avant-garde reactionary cosmopolitanism. Cosmopolitanism is an Orientalist, nineteenth-century colonialist concept privileging the world metropole: Paris, London, Berlin. Thai *transpolitanism* benefited from centuries of both Indic and Chinese contacts and diasporas, its resistance to colonial occupation, maintaining a sovereign state among bordering English, French, Dutch, Portuguese, Spanish, and American colonialism, and its more recent global alliances through global trade and tourism. *Transpolitan* Bangkok is primarily transformative. Contemporary Thai urban research at Chulalongkorn University and the Cornell Thailand Project both demonstrate the dynamic capability of Thai urbanism. Sociologist Richard O'Connor has demonstrated how, in Thai society, a person can choose his or her affiliations, creating dynamic extended household structures rather than a fixed nuclear-family model. For O'Connor, Thai groups are fluid and overlapping. This fluidity is not incidental but integral to the organization of society.[18] The deltaic network city of greater Bangkok hints at a counter way of modern social development, one that allows for multiple options and mobility at the individual and household level.

15 Tachakitkachorn, 2005.

16 Clarence Aasen, *Architecture of Siam: A Cultural History Interpretation*, (Oxford: Oxford University Press, 1998).

17 Bernard Tschumi, "De-, Dis-, Ex-", in *Remaking History, Dia Art Foundation Discussions in Contemporary Culture #4*, Barbara Kruger and Phil Mariani, eds., (Seattle: Bay Press, 1989).

18 Richard A. O'Connor, "Heirarchy and Community in Bangkok," unpublished paper in the collection of the Thailand Information Center.

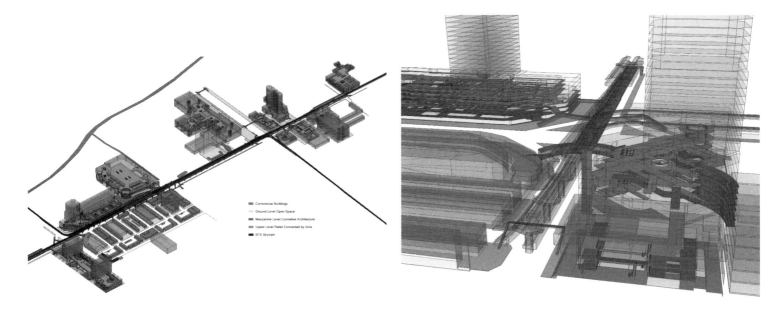

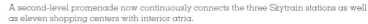

Bangkok has no CBD, but a central shopping district has formed around the intersection of the two Skytrain lines from National Stadium to Chitlom stations.

A second-level promenade now continuously connects the three Skytrain stations as well as eleven shopping centers with interior atria.

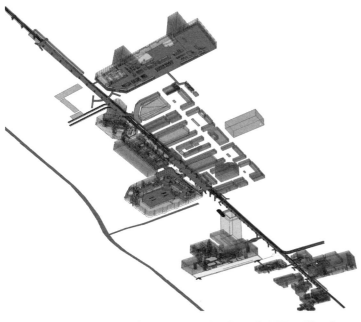

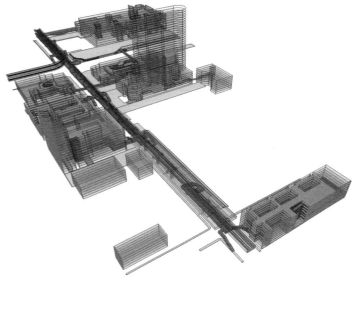

Travelers from National Stadium Station can enter directly into the MBK and Siam Discovery shopping centers from a mezzanine that crosses a busy Pathumwan intersection.

Businesses near Ratchaprasong Intersection collaborated to build an extension of the mezzanine from Chitlom Station to provide direct access to several small shopping malls.

Opposite National Stadium is Soi Kasemsan, where street vendors, small guest houses, and an ice maker serve the larger commercial enterprises around the corner.

Crushed ice is still delivered by *samlor* from nearby Soi Kasemsan.

Simultopia

The grand opening of Bangkok's latest glittering shopping mall, Siam Paragon, was broadcast throughout the kingdom in December 2005. The mall replaced the verdant Siam Intercontinental Hotel, torn down in 2002 on Crown Property Bureau land next to the royal gardens of the Srapatum Palace, just west of Wat Pathumwanaram. The grand entrance of the mall is a faceted glass "jewel," meant to glitter like diamonds in the day and glow with the colors of gems—ruby, sapphire, emerald, topaz—in the evening. Inside Siam Paragon are car showrooms, a food court, fountains, and the largest aquarium in Southeast Asia, Siam Ocean World. The mall

has nine different sections: Luxury, Fashion and Beauty, Digital Lifestyle, Living and Technology, the Exotic East, Dining Paradise, Paragon Gourmet Market, Paragon Department Store, and the Paragon World of Entertainment. The mall expects to draw 100,000 visitors a day and make Bangkok a shopping destination eclipsing even Hong Kong and Singapore.[19]

While the spiral ramps to Siam Paragon's 4,000-car parking garage loom above Wat Pathumwanaram's western flank, the expansive construction site of Central World Plaza rises to the east. According to the project architects, Altoon and Porter, Central World Plaza is being redeveloped as a mixed-use center that will include a seven-story-high, 350-meter-long digital Media Wall, with the capability to project multiple LED images, ticker tape, and lasers. The new high-tech face of the greatly expanded center looks out on a revitalized plaza that, like New York's Times Square, serves as the gathering space for the annual New Year's countdown; in the cool winter months, there are enormous German beer gardens, complete with fountains and gardens. The architects say the new offerings will include a variety of retail "rooms," or precincts—an Olympic ice rink, bowling, a fitness center, a convention center, a high-rise hotel, fifty-story office space, and multiple entertainment spots. The redesign turns the eight-story mall inside out by moving the vertical circulation—stairs, escalators, and elevators—to the interstitial space between the wall of the building and the media screen, which hangs from the existing façade.[20]

Siam Paragon and Central World Plaza are just the latest incarnation of a thirty-year series of architectural and social experimentation along this stretch of Rama 1 Road. The area first became a modern shopping destination with the construction in 1975 of Siam Square, built on Chulalongkorn University property along the south side of the street, just east of Pathumwan Intersection. Siam Square, a gridded enclave of blocks containing small shops, offices, movie theaters, and bowling alleys, was innovative and experimental in its use of French prefabricated, precast-concrete technology and its adoption of American-style park-and-shop convenience. It became a youth-centered district filled with restaurants, coffee houses, boutiques, and "cram" schools—private after-hour schools which supliment public education—due to its proximity to Bangkok's first university. Siam

Center, a mall of small boutiques clustered around three atria, was developed north of Rama 1 Road with support from the Thai Tourist Authority. Two pedestrian bridges were constructed across the wide boulevard, and Siam Center became an extension of Siam Square's youth market by the early Eighties. In 1985, wealthy rice merchants built Mah Boon Krong Center on land leased from the university across from Siam Square. MBK Center is a huge, mixed-use complex comprising a seven-story shopping mall with two atria, a department store, a hotel, and office building. MBK mall was linked to Siam Square by a futuristic, elevated pedestrian tube with an inside moving sidewalk across Phayathai Road.

MBK was overshadowed in 1990 when the first phase of an even larger mixed-use mall, office building, and hotel project called the World Trade Center opened one kilometer down Rama 1 Road. Its construction anchored a second shopping node at Ratchaprasong Intersection by complementing smaller shopping centers and hotels east of this intersection; Amarin Plaza and Sogo Department Store connected to the Erawan Hotel, and Gaysorn Plaza connected to the President Tower and Le Meridean Presidential Hotel. The owners of Siam Center responded in 1996 with the completion of an office building and high-end shopping mall on the northeast corner of Pathumwan Intersection called Siam Discovery Center. A raised plaza and fourth-level bridge connected the two shopping centers, while multiple bridges communicated both to a new multilevel parking deck. The rapidly escalating scale of commercial construction was evenly paced, as every five years a new mall was built. All the later shopping centers built large parking structures and relied primarily on automobile access. By the mid-Nineties, walking between malls was difficult and unpleasant given the heat and pollution, and Bangkok's legendary traffic jams made it difficult to drive to one shopping complex and impossible to visit a second. As a result, the malls were engaged in a competitive Darwinian struggle of outdoing the previous commercial enterprise, and fickle Bangkok shoppers abandoned one mall for the next. A new exclusive mall, the Emporium, opened much farther east of this district and seemed to promise the premature decline of the entire Rama 1 Road shopping district.

The catastrophic Asian economic crisis of

19 See http://www.siamparagon.co.th/.

20 See http://www.altoonporter.com/ and http://www.centralworld.co.th/.

Following the construction of the Skytrain, Siam Square and Siam Center reclad their opaque concrete buildings with acres of glass, providing a shimmering spectacle for travelers on the BTS night.

1997 began with a real estate bubble, bank failures, and currency speculation in Thailand. Between 1985 and 1995, Thailand was the world's fastest-growing economy, and its glittering commercial buildings symbolized the promise of national prosperity. After 1997, they turned into the countersymbol of economic depression, as hundreds of commercial developments in central Bangkok were idled by bankruptcy, shoppers disappeared, and the city became known for its hollow concrete shells. The fears of isolation and abandonment identified by Lucien Hank here became manifest in the symbolic heart of the modern city.

The millennium celebrations were a happy distraction for Bangkok, with a grand countdown and a fireworks display in front of the bankrupt World Trade Center development, distracting attention from the view of its unfinished office tower. But in the fallout from economic collapse, there were tangible transformations in the city's psyche. A national soul-searching took place, with the king supplying a message of Buddhist self-sufficiency and a new political party named "Thai Love Thai," led by telecommunications billionaire Thaksin Shinawatra, achieving government control. The millennium also brought the first phase of city's long-delayed mass-transit system: two lines of the elevated Skytrain, the concrete viaducts which forcefully torque and slide by each other, then meet at Siam Central Station on the long block of Rama I Road between Pathumwan and Ratchaprasong intersections. The Skytrain initiated a renovation and building boom for a glamorous shopping district lined with constantly reconstructed shopping centers. Rama 1 Road is now covered by two massive train lines converging at Siam Central Station.

MBK Center was the first of the malls to realize the potential of both the millennial optimism and the new accessibility the Skytrain provided at their doorstep. Metallic silver defined the twenty-first century, and the mall was reclad in aluminum panels and a giant elliptical illuminated sign. Additionally, the interior of the shopping center was connected directly by second- and third-level bridges to the Skytrain's National Stadium Station mezzanine, which extends a large, elevated public platform eastward across Pathumwan Intersection. However, the greatest new potential was in the social change the new political philosophy of Thaksin ushered in: unrestrained, credit-based optimistic consumerism. Thaksin made shopping a national duty at all levels of society.

The immediate success of MBK's renovation started a chain reaction of architectural makeovers, as Gaysorn Plaza and Erawan refurbished in concert with new skybridge connections to Chit Lom Station's concourse. Now, a massive construction site stretches the entire length of Rama I Road between Pathumwan and Ratchaprasong as the two largest shopping-center and mall developers in the country both have completed flagship developments east and west of Wat Prathumwanaram. The Mall Group recently completed the superluxury Siam Paragon and is renovating Siam Center and Siam Discovery Center as one integrated complex directly connected to both National Stadium Station and the Skytrain's main junction at Siam Central Station. The Central Group has assumed control over the former World Trade Center, and the renamed World Central Plaza has completed the first phase of the long-abandoned office tower, a glass lantern with flat reflecting pools facing the Skytrain. The World Central Plaza created a lengthy extension of the Skytrain's elevated walkway system, now connecting Siam Central Station through Chit Lom Station at Gaysorn and Erawan, with World Central's flagship at the opposite exit of Chit Lom. Confering status through shopping is the driving force in the Darwinian struggle to continually upgrade the architecture of Bangkok's malls.

Richard O'Connor has identified community and hierarchy as two keys to indigenous Thai urbanism and finds evidence in status displays of funerals and cinemas in contemporary Bangkok.[21] The shopping district of Rama I Road is a monumental symbolic representation of Thai urbanism, demonstrating indigenous ideas of cosmology, social rela-tions, and psychological states. Embedded within this layered and complex space is Wat Pathumwanaram, the monastery built as what Jumsai identifies as a "water chapel" similar to the temples that seem to float on islands in lotus-garden lakes at the center of ancient Sukhothai. The court of King Rama IV arrived at the water palace of Sraprathum and the temple by boat via the canal Khlong San Saeb, the same canal that continues on to Ban Chang, the village studied by Hanks and his colleagues at Cornell. The closed, illusionary shutters of Wat Pathumwanaram represent the rice-farming and watery scenes that reflect the remnants of the royal lotus gardens, alluding to Sukhothai but also creating sanctuary amid the commercial heart of Bangkok. Khlong San Saeb still connects the back of the malls to the Royal Rattanakosing enclave and the Chao Phraya, but it also continues beyond the Outer Ring Road to the agricultural fringe of Greater Bangkok.

Early in the morning, before the shopping malls open, one can find the doors of Wat Pathumwanaram open. The first temple houses a giant Buddha image, and a monk accepts offerings and gifts from local visitors. Behind the first hall is the white stupa containing the relics of the Lord Buddha. The last hall is the ordination hall for monks. Most mornings it is a quiet place for meditation practice. The columns and walls are filled with kneeling figures, eyes closed and hands in prayer. A lone meditator is present, and as he finishes his quiet examination of his mind and body he glances up. The upper frieze of the hall contains a giant mural of the royal barges circumnavigating the entire interior of the hall in a stately procession; the representation recalls the annual visit of the king to various temples along the rivers and canals of Bangkok. The wheels of the Skytrain can be heard over the silence of the boats encircling the hall.

Simultopia is a purposely ambiguous term coined to give meaning to the complex experience of place in late-capitalist cities. While *-topia* means place, the prefix *simul* implies many things: the modernist dream of *simultaneity* as the ability to understand

21 O'Connor.

The interior piers in Wat Pathumwanaram are adorned with portraits of expert meditators.

This attic fresco depicts the annual Royal Barge Procession, when during Buddhist Lent, the king distributed new robes to monks living in temples.

multiple actions in one place, and *simulation* and postmodern theories of the *simulacra*, which refer to copies without an original. *Simultopia*, therefore, describes the mediated experience of contemporary space that differs from the experience of speed, movement, transparency, and simultaneity that captivated historical modernist aesthetics and revisionist notions of the phenomenology of place that grew in reaction to the "placelessness" of modernist technological space. The term resonates critically in two directions: toward regressive utopian modernisms that still imagine heroic possibilities of human physical overachievement, and theories of place that are inadequate in describing the mediated experiential possibilities of contemporary environments, societies, and psyches. In this sense, *simultopia* resonates between Jean Baudrillard's concept of the simulacra and the vast knowledge embedded in Bangkok's Theravada Buddhist scriptures and practices.[22] *Simultopia* also dreams of inventing new paradigms for city production, ones which neither transcend nor simulate place but inhabit space as different layers of reality. Furthermore, *simultopia* embraces a philosophy of the new and the now, understanding a world of changing perceptions and experience, rather than symbolically fixed representations and signs of place.

According to Roland Bogue, the philosopher Henri Bergson found himself split into two individuals, one who observes the other as if on a stage and the other as the actor in his role—the automata and its spectator, free and real. For Bergson, time and memory are not inside us, but it is the interiority that we are in, in which we move, live, and change. The actual and the virtual, physical and mental, present and past, are inseparable, ongoing coexistences.[23] Theravada Buddhist meditation practice likewise enables the attainment of such perception by the development of a separate consciousness that surveys centered, sensory-motor existence from a floating, detached, nonreacting vantage point. This practice is most ideally developed in isolation. The most learned priests in Sukhothai were in the forest monasteries to the west. In modern Thailand, wandering ascetic monks still seek enlightenment in the forests, equipped only with a tentlike umbrella and an offering bowl, or they make their rounds in the small streets leading to Rama 1 Road before the malls open and commuters from Bang Chan file off of water taxis on Khlong San Saeb.

22 Jean Baudrillard, *Simulacra and Simulation* (Ann Arbor: University of Michigan Press, 1994). Walter Benjamin, "One Way Street," in *Reflections* (New York: Harcourt Brace Jovanovitch, Inc. 1978).

23 Ronald Bogue, *Deleuze on Cinema* (New York: Routledge, 2003).

Before the shopping malls open, a monk from Wat Pathumwanaram crosses Pathumwan Intersection in the early morning as he accepts food offerings from local residents and merchants.

Conclusion: Attentive Circuits

Early in the morning, Wat Pathumwanaram remains a meditative retreat within the heart of Bangkok. The temple, originally built outside the city, was established from the start as a meditation training center, and one can find area residents and workers sitting on the floor under the frescoes of past meditation experts. Glancing up, the attic frescoes depict the royal barges floating on all four walls. They remind viewers of the king's annual procession to bring robes to temple monks during Buddhist Lent. The painted images seem to gracefully move, but the sound of the Skytrain can be heard through the temple walls. Outside, a monk crosses the eight lanes of Rama 1 Road in order to accept food offerings from area residents. Ice is crushed in order to fill all the soft drinks consumed at the many area fast-food outlets. The billboards outside the Central World Plaza construction site next to the temple promise inner strength through shopping as a new form of meditation.

Liquid perception, transpolitanism and *simultopia* are three conceptual ecologies derived from research in Bangkok as a means to address contemporary crises in the environment, urban society, and the hu-

man psyche as articulated by Felix Guattari. Urban ecosystem studies require long-term, attentive research and observation. Concepts on the contemporary city based on globe-trotting can only remain superficial impressions. More in-depth transnational and transdisciplinary urban research tools must be developed. To Walter Benjamin's admonition that you cannot know an urban site without encountering it from four directions, we must add that this knowing is the result of not just diverse directional vantage points but from a synchronic, temporal dimension as well. What ties together *liquid perception*, *transpolitanism*, and *simultopia* are reflections on urban ecosystem processes: patterns of architectural and landscape difference transforming over time.

Benjamin has described architecture as experienced in a state of distraction. However, according to Bergson's concept of *attentive recognition*, when we consciously reflect on an object, we summon up a remembered image and superimpose it on the perceived object. Bergson carefully analyzed the connection between recognition and attention. To recognize an object is to revive a past memory of it and note its resemblance; presupposed is a reflection, an external projection of an actively created image onto an object.

Attentive versus automatic recognition do not differ qualitatively; in both we summon up a memory image and project it onto the object. In attentive recognition, the object and each memory-image we summon up together form a circuit. As we pay closer attention to the object, we summon up memory-images from broader and more distant past contexts. Deeper, reflective attention represents a higher expansion of memory and deeper layers of reality.[24] An architectural understanding of circuits of recognition, attention, reflection, and memory is evident in the great monastery architecture and planning of Siamese cities. No greater evidence of architecture built to create distraction exists in contemporary, themed commercial space. Bangkok seems poised in between these two conditions of distracted and attentive reflection. The question Bangkok's three ecologies pose is, how can architects make contemporary sensate environments in a world that is more and more mobile, fast-paced, and mediated? Contemporary architecture provides a wide array of attention-grabbing forms as well as new materials and technologies. The question ecosystem science poses for contemporary architecture is, how can this newly attentive urban citizen be directed to larger systems and processes to create new urban models based in new urban experience? The opportunity to connect these worlds, these ecologies, is everywhere present. In the heart of Bangkok, they can be seen in the water gardens of Wat Pathumwanaram and Khlong San Saeb that sit beside and behind giant shopping malls that deploy water and media as themes and signs. But along the Outer Ring Road, every few minutes another bridge crosses a canal and passes a water-based world connected only by the vertical posts of huge billboards. These are the sites in which to create the architecture of Guattari's three ecologies.

24 Henri Bergson, *Matter and Memory* (New York: Zone Books, 1988).

Students stroll through one of Siam Square's three atria. Consumerism and education are tightly linked near Siam Central Station.

Texting Beijing

Tina DiCarlo

**with Cao Fei, Sze Tsung Leong, Ou Ning,
Ole Scheeren, Yan Lei, and Zhang Jinli**

PreTEXT
by Tina DiCarlo

In the past five years the buildings on Beijing's Chang An Avenue, the city's major east-west axis, have doubled; the skyscrapers in the Central Business District (CBD) have more than tripled; magazines have gone from five or ten dusty copies sold from the back of a bicycle to hundreds of glossy editions sold at news-stands; fashion searches for style and expression; clubbing pushes beats into jam-packed crowds every night; the monochrome red-white-black palette of the street (the only color of cars until a few years ago) now includes yellow, green, and blue. The skyscrapers that rise against the once-horizontal city collapse, overlay, and intersperse a myriad of cultures: an apartment next to a Chinese interior-design office across from a Japanese girls bar, an old lady's residence, and a cosmetic surgery salon, all on a single inconspicuous floor overlooking eight- to ten-lane-stacked flyovers, suspended above twelve- to fourteen-lane ground-level intersections. Noise, smell, acrid air, demolition, dust, and the impact and displacement of Beijing's social environment exist alongside new design and construction at a pace and scale heretofore unimaginable.

This emergent culture is physical and psychological; it subverts and exceeds the historic structure of the city. This change translates to a quality of life defined not as increased comfort and convenience or desired coherence and a simplistic sense of order; instead, it harbors within multiplicities and contradictions, as well as a certain harshness that accompanies rapid transformation. But there is also flexibility and adaptability, which promises tremendous potential for new conditions, ideas, and spaces.

The individual subject is emerging from new forms of collective enterprise. A new generation is well placed to explore spaces of freedom that might provide possibilities unthinkable in Western systems. In the context of rapid modernization architecture still plays a larger role than in stable environments.[1]

—"Culture of Change" by Ole Scheeren

Within China's twenty-year trajectory of economic expansion Beijing presents itself as a border condition in which an accelerated rate of change gives way to hybrid conditions that coexist at a magnified level: preservation and modernization; the low, horizontal city of the *hutong* and the vertical city of the skyscraper; the forces of the market and those of a closed political system; the new urban rich and the agrarian poor; the European paradigms of architecture and an Eastern culture embracing Westernization and twenty-first-century change; the positive effects of increased wealth, globalization, hygiene, and infrastructure alongside the negatives of rampant corruption, pollution, acid rain, and urban displacement.

Regarding Beijing, most know its new icons as they know those of its past—Tiananmen Square, The Great Hall of the People, and The Forbidden City; Riken Yamamoto's Jian Wei SOHO; Office for Metropolitan Architecture's China Central Television Headquarters; PTW's National Swimming Stadium (in the form of a giant water cube); Herzog and de Meuron's National Stadium (in the form of a giant bird's nest); Steven Holl's Linked Hybrid; Norman Foster's National Airport (whose shape and color recall a red dragon); and Paul Andreu's National Theater (which resembles a giant egg) are all poising Beijing for the 2008 Olympics.

To map these new developments against older paradigms as artifacts and monuments, or to portray them as digitally generated form would be to present the city as stable, rather than that which produces, and is produced by and within, a field of forces through a dynamic series of changes and active stresses.

As a city that is not complete but being re-invented, Beijing has an urbanism that must be written as a projective history of future potentials and emergent patterns. "Texting Beijing" relies on a Foucauldian notion of critique in which analyses and mappings of particular conditions and specific phenomena give rise to a more general understanding. Its methodology is empirical and curatorial, invoking choice and juxtaposition to disclose a broader condition. Its representation is active rather than static, temporal rather than ideal. It proposes no constitutive theory other than one of fluidity and obscurity with moments of clarity and revelation to instantiate a culture of change.

Beijing's historic city is a city of walls—a fabric turned inward, in which the street is denied and the inner workings of a compound (be it familial, political, or industrial) are sacrosanct. Its spatial syntax—compounded with its scale, concentric growth, the blur of its milky-white air, the lack of one vantage point (such as a river's edge from which one can see the skyline)—mean that one can never really see Beijing. This condition metaphorically speaks to a methodological problem of a purely visual means of representation, a problem that is endemic to urbanism in general but also one that is particular to Beijing. Beijing is a city reinventing itself through industrialization; yet to represent it according to those self-same paradigms—vision and spectacle, mass media and the street, or the bird's-eye view of the architectural plan—is to fall prey to nineteenth and twentieth-century Western precedents.

"Texting Beijing" presents a fictive anthology of individual voices through which multiple points of view converge to stage the city as an interface for performative action. "Text" here refers to a temporal medium, either images or text, implicit in which is a point of view. Each constitutes an imaginary construction or narrative, an immersive paradigm that conveys spatial and environmental effects—a psychological space of inhabitation rather than the omniscient, timeless perspective and visual distance present in traditional mappings. The focus is not on the form itself but on the effects of the spatial syntax, which become instantiations of the experience of Beijing, rather than merely its visual representation.

"Texting" as opposed to "text" is invoked to reference the current trend of SMS-ing (rather than structuralist or poststructuralist theories). As an active verb of engagement and creation, it reflects to a process of transformation, mutation, and participation. Texting has its own language, its own code. Time becomes place to supplant physical locale. It subverts traditional surveillance because it slips under the radar. Its content is short, abbreviated. In a country that currently has the most mobile phones in the world, texting becomes an expression of individual agency (albeit in a somewhat generically represented way within the digital text) and a decentralized means of organization.[2] As a message "the text" is generative of a cluster of convergences. Order is neither imposed nor planned but productive of overlaps, interludes, collisions, divergences. These convergences have their physical counterparts in emergent urban phenomenon such as traffic or pollution. Really they manifest themselves in the impromptu parties staged at Urban Love Island (Beijing's gay club) where "clusters of culture outside the mainstream find their own places of belonging" or among the urban youth who use SMS-ing to organize the staging of their performances against the backdrop of the city.[3]

Beijing's historic spatial syntax of walled compounds, modularity, and repetition—reflected in the Imperial City and the courtyard house—its underlying grid that produced what was believed to be a harmonious society, reflected not the modernist subject as we know it in the West but embodied and produced collective subjectivities or collections of collectives, rooted in Confucian ideology and the social ideals of the People's Republic of China.[4]

Hence the reference to the digital age and to "telematics" does not propose a networked or an informational paradigm of the city. Rather, it proposes that technology alters the way in which we inhabit the city, navigate through it, and even build in it. While there exists, for example, a "great firewall" set up for the comprehensive control and censorship of the Internet—approximately 40,000 official wall monitors search the mail and homepages for suspicious-looking content and effectively cordon off the country—the bloggers are faster than the Internet police. The hidden alley escapes the authorities' view long enough to post a protest.[5] Organizations such as the Alternative Archive, a dispersed film collective of over 800 members, are springing up.

Cao Fei's Cosplayers films Chinese urban youth enacting Japanese comics. These actors use the SMS or "text" to organize their performances. The new city—now not Beijing but the artistic center of Guangzhou—in which contemporary artifacts such as the abandoned roadbed that floods every time it rains and thus appears as a lake, is appropriated as the set. The city becomes an interface for performative action and enactment. These enactments not only manifest themselves in artworks; but in the most minute levels of the street, such as the space where Zhang Jinli posts his protests.

Curation as method and text as media are used as paradigms of mapping to trace dynamic change and reveal invisible (or overlooked) yet defining phenomena and patterns. The voices invoked here are specific, representative of perhaps larger collective voices. They include the documentarian photographer (Sze Tsung Leong), the tourist (Tina DiCarlo), the Western architect practicing in Beijing (Ole Scheeren), the Chinese, Guanzghou-raised artists now re-located to Beijing (Ou Ning and Cao Fei), the resident of the *hutong* (Zhang Jinli), the Chinese painter unknown outside of China (Yan Lei), and the Chinese scholar whose works and knowledge of Beijing's spatial and collective structure has served as a primary historical reference (David Bray). The voices are passive and active; the narratives and images have been collected over the last two years. The graphic layout is intended to evoke a discrete spatial structure: the old city, colliding and effaced by the new in an ad-hoc accumulation within a peripheral order.

The various voices analyze five objects which reveal the transformation of the city: tall buildings, toxicity, toilets, walls, and telephones. They suggest that Beijing's urbanism is best represented through specific but largely invisible phenomena that organize the city and precipitate behavioral or performative patterns, whether they be the interior of the tall buildings, the air quality that permeates every aspect of daily life, or the toilet, credited in the West as defining the autonomous subject.

Six parallel columns contain six parallel texts, that unfold alongside one another across nine spreads. The texts have no particular order. They overlap, comment on one another, diverge, contradict. Ole Scheeren's story of CCTV unfolds alongside Zhang Jinli's tale of displacement; Sze Tsung Leong speaks of a certain beautification, of which the tourist finds none; Georges-Eugène Haussmann's modernization of Paris seems to provide a datum; Cao Fei and Ou Ning reflect the digital age through different media.

The texting of these multilayers reflect Beijing's new spatial syntax, in which local patterns of inhabitation still preside. The city can be found in the building, where harshness becomes a qualitative beauty: instability is a fixed condition; the underlying grid has been effaced, and order is ad hoc. They evoke something of its contemporary quality through which specific phenomena delineate (probe) political, cultural, socio-spatial histories and practices, new behaviors and ideas, a radial structure of a still largely inward-looking city, in which discrete clusters exist within striated urban space. In the absence of one particular vantage point, six viewpoints converge, allowing dialogue and positioning of the city as a temporal construction of parallel histories, proceeding forward without the ability to replay or rewind.

1 "Culture of Change," was excerpted from "Judge Beijing by its Skyline," by Ole Scheeren with Tina DiCarlo, originally published in *Monocle* vol. 2 no. 6 (July 2007).

2 Gregor Jansen, "Let the Wind Blow," *Totalstadt. Beijing Case: High-Speed Urbanisierung in China.* (Köln: Valther Konig, 2006), 307.

3 Ou Ning, "Street Life in Da Zha Lan," http://www.alternativearchive.com.

4 David Bray, *Social Space and Governance in Urban China: The Danwei System from Origins to Reform* (Stanford: Stanford University Press, 2005).

5 Jansen, 307.

Background image:
Rulai 13 (part a), 2005
Acrylic on canvas by Yan Lei

Yan Lei's paintings involve infinitesimal color separations painted in banded striations. Coded as a paint-by-numbers, they are industrially produced by a host of gallery assistants. Paintings ranging from abstractions (as shown here) to icons, portraits, and urban scenes in which the almost topographical striations of color radiate an atmospheric effect.

DA ZHA LAN: Offline City
by Ou Ning

The road separating Beijing's eastern districts, with their whiff of modernity, from Da Zha Lan on the city's south side is not long, and yet it is as though the two areas were separated by an age. Da Zha Lan, this isolated city district, has become a place unto itself, banished to the horizons of the world. The slow cadence of centuries past live on here, as though Da Zha Lan has been cut off from all other signals. Few of the upper-crust people who live on the east side have ever been to Da Zha Lan; it's is too old, too underclass, too remote.

Entering the deep and silent places of Da Zha Lan is like a journey through several ages. Refugees fleeing the destruction of the imperial capital in the Jin Dynasty (A.D.265– 420) carved out these slanting streets, carrying their pain and travelling to the new capital city of the Yuan Dynasty (A.D. 1271–1368).

There's no denying Da Zha Lan is an aged world. The people here live in homes from the late Qing Dynasty, walk along roads from the Republican Era (1911-1949), and use electrical wiring dating from the Liberation (1949). The young are seduced by modern life, stifled by the pace of Da Zha Lan. They have moved to the new city suburbs expanding outward, ring after ring.

As the new grows newer, the old grows older. The rise of increasingly newer urban areas in Beijing accelerates the ruin of the old. Economic disparities and historical protectionism between various administrative districts impede policy changes, undercutting renewal and development in Da Zha Lan. Forgotten by the upper crust and nouveau riche, migrants flocked here in huge numbers. Da Zha Lan's low cost of living drove massive population growth, and density eventually rose to 4.5 people per square meter, more than twice the average for the capital's city center. All were low-income workers from poor regions all over the country. They lived on average on eight yuan, or one U.S. dollar, per day. Da Zha Lan became known as a slum for Beijing's poor.

As populations from various regions of China mixed in Da Zha Lan, new forms of social organization began to form under its surface. Beyond the reach of the authorities of the district—the street agency and residential committee—people formed interest groups on the basis of regional connections. People from Henan collected recyclables, people from Hebei sold fruit, people from Shanxi opened boarding houses, people from Anhui worked as housemaids, people from Sichuan opened res-

The Authority of Beauty
by Sze Tsung Leong

Cities attain a state of beauty—however subjective, contested, or difficult to define—either as a result of a long, unplanned process of evolution or by being constructed according to particular definitions of beauty. Unplanned beauty emerges out of an organic process of growth where a city or town reaches a state of aesthetic and structural harmony, not through any willful design but through the slow accretions of time. The general agreement that medieval street patterns or traditional hillside towns are beautiful relates to the aesthetics of the natural order, which is one of the most accepted forms of beauty. In other words, these streets and towns are regarded as beautiful because they have reached a perceived harmony with the natural. Beauty in these situations is not so much intended as evolved.

On an urban scale, planned beauty is another aesthetic that has achieved dominance because of the forcefulness necessary for its execution. It conveys the idea of harmony but, unlike its counterpart, it does not necessarily align with the natural; instead, the aim is to reach an ordered harmony with ideologies, forms of power, or social structures. More often than not, the scale of forces needed for this type of urban planning and design means that the definition of beauty rests with those with the power to construct it.

The belief that beauty can be conflated with social ordering in the urban scheme has historically formed one of the main goals of the discipline of city planning. In China, the tradition of the Imperial City plan was seen as a form within which society could be organized. The urban plan was considered beautiful primarily because it reflected the structuring of society within a divine order: the plan was centered on the palace, the symbolic form of the emperor as the personification of heaven, around which tiers of society were arranged in hierarchical order within a planned grid. In Europe, the concentration of monarchial and military power, which developed prominently during the seventeenth century, enabled the planning of cities not only as symbolic forms of authority, such as Versailles, but as tools to facilitate control over society.

This lineage of beauty as a way to represent and foster social harmony and control forms the basis of "urban beautification," a term now widely in use and synonymous with urban regeneration and redevelopment. Planned beautification, which began in the domain of the imperial and monarchial, expanded its development through the social changes of the mid-nineteenth century that underlie modern society. During this time, Europe and the United States were

Toilets and Toxicity
by Tina DiCarlo

July 2005.
I arrived at Beijing airport from Shanghai at midday and took a 1.20 yuan red taxi to the China World. I had a street address but no idea where the hotel was within the city. I did not contact any one when I arrived. I did not read a guidebook, although I had two in my bag. I simply and intentionally placed myself there anonymously and alone, to wake the next morning and walk the city.

At first I could not find the street. Once I did I found no signs, and the map proved useless. I knew four things: the city aligned itself to the cardinal grid, there were five ring roads, the innermost ring was considered the wall of the Forbidden City, my hotel (which was circled on the map) was located near the Third Ring Road and the major east-west axis. I turned and began walking with the sun to my back. It was 9 a.m. I reached Tiananmen Square and the central gate to the Forbidden City at 10:30.

I turned right and walked along the north-south axis that runs through the Forbidden City. I reached the north wall at 11:40. I continued north through the hutongs that comprise old Beijing. I lasted less than an hour because of the stench, and took a 1.60 yuan blue-and-yellow taxi back to the China World. I arrived at 1 p.m. filthy from the pollution and heat.

May 2007.
I have been to Beijing nine times. Few red taxis remain; most are now 2.00 yuan and blue-and-yellow or black. The pollution has markedly increased; so has the traffic. The din of twenty-four hour construction and smell of sewage still hang in the air.

Piero Manzoni canned it in 1961. Wim Delvoye constructed a machine to produce it. Kiki Smith sculpts it in papier-mâché. Dominique Laporte chronicles its history. In Beijing you smell it.

It could be argued that one alternative history of urbanization is the history of defecation, or as Dominique Laporte terms it the "history of shit."[1] Laporte contends that: "Human waste is crucial to our identities as modern individuals, including the organization of the city, the rise of the nation-state, the development of capitalism, and the mandate for clean and proper language." Long before Georges-Eugène Haussmann, and perhaps culminating in his urban plan of monuments and boulevards that implemented the revolutionary sewer system, the modernization of Paris was thrust forward by an increase in hygiene and sanitary conditions. When the edict of 1539 "forbid all emptying or tossing out into the streets and squares . . . of refuses, offals, or putrefactions, as well as all waters whatever their nature" and commanded that "all stagnant and sullied waters and urines" be retained "inside the confines of your homes," it outlines

Walls
by Tina DiCarlo

The walled city and the walled compound were the two most significant spatial realms in traditional China...in its simple grid design it provided a template for the ordering of everyday social life. The grid was the foundation for the li-fang system of walled neighborhoods that inscribed communities within a clear spatial realm.[1]

—David Bray, *Social Space and Governance in Contemporary China*

As an imperial city Beijing was aligned to the cardinal grid.[2] The walled city—today known as the Forbidden City—formed its center and was the unit that corresponded to the imperial government. The walled courtyard house, or *siheyuan,* formed the unit that corresponded to the Confucian family. Situated outside the walls of the Imperial City, and confined within another set of walls that today is demarcated by the Second Ring Road, they formed the fabric of the historic city. Like the Imperial City, the *siheyuan* were aligned to the north-south axis.

Clusters of walled compounds formed blocks that were situated between a grid of avenues. Narrow lanes and alleyways, or *hutongs,* measuring nine meters or less in width, ran through these blocks of walled compounds.[3] Defined by the circumferential walls of the compound that comprised an exterior volume of inhabitation rather than a passageway, the *hutongs* were blind, permitting neither a view in or out.[4]

In its most basic form the *siheyuan* comprised four structures surrounding a central courtyard. The most privileged structure, the *zhengfang,* lined the north wall and faced south, thereby receiving the most sunlight. It maintained a tripartite construction: the central room, or *ting,* was used to welcome guests or for ceremonies and rituals. The rooms to the left and right, the *jian,* were generally used as bedrooms. Unlike the *ting* that had a central door opening to the courtyard, the *jian* had no access to the exterior. Occupied by the seniormost male of the household and his wife or wives, the central location of both the *zhengfang* and *ting* gave the patriarch oversight over the entire compound, and his wives.

The *xianfang* flanked either side of the *zhengfang.* Smaller in scale and lower in height, they were typically occupied by the second- and third-ranking males, respectively. The fourth side of the compound, the *daozuofang,* was the least important. Lining the south wall and facing north, it received little or no sunlight and was often separated from the main courtyard by an internal wall. It functioned to accommodate servants, house the kitchen, storage, and toilet.[5]

Made in China
by Ole Scheeren

This text was excerpted from two lectures: the first was given in Shanghai in September 2005 and the second in Stockholm in winter 2006.

The lecture is called "Made in China." This is obviously a label that we all recognize on things that come from there. These Chinese goods usually come from the low end of the spectrum of quality and production, but I think they are currently in the process of ultimately reversing that. The country has started to change not only its intentions, but also its position, to potentially go beyond being simply a center for cheap goods, but actually a global center in itself.

The first time I visited Beijing and looked at the site of the project that we are doing now, there were old motorbike factories on the site, and inside the production halls there was a sign which read ADJUST DURING DEVELOPMENT, DEVELOP DURING ADJUSTMENT. This was one of the old slogans not of Mao but of Deng Xiaoping. It was a sentiment that became symptomatic for the entire undertaking there, for a process that required people to change as much, if not more, than their environment. There were obviously other prophecies. In 1978 Deng also phrased the famous quote, "To get rich is glorious," and it is another prophesy that China is following right now, and you sometimes wonder how well understood or misunderstood some of those ideas are and where they can actually lead. There is a billboard on Chang An Avenue in Beijing that offers a third slogan after "To get rich is glorious." It reads, OCCUPY THE CHANG AN STREET. MONOPOLIZE THE WHOLE WORLD. Obviously, this is only a developer's billboard for a housing project along Chang An, and it is saying, "If you live here you live in the center of the world." But what comes out in the process of translation is obviously an entirely different meaning, and I think that this is symptomatic of the risks and dangers of this process of translation, not only in linguistic terms, but also in cultural terms. This is one of the most critical aspects of working in China.

In early 2002 OMA was invited to participate in two competitions: one in New York for the rebuilding of the World Trade Center and one in Beijing for the rebuilding of the China Central Television (CCTV) Headquarters. We had to choose between the two projects. One side was associated with the trauma of aggression, destruction, and retaliation, both physically and symbolically, if by tragic implication or by choice, and entrenched in a financial and architectural compendium of intricacies that seemed to make its outcome predictably compromised and a symbol of a conservative order trying to maintain its status by all means and methods. On the other side

117 MEISHI STREET
by Zhang Jinli

As the host of the 2008 Olympic Games, the Beijing Municipality decided to transform about three hundred "villages-amid-the-city" and urban "corners" that are considered dirty, chaotic, and impovershed. According to the sixty-first work meeting of the Beijing mayor in 2004, the number of localities in question was 343, and the Da Zha Lan area was one of the first on the list. According to the "Investigation of Urban Corners in Beijing," a report published by the Beijing Academy of Social Sciences in July 2005, in the Da Zha Lan area, the population density was 45,000 persons per square kilometer; the housing was overcrowded, with many old and dangerous buildings posing a serious fire threat; there was a shortage of water and electricity supply; the hygiene was deplorable; the public security situation was worsening; the market was inundated with counterfeits; and there was a huge number of migrant works living on less than eight yuan (one American dollar) a day.

In short, the Da Zha Lan area had become a typical slum. Owing to its location adjacent to Tiananmen Square, Da Zha Lan's problems became even more acute. The first measure taken by the Beijing Municipality was to improve the infrastructure and relieve the traffic.

As the government's relocation work began in Da Zha Lan on December 27, 2004, affected households opposed to relocation held their demonstrations amid the chaos, hanging banners from their rooftops, putting posters over their doors, and handing out leaflets to grab the attention of passersby. They had tried all legal means available to them, going to various government offices to voice their concerns, but in the end they could only place hope in gathering public opinion to their cause. This was the most direct means and the oldest, a centuries-old tradition of urban street life. As urban public space, streets are a place not only for flourishing commerce but also venues for public expression by citizens to exercise individual rights that lead and initiate contact between citizens and the government, inviting the participation of mass media, nongovernmental organizations, and social volunteers.

In June 2005, the Beijing Board of Renovation and Development declared that the width of Meishi Street would be increased from 8 meters to 25 meters for the 2008 Beijing Olympics. The area on either side of the street to be clear was declared the Red Zone. Zhang Jinli was a resident of 117 Meishi Street.

—Ou Ning

Curator's note: In the summer of 2005, Guangzhou-based artists Ou Ning and Cao Fei conducted research on fifteen villages within Beijing. As part of their 2007 Da Zha Lan Project, they gave Zhang Jinli, restaurant owner and resident of 117 Meishi Street, a video camera. If the house reduced to rubble implies catastrophe, then its looming destruction despite an apparent state of squalor urges upon its walls the politics of the collective individual [See Eyal Weizman, "Architecture, Power Unplugged: Gaza Evacuations," *Log* 6 (Fall 2005)]. The excerpts below were drawn from Zhang Jinli's video. They are translations of his banners and texts he posted in the street and on the walls of his restaurant, as well as commentary by other owners in the area that chronicle the events from 2004 to 2006.

Top three images: Da Zha Lan, September 2005, by Ou Ning. Bottom (left to right): *Siheyuan*, Wangjing Xiyuan Third District, C-Print by Sze Tsung Leong; Chaoyang District, Beijing, 2003, C-Print by Sze Tsung Leong; and Xi'erqi III, Haidian District, Beijing, 2002, C-Print by Sze Tsung Leong.

taurants, people from Jiangxi ran salons, people from the northeast cooked up small-time investment schemes or worked as pimps. All formed themselves into industry groups, defending their mutual interests. Native accents or dialects became an important way of distinguishing various groups. Only through Mandarin interpretation could one communicate with those outside their circle, reflecting the expression of China's ancient guild culture.

Individual rooms are generally the basic unit of service at upscale hotels, which also promise a range of intangible products, such as privacy, comfort, a sense of identity, of richness, and so on. By contrast, the small boarding houses of Da Zha Lan break rooms up into bed spaces and rent these out. Many of the boarding houses here are still in the style of the early Republican Era: old whorehouses with two open inner courtyards, often covered over with metal canopies to keep out the sun and rain. They advertise themselves with electric signs that say, BEDS AVAILABLE, drawing in guests from the street. This powerful advertisement bursts through the distinction between public and private space. It might be a sociopath sleeping in the bed next to yours, but it is 10 yuan a bed nonetheless, and you can sleep and dream more deeply here than out on the street. With so many beds lined up in rows, the very notion of the room dissolves, the boarding house itself dissolves, and in the night Da Zha Lan becomes a sea of snoring sleepers. The next day everyone awakens, and all return to the streets, continuing their push ahead with their lives.

The streets in Da Zha Lan have preserved the original pattern of the Ming and Qing Dynasties. Small and narrow like those in Lang Fang Er Tiao, they were the natural enemies of speed when the city ex-

rapidly transforming into societies driven by the market economy, and urban environments had to be adjusted to accommodate the new life.

Beautification was seen as a method to package and deploy the significant urban changes required by the new society. One of the clearest expressions of beauty imposed on an urban scheme was Baron Georges-Eugène Haussmann's "strategic beautification" of Paris in the mid-nineteenth century, under Napoleon III. As opposed to the imperial urban plans of China or Versailles, which were built from blank slates, Haussmann's beautification was a strategy to transform the existing city using two of the most influential tools of urban beautification: slum clearance and the widening of streets. What constituted a slum was defined by those with the power to transform urban areas, and the arguments for slum clearance were linked with the perception that urban configurations characterized by tight, medieval streets promoted disease, social degeneracy, poverty, and crime. Demolishing these areas, perceived as difficult to police and control, was seen as a way to promote sanitation and a healthy society.

The visible manifestation of urban beautification was achieved by the boulevard, which provided the city with visual and formal consistency. In Paris, boulevards were lined with uniform façades and punctuated by monuments such as the Opéra, Arc de Triomphe, and the Louvre. Yet the purpose was not merely aesthetic, for the functions of beautification transcended the visible. The boulevards were intended to give the city a symbolic structure by connecting and clarifying the hierarchies of urban institutions, to allow rapid movement throughout the city for the many forms of traffic (official, military, commercial, and public), and to aid in the policing of the city by the elimination or containment of labyrinthine urban districts.

what Freud contends are the cornerstones of civilization: cleanliness, order, and beauty.[2] This new "olfactory economy," as Laporte terms it, is constitutive of a new bourgeois subjectivity, the effects of which are found and sought in the transformation of the built environment.[3]

Laporte holds that the odorization of fecal matter gave rise to the "individualized body." Its domestication, he claims, "branded the subject to the body, and prefigured . . . the Cartesian ideology of the I."[4] Moreover, sanitary systems resulted in a deodorization and beautification of the city in a state of good health—improved ventilation, water and sewage circulation—transforming the urban family home into a privatized social space. "The provision of clean, piped water and a reliable sewer system for each individual household, a major innovation achieved under Haussmann's planning, had a profound effect on the urban pattern of life . . . [in which] the urban family home transformed into privatized social space."[5]

If the "I" is bound to the individualization of shit and its domestication is tied to privatization, could a corollary hypothesis result that binds the rise of the communal or collective ideologies of Mao Zedong to the public toilet?

The toilet was historically part of the *siheyuan* and located in the southwest corner, opposite the entry gate at the southeast corner.[6] Refuse was deposited into holes in the ground and collected nightly by the lowest ranks of imperial China's social hierarchy. This "night soil" was carted into the countryside, where it was used as fertilizer for agriculture.

The dissolution of the private toilet coincided with the dissolution of private ownership. From the 1950s through the 1980s, the rise of the PRC in China saw a drastic change in the urban landscape: vast spaces for industrialization including factories, schools, and bureaus were constructed just outside the second ring road, with mass housing in the form of low-rise slabs or row houses, modeled on the Soviet prin-

Top three images: Da Zha Lan, September 2005, by Ou Ning. Bottom (left to right): Jiangbeicheng, 2003, C-print by Sze Tsung Leong; Central Building District (computer rendering at the time of the 2002 CCTV competition); Unfinished Elevated Highway, Ciqikou, Shapingba District, Chongqing, 2002, C-Print by Sze Tsung Leong.

The courtyard house varied in size depending on the family's wealth—one courtyard was indicative of the lower classes and two or more courtyards reflective of a higher social standing—yet in each case the *siheyuan* defined a unit for the family. The modular courtyard plan and horizontal section seems abstractly akin to Western modernist domestic space of the individualized subject.[6] Yet their construction, as Bray notes, did not "result in the creation of private realms. On the contrary, it placed each family member visibly within the hierarchical order of the social group."[7]

With the rise of Mao Zedong and the People's Republic of China in 1949 came the first wave of modernization and industrialization to Beijing. Unlike Paris, where the medieval structure of the city gave way to a new spatial order, in Beijing the spatial grammar was not elided but transmuted. The wall became the defining element of the industrial form of the *danwei* and the paradigm of a new social order, that of the PRC.

In the broadest sense, the *danwei* is the generic term for the socialist workplace, referring to anything from the factory, shop, business, school, hospital, research institute, or party organ. Modeled on the Stalinist notion of the "social condenser" in which "productive labor was wedded to everyday life,"[8] the *danwei* incorporated housing and services into the place of work.

The *danwei* could be large or small. Some, such as the Wuhan Steelworks, took on the scale of a small city, incorporating its own hospitals, canteens, colleges, administrative offices, cinemas, community services, and residential compounds, all situated adjacent to the industrial plants and administrative offices. Others, such as factories, schools, or offices, were smaller in size and combined with residential space and community services.

stood a context of a complicated history and an undeniable struggle with many of its remaining conditions, but also one that had set out to engage in a process of transformation, set in the context of the 2008 Olympic Games and an enthusiasm for change within the country. We decided for China.

While the West is still facing the consequences of the "YES" regime, the Chinese situation is different. There is still a strong state, but also the arrival of a new economic power and a market economy. The emerging hybrid has no historical model or precedent. Most other socialist or communist states have followed a very different path. I was born and grew up in Germany. The unexpected historic moment in 1989 when the East and the West reunited was a very beautiful moment; it was one of the few peaceful revolutions in history. But it was also a very traumatizing moment, because the eastern part surrendered all of its beliefs to cross over and embrace the western regime. In my view, the country is still struggling today with an undigested divide that exists between East and West, with people realizing that what they gave up was not nearly as bad as what they ultimately got.

So I follow with great interest the path and development of China as a country that seems to search for a different way of embracing what might be the inevitable but perhaps not leaving everything behind at the same time. In Beijing's center is the Grand Palace, known to Westerners as the Forbidden City. The historic fabric of Beijing is essentially composed of *hutongs* and courtyard houses **(fig. 1, p. 47)**. In 1949 the People's Republic was formed, and the 1950s were marked by the erection of factories and increased industrialization. From 1958 to 1959, Mao commissioned the Ten Great Projects **(fig. 2, p. 47):** ten pieces of architecture, each one of an enormous scale of about 100,000 square meters, all designed and built within a single year. So the speed we

July 4, 2005: Fifty postal receipts posted on restaurant wall that never resolved anything.

September 5, 2005: *Attention to those willing to carry out removal. I am willing to talk about compensation.*

Red banner above restaurant:
THE DEMOLITION AND REMOVAL COMPANY HAS FALSIFIED DOCUMENTS. ORDINARY PEOPLE DO NOT HAVE A CHANCE.

Red governmental banner:
RELOCATING PEOPLE IN STRICT ACCORDANCE WITH THE LAW TO PROVIDE FOR PRESERVATION.

Red banner in restaurant:
CULTURED WORK UNIT.

Zhang Jinli: *"Aside from the compensation for the demolition of my property there is nothing to talk about."*

Zhang Jinli: *"Not about money for us common people"*

Residents of Meishi Street #53: *"They use this as an excuse to demolish as much as they can—now we have a shop front. In the new area we will have all south-facing rooms. They sweep everything unfair under the rug—they bury everything. Today they demolished two more homes, five people in each."*

Residents of Meishi Street #76: *"The government has abused its power, illegally relocating . . ."*

Banner in the street:
EVERYTHING MUST GO . . . NAME BRANDS AT ROCK-BOTTOM PRICES.

Zhang Jinli: *"The constitution guarantees legal rights to properties . . . we demand justice."*

isted at a smaller scale. People experienced the labyrinthine streets with their own two feet. Only in places like Lang Fang Er Tiao—lined on each side with shop fronts and jammed in with people—could speed be annihilated. Qianshi Hutong, once packed full of small banking houses, is only 80 centimeters at its narrowest point and a natural enemy of speed. Wide enough for just one person to pass, its narrowness meant it was easier to catch thieves and protect the old-style private banks.

Rather than the automobile, the vehicle most suited to the streets of Da Zha Lan is the three-wheeled pedal cart that preserves the ancient pace of the district. In the past these vehicles were used to transport pleasure seekers to Da Zha Lan's Eight Hutongs (Beijing's old red-light district) or to take prostitutes to clients elsewhere. Today they carry tourists on pleasure cruises through the hutongs, their purpose evolved from the utility of passenger vehicles, to a passenger vehicle of entertainment. In a society that puts a premium on speed, slowness becomes a curio, a rarity to be enjoyed and appreciated. Collectors of these pedal carts will stop at no expense, putting gold on the handlebars, adding bronze bells and

(Cont'd p. 46)

The elements that came to be accepted as requirements for urban development—slum clearance, wide avenues, and uniform façades—were the basis of one of the most explicit movements to impose particular ideas of beauty on the city, the City Beautiful movement. This movement was manifested most clearly in built form at the 1893 World's Columbian Exhibition in Chicago, also called the "White City." Its main proponent, the architect and city planner Daniel Burnham, believed that the unsightly aspects of city life exemplified by crowded tenements and narrow streets should be cleared away and replaced with airy, ordered avenues, and uniform fçades in the Beaux-Arts style; in turn, it was hoped that social ills of poverty, disease, and crime would be eliminated through the elimination of their environments.

Like many social constructions, beauty is a product of its time. In the urban context, one era's idea of beauty is imposed on past notions, and the form that this takes, as in Haussmann's Paris and the City Beautiful movement, is through the demolition of the past. Currently, there is no clearer example of this tendency than in contemporary China, where the combination of unchallenged, centralized power and extreme economic development have enabled one of China's

(Cont'd p. 42)

ciples of economy, simplicity, and industrialization. These housing units initially took either the form of dormitory or apartment styles. In 1955, a radical Chinese re-thinking of the Soviet model based on cost, economy of space, and division of living quarters and rooms resulted in "70% of households occupied by only one room, and multiroom apartments that accounted for only 20% of the living space. Per-capita living standards were reduced from nine square meters to four, and space was further economized by sharing of cooking and toilet and washing facilities—two to three families per kitchen and four to five per toilet."[7]

The *siheyuans* likewise resulted in overcrowding. Previously occupied by a single family, they were now occupied by eight to ten families. Ad-hoc structures to accommodate overcrowding filled in the courtyards. This coincided with the inception of the first public bathrooms in the 1950s, located in communal areas of the *hutongs*, where the streets widened to accommodate small buildings. The 1950s buildings were functional and efficient, issued from a uniform, governmental design; but in the 1980s they became more elaborate and stylized structures—bisected basilica, Greek, Suzhou garden, imperial, and modernist—as China prepared to improve its public image after opening its doors in 1979.[8] It is these

As in the Imperial City and the *siheyuan,* all key elements of the *danwei* were aligned along a central axis, while lesser subsidiary elements were arranged or grouped on either side. Its hierarchy reversed the traditional Confucian order, progressed from most to least important structure (rather than least to most privileged). In staging the monumental structure at the entrance, the power of the state was immediately apparent, its organization reproduced in miniature through the structure of the *danwei.* Such an order reflected the absorption of the Soviet paradigms into that of Chinese socialism.

Yet the most defining feature of the *danwei* was the high wall that encompassed it. In this sense the spatial structure of the *danwei* was an extension of the *siheyuan,* historically the basic unit of social and urban spatial organization and in which one's sense of social belonging and identity resided within the family. Likewise for the *danwei* the wall not only delineated its boundary but codified the *danwei* as the fundamental social and spatial unit of urban China under socialism. As Bray notes:

Not only was [the *danwei*] the source of employment, wages, and other material

are facing today has historical precedent in this country. Maybe one could say that the Ten Great Projects were one of the first modern architectural movements in Beijing. They were largely influenced by the style, technology, and support from the Soviet Union. Although here the connection might have been more ideological than purely technological, there is a precedent for foreign collaboration on the architecture in China.

During the 1980s Beijing expanded outward, with large housing developments and flats built to accommodate the rising population of the 1970s baby boom **(fig. 3, p. 47).** Ring roads formed lines of modernization as the city expanded concentrically. The third ring road was completed only about twelve years ago. By now, the fourth and fifth are fully used, the sixth is almost fully complete, and the seventh is already in planning **(fig. 4, p. 47).** When OMA arrived in Beijing, we had to ask ourselves how to build a building in this city. How do you build in a place that has such a political coherence, in which the old city of the *hutong* contrasts with the new city (essentially a huge infrastructural node)? Where the national architectural task looked like this only five years before we started CCTV, and where apparently the only vision provided by foreign architects for the future was Paul

Red governmental banner:
IN UNISON, PEOPLE ACTIVELY SUPPORT DEMOLITION AND REMOVAL N STRICT ACCORDANCE WITH THE LAW PROMOTING PRESERVATION.

Painted banner:
TO BUILD A HARMONIOUS SOCIETY GOVERNMENT, PEOPLE MUST USE THE LAW AND REASON.

Painted red Chinese character, circled:
DEMOLISH

Zhang Jinli: *"This house was forcibly demolished. About one hundred authorities came to oversee it."*

Zhang Jinli: *"I sent more than fifty letters. No one did anything about it. Only then did I hang the letters."*

Residents of Meishi Street #76: December 15, 2005: *"Family will be forced out."*

Residents of Meishi Street #76: December 16, 2005: *"Family evicted."*

Residents of Meishi Street #4: *"Our rights go back to before the Cultural Revolution."*

Xuanwu District, Beijing, 2004
C-Print by Sze Tsung Leong.

public toilets that are still used by the residents of the *siheyuans* today. As of 2000, about two thousand remained and were still used within the historic areas of the Second Ring Road.[9]

Like their domestic counterparts, these public toilets have no internal plumbing; all the refuse falls into a pit and must be manually cleaned out. There are usually no dividing walls between toilet holes, reinforcing the communal over the individualized body. In light of the absence of any social center or open public space, they became like the *hutong,* an area for communal interaction. Ironically, urban expansion did not bring the eradication of the public toilet but rather its increase and improvement. Modern plumbing was implemented, air circulation increased, and sanitary conditions improved. Between 1995 and 2000, twenty new public toilets were built and seventeen refurbished in Beijing.[10]

Laporte equates the disposal of fecal matter and the deodorization of the city with the beautification of the Western city. These tropes of increased hygiene brought along with them the improved quality of air through even the simplest means of renovation. Openness and green space that increased circulation and sunlight overcame the dinginess, overcrowding, and filth of the narrow streets of the medieval city, as Lewis Mumford notes, and became a defining characteristic of the modern city.[11]

As a modern city, however, Beijing's air quality—measured by the air pollution index, or the API, established in 1998—is some of the most toxic in the world. Sulfur dioxide, nitrogen dioxide, and suspended particulate matter are measured on a scale ranging from zero micrograms of particular matter per cubic meter of air (mgr/m^3), or grade 1 (excellent), to 300+ mgr/m^3, or grade 5 (seriously polluted). On December 12, 2006, the API for Beijing exceeded 500 for over twenty-four hours—what one blogger said was the worst he had ever seen and what another said was the third day above 500 and the seventh above grade 5.[12] The *Insider's Guide* to Beijing warns that going outside during levels of 150 mgr/m^3 is dangerous. Australian and German governments see the critical level as being 50 mgr/m^3. These levels can be exceeded only 35 days per year in Germany and five days in Australia. In Beijing in 2006, 347 days exceeded 50 mgr/m3 of particulate matter, leaving roughly 20 healthy days.[13] On the days when the API reaches grade 2 or above, the air becomes increasingly milky and increasingly acrid, until it literally burns one's throat as if having smoked two or three packs of cigarettes.

Such poor air quality is the product of geography exacerbated by the rate of rapid expansion combined with pollution producing antiquated technologies. Located inland in the northeast corner of China, Beijing is characterized by an benefits for the vast majority of urban residents, it was also the institution through which the urban population was housed, organized, regulated, policed, educated, trained, protected, and surveyed....As the basic unit of urban society, each *danwei* became a community, provided its members with an identity, face and social belonging.[9]

Bray's thesis that the wall in China is a marker of social space, as well as a productive mechanism of a collective subjectivity and societal order (rather than solely symbol of a closed and xenophobic nation), argues for a unique socio-spatial paradigm.[10]

In the West, the paradigm of urban modernization is generally indebted to Georges-Eugène Haussmann's nineteenth-century plan for Paris and its ideology imbedded in the notion of a tabula rasa. Its imperative is often solely attributed to increased hygiene, air, and light in order to eradicate disease. Yet these effects were a result of a far greater overarching plan of increased communication and circulation that pervaded every aspect of the city, from the development of the modern sewer system to larger avenues that created visual and spatial axes connecting discrete points of the city in the most efficient way to the expansion of the railway network.[11] Such an objective was in line with Marx's prediction that increased values of exchange increased the physical conditions of exchange: the means of communication and transport.[12] Paris's plan precipitated the networked model of the city, where transfer points between demarcated or designated nodes of exchange increased circulation and thereby the economies of exchange, hygiene, transportation, and surveillance.

In Beijing, however, the paradigm was markedly different. The wall became the single most defining element of its spatial syntax. It not only represented the traditional Confucian order, marking and regulating the collective unit of the family and the imperial order of the city, but fostered the creation of a collective subject, first produced within the family compound and later aligned with the workplace and state. It produced behavioral patterns, where local patterns of inhabitation and circulation, precipitated within family compounds, were codified and reinforced through the rhythm, routine, and spatial form of the *danwei*.[13] Modern urban society thus emerged as a collection of *danwei*, or a collection of collectives. As Bray concludes, "This factor was to bestow a unique character upon the cities of China. The Chinese city was to develop more as a collection of self-contained and spatially defined communities than as an integrated urban network.[14]

Andreu's National Theatre in the form of a giant egg. CCTV is currently located west of the city, at the intersection of the Third Ring Road and Chang An Avenue, and will move toward the east, basically mirrored across the Forbidden City into the new Central Business District (CBD). CCTV is in the area of Beijing planners call a "dedicated community." The site of 20 hectares in the center of the city was made a tabula-rasa through the demolition of the derelict motorcycle factory located there. The only thing we had was this empty piece of ground and an image that was given to us at the time of the competition by the Beijing city planners: the vision of a vertical skyscraper city that was to be built in the next ten years. So we knew this was not only about CCTV but also about the skyscraper.

We wanted to ask ourselves at this point in time what could one do with building a skyscraper, and what has the skyscraper become? When it was created it incorporated and accommodated a vast amount of different urban programs, propelling city life and existing in density, crammed together in a small island; ultimately, it generated the city itself, as well as an intense life for the people inside the city. The skyscraper today is empty, a tool to create generic office space for undefined users and a tool for developers to maximize profits on a small piece of land. It lacks identity, and it looks the same from all sides, so what usually happens is that it gets stylistic additions, either flower-style, pagoda-style, or more modernist compositions on the top that try to compensate for its lack of development on the inside. When we started the project, it was also a time when, for the first time in history, Asia had more skyscrapers than the West, so this typology was clearly adopted as the triumphant symbol of its modernization. We wanted to imagine something different, to search for a form, a shape, a building, and a program that could re-engage space and the city.

CCTV is already one of the largest media organizations in the world today. It has fifteen self-produced channels, and, with the completion of the new building, it will be capable of broadcasting more than 250 channels. Television is actually younger in China than anywhere else in the world. The first broadcast was in 1958, the same year as the Ten Great Projects, so there was great momentum at that time. Obviously since then CCTV has developed rather quickly, and it is ready to take on the largest scale of any television company in the world. As the state broadcaster it is obviously also an organ that has been tightly connected to a political vision of information distribution or, in certain cases, information retention. The first live broadcast on Chinese television in 1998 was a sensitive

Jinli painting in red:
DEMOLITION AND RENOVATIONS HAVE FALSIFIED DOCUMENTS.... THE HOUSE IS OUTSIDE THE RED ZONE ... FORCING DEMOLITION AND DESTROYING A HARMONIOUS SOCIETY.

Zhang Jinli: *"Abuse of power crushes the common people."*

February 16, 2006: *"Bulldozer crushing building."*

Document 1006: *"Those being evicted are supposed to be settled first."*

Zhang Jinli: *"I understand government demolition and removal. But according to Mao, demolition and removal cannot violate legal rights of citizens. The government must protect the legal rights of citizens."*

February 27, 2006: The government tears down all banners and posters posted on outside walls.

March 14, 2006, 8:40 a.m.: Police arrive. Getting measurements of room that is contested.

Residents of Meishi Street # 117, statement read by police: *"Eviction to be carried out—formal reading of ruling forcibly relocated."*

March 14, 2006, 8:43–8:45 a.m.: Government packs Zhang Jinli's belongings onto a truck, which begins taking them away. Demolition begins with jackhammer in the restaurant. Zhang Jinli signs his name on inventory list, as instructed.

Tiantong Xiyuan Third District South, Changping District, Beijing, 2004
C-Print by Sze Tsung Leong.

公共流线
Loop

厨房
Kitchen

健身室
Gym

most significant and extensive urban transformations.

The tradition of authoritarian power that enabled the uniform construction and ordered layouts that once defined Chinese cities is also the tradition enabling their destruction. The rationale for the large-scale demolition of traditional urban fabrics is not so different from the goals expounded by the urban beautification movements in Europe and the United States. In Beijing, many traditional neighborhoods have been officially labeled as "dangerous" and "dilapidated." The decay of traditional neighborhoods is the result of an ideologically-driven reconfiguration of the original fabric. The Communist Party, in the early years of its new state, ordered traditional homes to be transformed from private family households to multifamily compounds. As a result, unregulated constructions and additions dismantled the architectural integrity of the homes and filled the courtyards with haphazard shanties. The decades of state-sponsored disdain of history during the Mao era effectively turned urban fabrics once symbolic of Chinese culture and society into slums.

In most cases, the demolition of traditional urban fabrics is total. With little or no historical encumbrances, new street patterns and buildings with uniform façades can be imposed on a blank slate. The rationale for this process is primarily economic. As in Haussmann's Paris, the new city gives an urban face to the new society, while driving out the poor from the city centers. The social order and its corresponding aesthetics is one based on giving an urban face to the new wealth, the departure from an uncomfortable past, and the pursuit of the new goals and requirements introduced by the market economy. The form that urban beautification takes in China is not the adjustment and modification of existing fabrics, but is most often the complete replacement of the past with the new. The urban beauty of the socially ordered, imperial past, decayed through ideological neglect, has become a casualty of a new form of beauty. To ask whether this new reality is beautiful or not is irrelevant. The more significant question is to whom does this beauty belong?

arid climate. Dust storms regularly blow in from the northwest, amplified by unrestricted use of land, deforestation, and loss of grassland cover. Summer provides approximately 70 percent of the annual rainfall, and the rate of annual precipitation has declined since the onset of rapid urbanization, particularly after 2002. In 2006 rainfall was below the yearly average of 600mm, and the dust was so bad that the clouds were at times seeded to produce rainfall.[14] The dust is compounded by the uninsulated *siheyuans* that lack central heat and are still reliant on coal, the continual construction at over 6,000 sites, and the pollution from cars, whose number increases by five to ten percent annually.[15]

To walk Beijing is to be subject to its stench. Mapping these areas reveals an antithetical corollary to Laporte's thesis: not areas of beautification but rather areas of impoverishment—the remaining pockets of *hutongs* to the north of the Forbidden City and to the southwest of Tiananmen Square—are rooted in the merging of a market economy with a socialist state. To be immersed in its milky-white air is to reveal an invisible yet pervasively present phenomenon of a culture of change.

1 Dominique Laporte, *History of Shit*, trans. Nadia Benabid and Rodolphe el-Khoury (Cambridge and London: The MIT Press, 1993). French edition originally published in 1978 under the title *Historie de la Merde*.

2 Ibid., 11,27.

3 Rodolphe el-Khoury, Introduction to Laporte, x-xi.

4 Laporte, 31.

5 David Bray. *Social Space and Governance in Urban China: The Danwei System from Origins to Reform*. (Stanford: Stanford University Press, 2005), 74.

6 Bray argues that the *siheyuan* does not create the private realm but institutes the individual as part of the collective whole.

7 Bray, 151.

8 Tim C. Geisler, "On Public Toilets in Beijing," *Journal of Architectural Education*, (2000), 216-219. Geisler notes that within the PRC the lavatory maintenance worker—representative of the overthrow of the bourgeoisie and the rise of the working class—were some of the most admired, publicly greeted, and heraled by Mao as model citizens.

9 As late as 2003 there were 3.18 communal toilets for every 10,000 citizens in Chinese cities, up from three per 10,000 in 1995.

10 Quoted from Zhang Yue, deputy director of urban construction department of Ministry of Construction, Beijing. *Peoples Daily Online*.

11 Bray, 44. Lewis Mumford, *The Culture of Cities* (San Diego, New York, and London: Harcourt Brace & Company, 1938), 428.

12 See http://www.danwei.org/beijing/baijing_air_pollution_off_the.php#comments.

13 Ibid. See also http://www.zhb.gov.cn/english/air-list.php3.

14 See http://www.china.org.cn/english/2006/Jul/176117.htm; http://www.cbc.ca/world/story/2006/04/18/china-cloud-seeding060418.html.

15 Because no infrastructure underlies these districts, the most efficient way of preservation means demolishing and rebuilding them exactly as they were, with modern facilities.

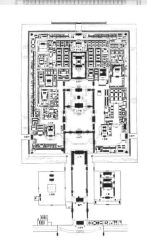

Plan of the Forbidden City.

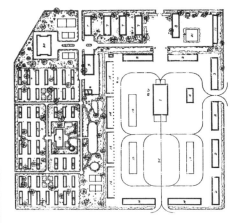

Plan of tractor repair station, Beijing.

In his tongue-and-cheek text titled *Programming,* Yung Ho Chang notes that the Chinese stack their dishes at meals, rather than serving them in courses like Westerners. The dishes pile up, accumulate, and elude practicality for expression in which stacking is a process that produces overlap.[15]

Beijing's historic city is largely being demolished: The center has shifted east, already symbolized by the China Central Television Headquarters, designed by OMA, located within the Central Building District. Chang An Avenue constitutes a major east-west artery that diffuses the north-south axiality of the Confucian order. Of the 6,000 *hutongs* comprising the historic city, approximately 450 or less remain, concentrated in the areas to the north of the Forbidden City and to the southwest of Tiananmen Square. The *siheyuan* that surround them reflect the overcrowding from the PRC—ad-hoc, accretive structures fills courtyards. Industrial structures and housing blocks of the post-1950s city are giving way to new construction, and, as of summer 2005, the last remaining communal housing block—one of two constructed from

political issue that might seem like a very small step. On the other hand, we remember what happened several years ago in the U.S. at the Superbowl when Justin did this thing to Janet and everybody was incredibly traumatized. We also know that now all live broadcasts like the Oscars are on a three-minute delay so that anything improper can be edited out. So the relevance of "live" is still an interesting subject. Also, while CCTV is a state broadcaster and receives subsidies from the state, the reality is that it is becoming separate. CCTV is making so much money from advertising revenue that what it pays in taxes is many times higher than the subsidies it receives, so actually CCTV is an entirely independent organization. Its revenues are so enormous that CCTV can pay for the entire building project in a single year.

The program brief contained a very crucial element: about one quarter of the building was to be dedicated to the public. While the current site is largely a gated and secured plot of land, cordoned off with barbed wire to prevent public access, in the future enormous parts of this project will be open to the public. The loop of circulation that we created for the staff and occupants is coupled with a second internal circulation route for the public and visitors. The public is admitted to the building and can follow a path that not only allows CCTV to introduce itself as a media organization, but reveals the production studios in the basement and all the different aspects of television production.

The new headquarters will integrate all the processes of television making into a single, nonhierarchical structure, in a continuous loop of 24-hour activity. The structure resembles a kind of living organism more than it does a classical building; it is not an empty generic container but rather a highly specific lifeform. It proposes solidarity instead of isolation, collaboration instead of opposition—a structure in which the brains know what the hands are doing and vice versa. Along this loop a multitude of cultural and communal spaces are positioned throughout the building, meeting spaces where people can gather from different departments and exchange information. The top of the building is not occupied by the senior management but is instead a staff forum accessible to all workers. The scale of the building exceeds many previously witnessed situations: there will be 10,000 permanent staff and several thousand visitors coming and going every day. There is really a sense that the building might be closer to a collective than a pure accommodation. This sense of the collective might also formulate an interesting alternative to many of the things that architecture produces today.

The main lobby has to process around

演播室
800/2000 Studio

播送区
Broadcasting

入口大堂
Entrance Lobby

PROPERTY LINE

Background Image:
China Central Television Headquarters (CCTV), Plan of Plinth
by OMA/Rem Koolhaas and Ole Scheeren

the leftover stones from the People's Hall—was slated for demolition.

Like the dishes on the table, Beijing's urbanism emerges not as tabula rasa but an ad-hoc accummulation of new construction stacked, overlapped, and radiating out in a set of complex spatial relationships that bear the birthmarks of its socio-spatial past. A collection of self-contained and spatially defined communities rather than an integrated urban network of circulation still characterizes the city, from the new-gated housing communities on the outskirts of the city to the repetitive housing complexes that vertically echo the grid-like pattern of the horizontal city to the skyscraper that absorbs the city into the building to the striated spatial structure of the avenues.

To walk Beijing is to notice that everything is walled: construction sites, new housing blocks, the Imperial City. The materiality of these walls varies, from fifty-foot-high steel placards to red-and-grey brick to improvised cinder-block constructions to looped white fences that line every sidewalk, street, parking lot, and Tiananmen Square. In each case, walls cordon off, limit the view, and control and direct movement.

Within the China World Hotel—the first building to be constructed in the Central Business District—one can finds the city: a hotel extends seemingly ad infinitum from high-end restaurants and bars in the lobby to clinic, gym, and massage parlor downstairs to designer shopping and Starbucks, to grocery store, to lingerie displays, ice-skating rink, a Subway sandwich shop, and so on. Riken Yamamoto's Jian Wei SOHO exists as one of the few non-gated communities. Turned thirty degrees off the cardinal grid, here workplace, commerce, and daily life overlap on all levels of its thirty towers. "Streets" nine meters wide weave through its multiple layers. Advertisements, signage, and curtains appear on all floors of the façade, deneutralizing the white, modernist grid, aged and graying after one year.

Forms of collective practice and signs of a new China are emerging. The Olympic structures are sited north of the Forbidden City, extending the imperial axis. CCTV proposes a kind of contemporary *danwei*. The program integrates administration, program and news production, VIP and actors' lounges, canteens, gym, and other services. CCTV bears in the planimetric form of its plinth a resemblance (albeit unintentional) to the modular socio-spatial structure of Beijing's Confucian and socialist past. As a centralized headquarters in which the form of a loop breaks down traditional hierarchies and integrates all the aspects of television making, it encourages a

14,000 people everyday, so it cannot be organized like a typical lobby. There are continuous plates on the ground, where people will enter from the ceremonial plaza. The lobby is located on three levels, with direct links to the parking deck on B1 and with a direct connection to the subway currently under construction on B3. The planning of the elevator systems was close to that of a subway network, in which there are trains of different lengths. We have single elevators, but we also have double-deck elevators that travel through the building to save space and maximize consumption of the floor-plate area. This, in combination with shuttles and sky lobbies, forms a complex system of circulation that makes all parts of the building accessible very quickly. At the top of the building, the 70-meter cantilever contains a 160-meter-high viewing deck that gives spectacular views across the city. At this scale, architecture really takes on the character of infrastructure.

Since the groundbreaking on September 22, 2004, the construction has continued on schedule. The foundations are complete, 1260 piles for CCTV are in the ground, and TVCC has fully completed foundations and is slowly growing upwards. When we started the project in 2002, Beijing had just been awarded the 2008 Olympic Games, and this has now become a deadline—for the city and possibly for the entire country, as well as for architects and builders—to implement a process of change.

Tussle from *The Cosplayers*, 2005
by Cao Fei

This video still captures teenagers in full costume enacting a Japanese comic using urban constructions within the city of Guangzhou as the stage set. A deserted roadbed, which floods every time it rains, becomes the "lake." Teenagers text to organize and stage the performance within the city.

brocade. The vehicles are worshipped at home, not as carts on which to fly through the streets but as obsolete sacrifices.

With the rise of the Internet, our world is now divided into the online and the offline. Da Zha Lan is a city offline. It abides by its own time and its own logic of survival.

The Da Zha Lan area is located outside the southwest corner of Tiananmen Square, bounded by Qianmen Avenue to the east, Nan Xinhua Street to the west, Zhushikou Xi Avenue to the south, and Qianmen Xi Avenue to the north. The typical layout of diagonal streets in this area was formed naturally, as people traveled in between the new and old capitals after the Middle Capital of Jin was destroyed and the Main Capital of Yuan was rebuilt. Unlike the neat and orderly design of hutongs in the Inner City, Da Zha Lan has a freely developed grass-roots style suitable for the outer part of the city and bears witness to its long history.

From the Ming Dynasty (1368-1644) through the Qing Dynasty (1644-1911) to the Nationalist Government and to post-Liberation, Da Zha Lan has always been the commercial center of Beijing. A great number of established shops and brands have existed here for hundreds of years. Transitions from Chinese handicraft industry to capitalist fair trade to socialist market economy can be seen as the paradigm for Chinese commercial culture.

As the city keeps expanding toward the suburbs, the infrastructure in such an old city center as Da Zha Lan remains underdeveloped. The cap on the height of architecture in this region has prohibited property developers from construction; it's impossible to trade second-hand houses. As a result, the elite class continues to move outward, and the risk of the area being vacant runs high; a great number of low-income immigrants move in from other places. Impoverishments and degenerations in this region are beginning to reveal themselves.

Although situated in the heart of Beijing, Da Zha Lan has a reputation today as one of the city's slum neighborhoods, owing to the rundown condition of its homes, poor public facilities, and high concentration of low-income workers from outside the city. The government's relocation effort is focused on commercially revitalizing this valuable stretch of property by renewing and reshuffling the neighborhood. All local governments in China regard urban poverty as a shameful mark that must be cleared out of sight of the city. Da Zha Lan's history of migration and habitation by the poor parallels the history of Beijing.

National Swimming Stadium, May 2006
by PTW.

National Olympic Stadium, May 2006
by Herzog and De Meuron.

CCTV, August 2, 2007.
by OMA / Rem Koolhaas and Ole Scheeren.

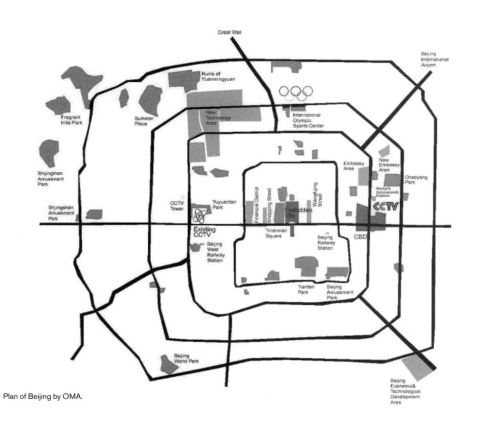

Plan of Beijing by OMA.

method of work that is more "communal and collective than atomized."[16] Taking on the scale of small city within the city, the loop absorbs the pedestrian street, introducing spectacle, increased transparency, and the potential for an individual and collective subject to emerge.[17]

To walk Beijing is to realize that its scale is too vast, the air quality too poor for the pedestrian. Movement is simultaneously chaotic from sheer numbers, controlled and directed. Local patterns of inhabitation still predominate, reinforced by continual and increasing traffic, fostered by digital connectivity and the city within the building.

1 David Bray. *Social Space and Governance in Urban China: The* Danwei *System from Origins to Reform.* (Stanford: Stanford University Press, 2005). This essay is largely indebted to Bray's study.

2 "The Rites of Zhou" specified that the imperial capital should be set out as "'a square with sides of nine *li*, each side having three gateways. There were nine meridional and nine latitudinal avenues, each of the former being nine tracks in width.' The emperor's palace was sited at the heart of the gird, facing south and approached by a long ceremonial avenue from the central gate in the southern wall." Bray, 22.

3 See http://www.urbanchina.org

4 "The term for street intersection reveals the traditional conception of the Chinese street as delineated rather than infinite space. Streets are seen not as abstract lines in space but as inhabitable rooms bounded between two mouths, or entrances." Sylvia Wallis, 'A Brief Lexicon of Chinese Urbanism, 2003," *32: Beijing New York*, issue 4 (2004), 17.

5 The square Chinese table takes on the same configuration, reflecting the hierarchical order of the Confucian family. See Yung Ho Chang, "Programming: II Dining Tables," *32: New York Beijing*, issue 2 (2003), 6.

6 See, for example, Ai Wei Wei's designs.

7 Bray, 34.

8 "Through its communal style of organization, the social condenser was intended to replace the family as the basic unit of society. Hence, ...workers were to sleep in dormitories, eat in collective canteens, socialize in public recreation areas, and attend lectures and discussion groups in communal meeting halls. [Here] the functions of the factory, workers' club, and communal house were unified in one spatial form of super collectivity." See Bray, 86.

9 Bray, 123–156.

10 See Bray, 124–5: "The predominance of walled spaces within societal China . . . is not indicative of a certain cultural closure of xenophobia . . . but rather shows the way in which modern social formations have redeployed an old architectural technique."

11 David Harvey, *Paris, Capital of Modernity.* (New York and Oxford: Routledge, 2006). See, in particular, 107–116.

12 Harvey, 207. See also Bray, 73–75.

13 Bray, 147.

14 Bray, 157.

15 Ole Scheeren, "Made in China" lecture, Shanghai, September 2005.

16 CCTV has provoked much controversy, the discussion of which is beyond this essay's scope.

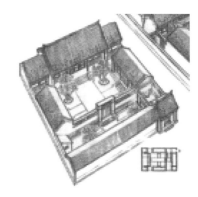

1 Left: Plan of Beijing showing remaining *hutongs;* right: typical *siheyuan.*

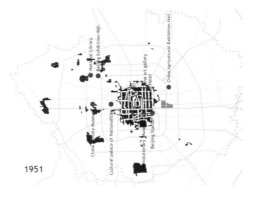

2 Left: Ten Great Projects; right: Great Hall of the People.

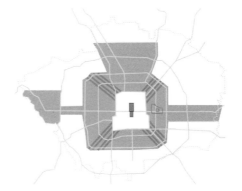

3 Left: Development 1970s-80s; right: Socialist slab housing.

4 Left: Recent urban development; right: Jian Wei SOHO.

Where Subversion Is Normal

Srdjan Jovanovic Weiss

National Bank of Serbia.

Almost thirty years after the death of Tito—and half as little time after Milošević's failed quasi-Titoistic rise to power—Serbian nationalism, Balkan wars, and severe tragedies and crimes emerged, and the territorial and political influence of Belgrade shrank from the city, once the main southern Eastern European capital and now only one of several resurfacing capitals of the recently and curiously named Western Balkan Territory.[1] This dynamic territory now is a political purgatory hoping to join the European Union. As a result, a network of Balkanized cities has emerged, casting new light over the shadow of crisis. They include new capitals—Ljubljana, Zagreb, Sarajevo, Skopje, Podgorica—and potential new capitals (Priština and Novi Sad), as well a booming capital outside of Tito's direct legacy, Tirana. All together, they represent the new network of cities that lack the qualities of a capital. As such, they strive individually to acquire them through different means in each case.

Different roles for these cities are taken on a first-come, first-serve basis. While Zagreb, capital of Croatia, does everything it can to solidify independent, creative, and critical action in the current government, Tirana in Albania has a higher GDP than Bosnia as well as an inventive architecture it promotes to progressive Dutch design firms; Belgrade has now become known as "Sin City" in the sphere of the spatial practice still reminiscent of cultural tourism. Dušan Grlja, one of the editors of the Belgrade critical theory journal *Prelom*, describes how people view this city as "some kind of carnival-like place: loud and flashy crowds of good-looking people swinging in a haze of tobacco and alcohol fumes; nightlife on river boats, spiced with the smell of grilled meat, where turbo-folk music meets deep electro, and gypsy brass bands play alongside hard-rock groups; a whole street crammed with bars, one after another called "Silicone Valley," due to the amount of plastic surgery implants that you can see on the women there; clubs, beer joints, street cafes, city squares—all saturated with a wild, almost manic and erotically charged atmosphere."[2]

1 Western Balkans is the cluster of Ex-Yugoslav states, excluding Slovenia and including Albania. Albania, Bosnia, Croatia, Macedonia, Montenegro, Serbia and Kosovo together constitute the Western Balkan region.

2 Dušan Grlja, "Sin-City Belgrade," published in *Lost Highway Expedition* reader, edited by School of Missing Studies and Centrala Foundation for Future Cities, (Ljubljana: ŠKUC, 2006).

The description goes on to further speculate that the image of the city we see is not accidental, nor informal, but that this image of the Sin City represents a good part of the official tourist attraction.

True enough, *The New York Times* in its "Travel" section, which usually presents the world as a beauty to a waking metropolitan mankind ready to fly anywhere, writes "Belgrade Rocks" and depicts the city as a destination for nightlife, drinking, partying, and having fun with the following rational:

> This night, with Mr. Milošević on trial in The Hague and Belgrade's doors open to the West, it's only the lights from [an] open-air dance floor that flash in the night sky. The club's thudding sound system, not bombs, sends ripples through the river.[3]

Or take this travel report from the same section, written in 2002, that gives another chilling but similarly related rationale:

> Visiting Belgrade is an especially strange experience for an American. Before Sept. 11, Serbians liked to point out the five or so NATO-bombed buildings in the city center and ask Americans, with more curiosity than hostility, "Why did you bomb us?" During a brief visit . . . . the comments I heard were more along the lines of "Now you understand."[4]

Common sense may say that there should be no place for worry because "any publicity is good publicity," and therefore the promoter, *The New York Times,* is by default on the winning side of the geo-political struggle and even helps Belgrade to capitalize on what it has and what it lacks. This means two things: first, Belgrade as a city has something that a New York as a metropolis lacks; second, Belgrade can save New York itself from the serious deficit of not being able to "rock" that hard.

An unrelated but simultaneous line of thinking is promoted by the presence of the foremost Dutch architecture messiah, Rem Koolhaas, who visited Belgrade for the first time in 2003.[5] At a four-hour brainstorming session organized by the Serbian Ministry of Culture on how to improve Serbian identity, he said to the hungry audience that Belgrade should not try to be a B or C version of a Western European capital; rather, Belgrade should capitalize exactly on its preeminent ability to

lower [urban] standards and offer this knowledge as a service to places that have higher standards than are necessary.

Thus, if we want to look at Belgrade's contribution to the creative subversion of inflated standards, first we need to point out the confident optimism that Tito had generated and left as his heritage to urban planners and architects. Then we must register the contrasting dearth of engagement in the public realm of the politics of Slobodan Milošević. Between the two, what happened? How did the culture of optimistic urbanism, which built new cities for the national liberators, become the culture of evasive and creative politics of violation and the solidification of temporality?

Tito passed away in the early 1980s. His grave is a white minimalist box planted in the central space of the so-called House of Flowers, built in the posh district of Belgrade where most influential figures, like Tito before, acquired urban villas and led socialist, aristocratic lives. Nearby is a modernist museum dedicated to the date of Tito's birth, May 25, holding a collection of gifts, as well as his personal collection of suits, including his wigs. Originally a must-see site visit for all schoolchildren and workers in 1960s and 1970s socialist Yugoslavia, the museum now hosts temporary fashion shows and contemporary art exhibitions.[6]

Although Tito opened spatial practice to new challenges of building cities like New Belgrade and New Zagreb, which were constructed mainly to house the partisan liberators, his true achievement was the success of capitalizing on the special political situation of Yugoslavia, which stood outside of both West and East. His leadership in creating the movement of Non-Aligned countries made a global impact on Serbian architects and engineers, hungry for commissions opening in Africa, South America, and especially in the Middle East.

In fact, both Serbian and Croatian architects and engineers followed Tito's paved road to the world of new commissions in the Third World. Including works from only Eastern-bloc countries, the expertise was often exported to the Middle East, especially in Iraq during the 1970s and 1980s. The full-color catalogue of Belgrade-based Energoprojekt, the socialist version of a Skidmore, Owings & Merrill corporate architecture firm, proudly presents projects like Al Khulafa Street Development, built from 1981 to 1983 and the Presidential Palace Complex, both built in Baghdad. With these designs that combined a late modernist cor-

porate style with a twist toward a fictional or Orientalist style, the Energoprojekt architects paved the way for other infrastructure projects—the underground bunkers and hideouts were not included in the catalogue — which were soon to be invaded by the U.S.[7]

Energoprojekt is the sole phenomenon that could house architectural talent created with the formula of expertise in heavy industry multiplied by a design-savvy corps, tailored for undeveloped societies that had basic infrastructure needs, but which, thanks to Tito and the Non-Aligned Movement, exceeded expectations, even with just the basics. A few conditions in former Yugoslavia made this a good working method, the main one being that the Energoprojekt model offered a solution to the difficulty of running private architectural offices within the Yugoslav communist system, which did not allow for private businesses such as architectural firms. Socialist corporations like Energoprojekt provided a cushion for practitioners by employing most everyone who proved talented during their studies and guaranteeing a safe stream of institutional commissions. This effectively abolished the need for some of the best Serbian architects to have a private office and avoided the resulting obligation to bow to a systematic course of architectural catering to the outside, like the Non-Aligned countries, in the great need of both technical and conceptual expertise.

The most productive architects who worked in this system are the couple Ljiljana and Dragomir Bakić. After finishing their architectural degree at the Faculty of Architecture, University of Belgrade, they first worked with Alvar Aalto in Finland and then earned collective employment at Energoprojekt back in Belgrade. Soon after, they were funded to travel to the Middle East and observe the new opportunities that were developing for the young, talented Yugoslovian architects who could provide what the West could never realize in Third World countries: generosity in design expertise and technical guidance for much less money. Thanks to Tito's logic of institutionalizing the impossible, the Bakićs had an open field laid out in front of them to design some of the most prominent structures in Nigeria and Zimbabwe. The couple even moved their office and residence to Harare during the 1990s but decided to abandon it when nationalism rose both in Zimbabwe even as it was culminating in Serbia.

Bakić architects were exactly what a state apparatus needed to simulate a status

3 Seith Sherwood, "Belgrade Rocks," New York Times, (October 16, 2005).

4 Neil Strauss, "Belgrade Relishes Life at Peace," New York Times, (February 24, 2002).

5 "World Famous Architect Rem Koolhaas in Belgrade," (November 27, 2003), http://www.arhiva.serbia.sr.gov.yu/news/2003-11/27/332112.html.

6 More information on the House of Flowers and the Museum of the 25th of May can be found on B92 Travel section: http://www.b92.net/eng/travel/index.

7 The company's web site reveals more information on its history and current activities: http://www.energoprojekt.co.yu/english/index_eng.htm.

equivalent to an architectural practice in socialist Yugoslavia vis-à-vis European or American modernism. But it was not all that the field of architecture needed from the state, which only promoted its products as a business to the Non-Aligned Movement of countries and ignored Western Europe and the Anglo-Saxon critical world of contempt. For example, in Kenneth Frampton's influential history of the modernist movement in architecture, there are no mentions of Yugoslav practice other than to point out its deprivations and conservative nature shown by the works by Josip Plecnik, a Wagnerian pupil, who was well-to-do in his native Slovenia; there were no mentions of visionaries like Nikola Dobrović, who built in Prague, Belgrade, and Dubrovnik in his highly original style, influenced by the philosophy of Henri Bergson; nor of Milan Zloković, a bourgeois who was the most creative in introducing early European modernism to the Belgrade urban landscape. Therefore, the couple Bakić can be seen as one of the first architects to be accepted and supported by the interior system who did not rely on the exterior critique. Because of that, possibly the exterior critical view did not register their achievement. They were well educated and with the best intentions; however, they suffered from a lack of critical history and theory of architecture in Serbia that would have strengthened their critical position in shaping new architectural visions in tandem with the might of Tito's masterfully created state, wielding international influence and domestic satisfaction through enhanced self-esteem.[8]

In short, the generation led by Bakićs had it all, with all the optimisms of the construction industry as the main carrier of the special socialist message. However, they could not rely on First World recognition of these efforts because, among other things and as paradoxical as it may sound, their effort was locally too pure to be accepted as globally true.

Why? That international social goodness was of course deviant by default because Tito's Non-Aligned Movement reached where neither American/English nor Russian influence could go so easily: Middle East, Africa, South America. How could anyone, even of the caliber of Charles Jencks or Kenneth Frampton, not to mention Bruno Zevi or even utopian Doxiadis, ever swallow Yugoslav infrastructural commissions in Libya with Gaddafi, in Iraq with the early regime of Saddam Hussein, or the architectural solidification of shady

business in Zimbabwe through one of the most cruel and most entrenched dictators, Robert Mugabe?

How could leftist theory on the rise at the time ever absolve Yugoslav engineering contracts for Iraqi and Egyptian atomic shelters and works in Saudi Arabia, and so on?

In their early careers, Bakić architects traveled first to Finland to work with Alvar Aalto in his later years but also traveled to Kuwait and the Middle East for an expedition equaling Aldo Van Eyck's African travels. They came back with similar energy to present their findings of different kinds of habitation to the late-modern architectural audience of the time. Bakić's sponsor and employer, Energoprojekt, was still there to create new jobs but did not see its mission as a publisher of research after all the trips that Yugoslav officials had made during Tito's best years; rather, the most influential socialist corporation believed its goal to be solidifying the infrastructure of the Third World, not to theorize about it. The lack of theorization of this gathered knowledge is responsible for the lack of general cultural knowledge of one of the most sincere engineering operations taking place at the time of the 1968 uprising in Western Europe.

Tito allegedly knew that promoting the Yugoslav architectural model in building new cities was of lower importance than spreading the word about the new socialist experiment in self-management and self-organization as a method, not as a result. Perhaps the reason why Tito's political structures did not fully support Bakić architects or their Croatian, Bosnian, and Slovenian counterparts is that his project was still the territorial one of establishing Yugoslavian identity through existing difference, not constructing sameness through architecture.

Energoprojekt was a solid guarantor for all projects that opened up in the geo-political territories where the United States and the USSR could not show their faces unharmed. At the same time, its strength masked the need for an independent architectural or urban practice that could develop autonomously and keep its portfolio intact and separate from political projects. In a way, as much as Energoprojekt empowered Serbian talents like the Bakićs to build, it did them a great disservice, because no autonomous architectural practice in a socialist state could be counted globally as a meaningful and critical one. Take the example of Oscar Niemeyer, who had all the benefits of the socialist state and could build for

Kubitchek and Brasília but moved to France to develop as a solo architect, eventually designing and building with few restraints for the leftist circles in power.

In stark opposition, we can now look at Slobodan Milošević, whose impromptu grave was arranged in the garden of his family house in Požarevac, a depressed Serbian town. If Tito never cared for roots and worked progressively to seduce the masses so that he could lie within their territorial space in such posh surroundings as Dedinje of Belgrade, Milošević opted for the come-back-home sanctuary, to be buried in the garden, below a family tree. This ground-loving enterprise, not that different from other nationalist leaders of the past who end up coming back to their own backyard as a viable space for contemplation, is telling of Milošević's role in the spatial practice of the former Yugoslavia.

His deep entanglement in the overall crisis of the Balkans can be seen in the way he held back the development of cities in each nation so that the anachronistic former official socialist urban planning schemes were weakened enough to be conveniently violated, meaning that any action in the city to fill this void was subversive by default, not by choice. As a result, subversions of this dying system came from self-organized populists, nationalists, and the emerging entrepreneurial class, which was the strongest in its will to capitalize on violating (and mocking) the loss of socialist and communist values in urbanism and architecture. Because these various entities joined forces to build more than a socialist city could ever do, Belgrade's main contribution to global subversion of planning is the production of a wide diversity of evasive interpretations of zoning, specifically in creative violation of architectural typologies.

This also made it possible for Energoprojekt to continue to accept commissions from the Middle East without ethical qualms. One such commission was with the military in Iraq for what became the representative architecture of the early part of Saddam Hussein's regime. The money was too good to be rejected, and it confirmed the business speculation that the Third World can act and build things on its own; further, the Third World can complete business transactions despite their being propelled by the economy of sinning, including prisons and palaces built on war profiteering and blood money.

Additionally, in the sphere of influence, a few other things have changed since Tito's

8 This missing history has recently been partially filled by a book by Ljilljana Blagojevic, *Elusive Margins of Belgrade Architecture 1919-1941.* (Cambridge: MIT Press, 2003).

"The man without passion," as Slobodan Milošević was called throughout the Balkan crisis by international journalists, did not choose to build Belgrade.

Non-Alignment Movement policies. Specifically, as Eyal Weizman has noted, Milošević's power never fossilized into architectural monuments or ceremonial urban schemes because the scale of his spatial politics was not the urban but the territorial. This politics was mainly concerned with carving out, expanding, and cleansing a Serbian national space. Indeed, all throughout the Yugoslav secession wars, the city of Belgrade, where the Milošević government was located and where it was bombed into submission by NATO in 1999, was firmly held by his (far too acquiescent) political opposition. Milošević's nationalist rhetoric celebrated an ideal countryside of Serb villages and the traditional values he believed they embodied; his spatial politics was exemplified by liberating latent psychic forces beyond the capability to harness and control them. The Bosnian countryside, a familiar European mountain landscape, littered with burnt-out and deserted hillside villages, and Sarajevo, a multi-ethnic city systematically destroyed by forces composed mainly of the rural population that surrounded it, are the material vestiges of an ideology that brings rural and urban into violent confrontation. Balkanization, as this phenomenon has come to be known, is thus a spatial-political concept, endowing fundamental social notions of conflict and enmity with spatial processes of territorial fragmentation and the shattering of social space into a multiplicity of enclaves that are internally homogenous and externally hostile to each other. The process of national fragmentation has unleashed as well a new class of shady, close-to-power real-estate entrepreneurs and their emergent populist architectural styles, a substitute for the official architecture and urbanism.

"The man without passion," as Slobodan Milošević was called throughout the Balkan crisis by international journalists, did not choose to build Belgrade.[9] For better or worse, he lost the chance to solidify his era of power in the architecture of his capital. There are no grand urban proposals to be found, no government buildings, no new cities, and no style that is identifiably "his" akin to the stripped-down neo-classical architecture of Stalin or Ceausescu in their origins of ideological and national power. Among his peers, Milošević is closest to his political soulmate and Iraqi ally Hussein,

earning the nickname "Serbian Saddam." Still, in spite of what many believed was quite a complimentary nickname, no palaces nor treasures like Saddam's are to be found.

With regard to architecture and Belgrade, Milošević could have done much better with his considerable power. Instead, when he gained control, he was known for blocking Tito's immense modernist axis spanning the width of New Belgrade. The axis that Tito planned to be a monumental free space for the workers, Milošević filled in with layers of military flats, shopping malls, and corrupt construction ventures. After the NATO bombing in 1999, Milošević's promotional drive to "reconstruct" the country (mimicking Tito's campaign after WWII) preferred spending state money on memorial plaques inscribed with his name, rather than on infrastructure. Still, of the few commissions Milošević ordered, only two materialized that we can call complete.

His first was a 1994 subway station for a war-immersed capital that did not even have a subway system. The analogy is extended: the station without a subway system is named "Vuk Karadžić," for the founder of modern Serbian, a language without a nation. The station's design acts as a double necropolis deep below the surface of the street, the only remains of the scrapped subway system and a foreshadowing of Milošević's larger failures to come. His second building project, a monument said to commemorate the "victory of Serbia over NATO," was erected in 2000, one year after the NATO victory over Serbia. Not only did the oxymoronic "Victor" display spelling errors on the plaque condemning the Western powers of crimes against Serbia, its white concrete lantern, containing an "eternal light" powered by electricity, was built at a third of its projected size in a stripped-down, neo-Stalinist style. The monument was quickly judged as debased as Milošević's own political rating: the eternal light was switched off with the popular uprising of October 5, 2000, and the lantern became a graffiti-plastered fixture in the park that Tito first laid out during the optimistic age of political nonalignment with neither the West or the East. An exception to this rule is Milošević's allowance to continue an epic construction of the National Bank of Serbia, following the plans from the 1970s. As with his

other two projects, the National Bank was being built contrary to common sense. During its construction, Milošević's Yugoslavia suffered one of the biggest inflations in the history of economy.

It is no wonder that intellectuals today in Belgrade see the "architect" Milošević in the same light as Fidel Castro of Cuba: preferring architectural self-castration in order to capitalize on political and policing power. Milošević may have learned from Castro, however his ultimate failure can be read as the reverse of Castro's successful hold on power. Castro was in fact Tito's, not Milošević's, ally. The lessons that Milošević missed were the dictator's credo. One: If you promise the future of the glorious past, you will have to build it to last. If you promise the glorious future alone, you do not have to do anything. Two: Never emulate your father (Tito) unless there is a biological connection.

In spite of the continued weakening of his ideology, Milošević was the most powerful politician in the Balkans. His disinterest in architecture opened a void for sources to flood in other than the top-down directives, enabling a sort of open-source, national-socialist anarchy, which, curiously, he knew how to navigate. His power was wielded not by public reappearance but by a steady flow of absence. The less Milošević spoke, the more he maintained control over the public.

In fact, the less Milošević built, the wider the gap opened for uncontrolled construction. The result is a dearth in the public realm; aspirations of the city are nowhere to be found, but its space is thickened like an oversized village. In spite of the political and economic isolation during the last fifteen years as well as lost wars with Slovenia, Croatia, Bosnia, and (with the world) over Kosovo, Belgrade has witnessed an explosion of construction. The estimates are that as many as 150,000 houses and buildings were built in Belgrade in the last decade and between 800,000 and 1,000,000 in all of Serbia. The quantity that evolved during this short time—twenty-eight buildings built per day on average for fifteen years—amounts to a brief, rapid history of a national architecture in the making. The intellectual elite, in opposition to Milošević, hated this architecture and in vain called for its removal. The

9 Misha Glenny, *The Fall of Yugoslavia: The Third Balkan War,* Penguin 1996.

Slobodan Milošević and Mirjana Marković, Eternal Fire.

main reason for such disdain was not so much its trashy postmodern appearance, a march of symbolic and empty rhetorical shapes, but the link of illegal construction to war and criminal activity that also gave birth to dominant cultural forms of not only how to violate the norms, but also how to normalize the violations, how to make it all business as usual.

Therefore, we are left with four dominant subversions in building that work within Milošević's isolating and passionless system. Each is an expression of a political opposition to the systematically emptied socialism of Tito. The first type is the bastard child of a glitzy-corporate and folk-nationalist architecture identified in the following text as "Turbo Architecture," sponsored by neo-liberal movements coming out of deteriorated socialist age.

Second is the vertical expansion of temporary structures subversively grabbing for air space that are identified as "Mushroom Houses." These were enabled by the immigration policies of the Serbian Radical Party, the most extreme nationalist movement that supported the relocation of Serbian minorities into the heart of Serbia proper. Third are out of proportion additions registered as the radical preservation of postwar modernism identified as "Housing Upgrades" and supported by a mix of entrepreneurial neo-liberals subscribing to the centrist Democratic Party, local moderate nationalists, and the remaining mafia, which target the young generation who are moving from out of town to the city to study. And last is the pixelated "Neo-Orthodox Landscape," made up of single standing shrines, churches, and portable miniature churches, built as con-

temporary copies of Byzantine iconic architecture. These forms are supported both by the emerging extreme right-wing parties and royalist movements and explained away by the official government structures as a normal shift in ideology.

1. Turbo Architecture

Milošević's deceptive absence and lack of clear vision resulted in an alibi for an army of self-appointed saviors of lost values from the Serbian past acting in the city. Middle-aged architects, the frustrated generation that came second after Tito's first and most privileged generation to build the communist city of New Belgrade, saw their chance to act. As Milošević bowed to popular participation in policy-making, which had been Tito's main taboo, architectural production derived from the taste of

TV Pink Studios.

newly composed folk music or simply neo-folk, which arose in villages and the suburbs as a substitute for authentic traditional values. Coincidentally, the first Neo-Folk building was constructed in the center of Belgrade in 1989, the year Milošević won elections in Serbia.

As a deviation of Neo-Folk from the late socialist times after 1989 into the times of wars and isolation, Turbo Folk was born from the immense copyright-free collision of traditional and contemporary music forms. It also served as a basis for Turbo Culture and other trends including crime, nationalism, and fashion. Finally, Turbo Architecture was Turbo's last and most concrete form. In fact, Turbo has neither a negative nor positive meaning; neither value judgments nor volition are ascribed to it. "Turbo" is inherently a neutral term. Turbo depends on the context; it is fed by the existing circumstances to push just beyond limitations.

In Serbia, under the oil embargo in an economy under sanctions and going backward, Turbo marked accelerated decline and a perverse speeding up toward the approaching crash.

The most contested example of Turbo architecture is the building of TV Pink Studios, the very place where Turbo Folk was produced and disseminated on the air to the public. The controversial station started in the early 1990s allegedly under the control of Milošević's wife, Mirjana Marković, broadcasting pirate editions of feature movies and pornography. The building's form is a direct interpretation of the complexities of both Turbo culture and the television medium in the changing politics of Serbia, it is indirectly Milošević's unclaimed architectural baby. TV Pink arose from a collision of disparate sources, yet it was rendered monolithically, wrapped in aluminum and reflective glass foil. Turbo architecture is

at its peak here, employing many elements of Byzantine style that allude to this past, yet rendered in steel, aluminum, and glass materials that belong to a high-tech look. The dome is a semicircular tower cut at the top to resemble the typical hat worn in Serbia during World War I. Although it was built without official paperwork on the outskirts of Belgrade in the vicinity of Milošević's house, this building became a dominant cultural force in the mainstream.

Milošević looked away as Turbo architecture became a dominant force to make up for the loss of a national identity. As with Turbo Folk music, the mechanism of this populist folk engine felt right for the situation because of its power to substitute for the actual world and authentic tradition. This is best demonstrated weeks after the NATO bombing of Belgrade in late spring 1999. Milošević saw his opportunity

The mushroom strategy is simple, cunning, self-organized, and wild. The typical mushroom builder is displaced and desperate.

to become a builder by reconstructing the country like Tito after World War II. He went about this in his particular way: by pushing someone else to do what needed to be done and shielding himself from criticism. In a somber, brown interior of a TV studio adapted to look like an office, a group of architects and planners presented drawings and computer renderings related to reconstruction that one could see day after day on the news. This is the peak of Milošević's transfer from political action into planning and the sheer exploitation of two of the most effective tools in the Balkans: deception and demagoguery, two shared main characteristics of Turbo architecture.

After Milošević's arrest and transfer to The Hague, the very same Turbo architecture that had become so controversial was promoted as a new national style at the 2002 Venice Architecture Biennial. The official Serbian selectors projected national pride at withstanding the destruction of NATO, which was incredibly small for Vukovar, by promoting a catalogue of buildings erected during Milošević's reign as a proof of endurance. The book itself has a front and back cover made of aluminum, like a bulletproof vest, and outfitted with the trace of a half-penetrated bullet. Further, its protective sleeves were cast in light concrete to appear like a concrete block, a sign of continuing desire for construction, in spite of the "West, who wanted to destroy Serbia." This armored catalogue reveals and embodies Milošević's urban legacy, which is devoid of passion and leaves behind a sense of crude pathos.

It was not until the somber days following the assassination of Zoran Djindjić, on March 12, 2003, two years after Milošević's handover to The Hague tribunal, that an official attack on Turbo was unleashed and made real. On March 13, the wounded democratic powers of Serbia dispatched a destruction squad to remove a building that belonged to one of the men accused of the murder. The building that was to be leveled looked like a mix of new romantic architecture with high-tech elements. In other words, it was a prime example of Turbo architecture in Serbia: a fanciful, stone-clad, bold four-story shopping center. All Serbian television channels aired live coverage of the pained efforts to destroy the building under duress. Although there were no apparent or recorded connections between Milošević and these criminal killers ensconced in the production of Turbo Folk, these images of clearing away the remains of heavy-duty Turbo architecture were

seen as an optimistic cleansing of the traces of Milošević's negligence and undoing of the city.

2. Mushroom House

Now take the example of the Mushroom House, a tiny, subversive housing type that proliferated throughout Belgrade during the crisis of the 1990s. We can be thankful to Milošević for this architectural gift, even though he did not plan for it. When he won wide nationalist support in Serbia and started to engage in the wars in Croatia in 1991 and in Bosnia in 1992, the United Nations imposed sanctions on Serbia. The following period of time was marked by one of the highest rates of hyperinflation ever: in January 1994, prices rose approximately 62 percent per day. At the same time, as a result of the wars in Croatia and Bosnia, a steady number of Serbian refugees and war profiteers flooded into Serbia. Milošević diverted them to Kosovo to increase the numbers of the Serbian minority there, but the plan failed. Instead, the outskirts of Belgrade were the preferred places for starting a new life. The extreme nationalist party led by the current prisonmate of Milošević, the Serbian Le Pen–Vojislav Šešelj, started offering better deals: for a small fee and a large bribe they offered city land, including sidewalks and land for future highways and commercial kiosk construction. With this bastard type conceived among the national socialists, today's kiosks became tomorrow's houses, blocking streets and highways.

The mushroom strategy is simple, cunning, self-organized, and wild. The typical mushroom builder is displaced and desperate. He comes quickly to the realization that a client-builder relationship is bound by equal ambition to expand in all directions possible, which the official system would not provide on paper. After obtaining "permission" to install a kiosk on public land, usually in the layer between modernist slab housing blocks and the street, a thin kiosk shell is either reused or rebuilt and plugged into electric networks. If the builder is quick, masonry walls are built from the inside while the commercial unit continues business-as-usual. A second level cantilevers as far out as possible, concrete is poured in place, and soon the tiled perimeter resembling a roof is put up. Cantilevering up to two meters on each side, the surface area of the captured space can go up to one hundred square meters, the size of the elitist socialist apartment. This will become living space for a family, a home office, or source of rental income. Distorted by the ex-

tended width of the second-floor interior space, the view from the side resembles a mushroom, and so this is how the type got its name.

The legal framework in the absence of systematic planning serves only to be violated in as many steps as possible so that it becomes normal. This set the norm for more "official" construction developments that fully embraced the mushroom strategy and gave birth to a wider and deeper entanglement of mixed use. More prominent examples of mushroom construction followed for private residences, banks, gas stations, and shopping centers.

The importance of the Mushroom House is that it shrank and displaced geo-political borders to architectural borders and similarly the idea of zoning to the reality of the pixel. Refugees from the Bosnian and Croatian wars flocking into Serbia made islands of their own space of survival through this speculative housing type. But more than that, by redefining the interior-exterior borders, they embraced the opportunity left by the postsocialist void and created a new type that acts like a pixel in the new city.

3. Housing Upgrades

Housing Upgrades are essentially two buildings on top of each other: a large new one on top of a smaller older one. They are solidifications of various gray capital currently in operation throughout the Balkan region.

Immediately after the liberation of Belgrade in World War II, a joint operation of Tito's partisan forces and Russian army volunteers quickly built new suburban housing in parts of the town to accommodate the liberators. Dubbed as Russian Pavilions, they were built following an automatic campus scheme: an array of autonomous, light single-story structures on an empty field. However, what soon became an aggravation between Tito and Stalin in 1948 left the pavilions without a clear owner. Much later, this lack of clarity protected the pavilions from the sellout of state property by Milošević when he was in need of money for his army and police. Additionally, because they were a rare example of early civilian urbanism built by the military, the pavilions fell under a special preservation law for protection of cultural heritage. After the wars and NATO intervention in the 1990s, these pavilions were offered one by one to private groups for development in return for bribes. Permits were issued as long as the developer preserved the original structure and secured permissions from current occupants.

In effect, the occupants gained their own right to stay in privatized property in exchange for the air rights and another building on top of their own. The success of the Housing Upgrades is determined by the degree to which the inventive interpretation of the permit multiplies the volume of the levels.

Depending on the position of the pavilion in relation to the street, new pillars are placed either next to the existing walls or spaced at a distance; after the columns are erected, the new platform is formed on top of the pavilion's roof. The new ground acts like an elevated tabula-rasa for a new building that is not connected structurally to the pavilion below. The process takes place while the original floors are still populated. The Housing Upgrade builders don't miss the opportunity to build at least two new levels before the new roofline is reached. Once it is reached, a mushroomlike mansard roof rises at least another two levels, and it can extend up to six hidden floors in the exaggerated roof section. The upgrade also gains in width by cantilevering to the edge of the bottom supports. Then, the customization of the two original bottom floors can take place as the inhabitants sign permissions for the Housing Upgrade in exchange for renovating their own floors. Many project their own balconies in between the pillars. The upgrade is then painted in bright yellow or pink, a pervasive preservationist color of compromise to legality and appearance.

The extension of Russian Pavilions is an emblem of the political transition in Belgrade from the Milošević era to the democratic era. As Miloš Vasić writes in his book about the assassination of Zoran Djindjić, the prime minister in power during the Housing Upgrade projects, the state was fragile because the majority of its operations were still ruled by the cartel connected to crime and profits from the gray market. The Housing Upgrade projects were given permits under the Djindjić government, even though he made plans to strike out against organized crime. His plans for arrests were leaked and instigated his own murder in March 2003. The devastated government responded by following Djindjić's plan so that housing projects were stopped, in some cases leaving structures partially built. Vasić writes that democratic powers had to deal with the Milošević heritage of criminals for some time after he was arrested and sent to The Hague.

Political transition and blurry ideologies gave Housing Upgrades the legality and a license to radically interpret what is allowed on paper. Here, legalization works beyond merely lowering standards of urbanism to match the actual condition; lowering standards was deployed as an outright strategy and proved effective in increasing density.

As the first upgrade finishes and the extension of the next house starts, it is clear that the system, not isolated incidents like the Mushroom Houses, is being deployed. The same principle of vertical extension was used in an area of thirty buildings that gave it the modernistic character of a great urban proposal. With the look of illegitimate architecture, the new objects were actually legitimate products of a bizarre but deliberate mishmash of transitional politics and entrepreneurial action.

4. Neo-Orthodox Landscape

The massive St. Sava Shrine in Belgrade, the central icon of the Serbian Orthodox church and the anchor in the chaotic skyline, is still under construction. Started in the middle 1930s, the work was stopped just after laying the foundations due to World War II. After the war, the shrine joined many other national taboos that Tito kept tight under his reign. Immediately after Tito's death, work on the shrine was continued with new money coming from the anti-communist diasporas mainly prospering in the U.S. as well as later significant support from the Serbian anti-Milošević government. Even though it opened for service late in the 1980s, its exterior was completed much later, in 2004, and the work on the interior, including the iconographic mosaics, is projected to continue for another four decades to come.

Originally, the shrine was intended to be the biggest Orthodox church in the world, bigger than its historical predecessor, Hagia Sofia in the former Constantinople. Because they are copied from the medieval sources, St. Sava and all recently built Orthodox churches are from the same mold. This cookie-cutter style of national neo-Byzantium includes a heavy, wide system of circular arches arranged to mimic what is called a "Greek plan," which supports the mandatory dome, a symbolic representation of heaven. Strictly tectonic, there are neither cantilevers nor projections, thus symbolizing stability and strong links to the Earth.

With such a megalomaniac dream project, it is the church and not the state that generates the character of public places left over from Tito's era. Neo-Christian orthodoxy has survived through the entire second half of the twentieth century of communist rule as a suppressed ideological empire and now retaliates by rebuilding icons and copies of Byzantium church architecture everywhere it can. The *main* neo-Orthodox character is generated by denouncing modernity; this is the politics of a clear and aggressive dismissal of the International Style supported by Tito's state. It follows the trauma of the generation of architects who embarked upon their careers just when Tito's modern-city building went into decline after half a century.

The heart of this generation of architects was broken three times. The first time was when a post-World War II generation of architects arranged with great luck to have steady socialist commissions for building new cities like New Belgrade. The second time it was caused by the effects of Milošević's disinterest in architecture as a way of recognizing those who supported him in the beginning of his political power. As a banker, he was stronger in postponing war equity and breaking the rules of the economy rather than having the courage to spend money on architecture.

The architects of the frustrated generation did not have a choice but to seek another ideology as a sponsor with the slight hope that the longtime suppressed Orthodox Christian values would rise as a patron in building the new culture in concrete and stone. It was assumed that the Orthodox church would come back as a soft cultural power, opposing the harsh communist-modernist alliance. However, the Serbian Orthodox Church was not as supportive as architects had hoped; funds do not come from the church's financial structure, as is the case with The Vatican. Real life proved that the funds flowed solely in one direction—*to* the church. Instead of becoming a patron, the church became merely a vessel for architecture. Quickly, it became clear for anyone practicing architecture in support of romantic and national values that the Orthodox church would not be much support. The Church is spending everything on its megalomaniac dream, not too differently from The Vatican's Middle Ages dream of domination when building St. Peter's Cathedral in Rome. One would expect some negotiation through reformist methods, but that would take on a model developed by the Western Protestant network. That could never be the case because Protestant ideology is even more detested by the fundamental Orthodox thinkers than The Vatican. With the architects' hearts broken twice, no passion survived for promoting architecture based on local Serbian tradition in order to advance a sense of belonging to the world as a sensible nation, the so-called true Serbia. Thus conditions made it possible for the very same late modernist architects who built office skyscrapers and the tallest buildings in the Balkans during the 1970s to embrace the indifference and the aberration of the all too copied and quasi-neo-Byzantium style.

The neo-Orthodox desire for architecture is scaleless, and it adapts any available

Amalgamation of modernism, clericalism and commerce: New Belgrade.

techniques for execution to complete a lost medieval dream. In 2005, a helicopter of the former communist army appeared in the air carrying an unlikely object: a small Serbian Orthodox Church, built in a harbor shipyard of Bar, Montenegro. The church was manufactured, pre-assembled, and welded with painted steel in the form of a small chapel with a single nave and a miniature dome. After a short ride, the helicopter delivered the metal church to its destination, a mountain site around a disputed edge of the Serbian Orthodox empire and the Montenegrin Orthodox empire. Ordered, manufactured, and delivered on a remote site in haste, the miniature Serbian Orthodox Church was quickly sanctified by a Serbian Orthodox priest council. One agent of power, the degraded military of Milošević, was subsumed by a rising agent of power: faith. It was not that faith looked for the military

protection, but rather the military was looking for a new ideology to fill its sails that were sagging after the fall of Tito's communism. The merger of the military and religion was so important that the canons the Orthodox Church cherishes so deeply—the sense of history in an object of spiritual love, medieval materials, tectonics, and appearance—were all forsaken for the metal church . . . by the Orthodox Church itself. The subversion of rules thus came from the very agent that set the rules. An icon of nationalistic origin merged with faith was efficiently reduced to a pixel of sanctity that was directly used to mark the edge of a territory. It is in this territory where throughout Milošević's passionless and pathological reign the lost passion itself became manifested in the centers of faith like Belgrade's St. Sava Shrine. Thus socialist cities were soon seen as the place where

violation was tolerated and was considered creative. Their creation was an emerging landscape, an amalgamation of modern urbanism, clerical architecture, and bland commerce. This landscape is perhaps the terminal phase in the process of postsocialist disenchantment with the city.

Brasília's Levitational Field

Sunil Bald

Tia Neiva (1926-1985), founder of Vale do Amanhecer (Valley of the Dawn).

Oscar Niemeyer, sketch showing floating eye, National Cathedral in Brasília (1959-1960).

In 1999, as the new millennium approached laden with apocalyptic scenarios, there were just over one million visitors to Brasília. However, most were not coming to pay homage to their country's capital, let alone its architecture. The city's tourism secretary, Marcelo Dourado, estimated that half were there to visit one of the more than 150 mystical New Age organizations and communities that have helped to make Brasília and its surroundings an important center for New Age culture.[1] Since the city's conception in 1957, individuals have remade themselves as they have made the city. One with a lasting legacy was Tia Neiva, a truck driver who founded the Valley of the Dawn just north of Brasília. Like most of the laborers who built Brasília, Neiva came from the vast northeast in pursuit of the purported prosperity that would accompany this city of the future. Her Valley of the Dawn is now a community of five thousand people who communicate daily with "a fleet of vessels from a far-off planet known to its inhabitants as Capela [chapel]" that hover a few miles above the valley.[2]

Near the Valley of the Dawn lies another New Age community, Eclectic City. The military pilot Lieutenant Oceano de Sa, later known as Master Yokaanam, founded Eclectic City in 1956. While flying over an area near Brasília's future site, Master Yokaanam received an assignment from a supernatural force to establish a new spiritual community on the ground below. A harrowing crash immediately followed these instructions, Master Yokaanam was convinced, and Eclectic City prospers to this day.[3]

While Master Yokaanam's flight and the hovering satellites of the Valley of the Dawn may seem peripheral or even oppositional to the technocracy and monumental symbolism of a national capital, both can be understood as alternate manifestations of Brasília's own mythology. Brasília's architectural objects sit in a dramatically expansive landscape and under a big sky that projects into "the beyond," a reference that can equally apply to the aspirations of the nation-state or the transcendence of individual consciousness. Those who came to build Brasília, those drawn by its promise, and their descendants who still remain infuse the city's monumental urban form with a particular vitality. Like Tia Neiva, many of the residents came from the vast northeast, a region that particularly reflects a tradition of religious and spiritual syncretism mythologized by Gilberto Freyre in his foundational national narrative *Casa Grande e Senzala*.[4] Within a generation, they have managed to mold this heritage into a local "Brasiliennese" identity that flourishes in this environment of state bureaucracy.

Consequently, Brasília supports multiple mythologies that contribute to the cult of the nation as but one of the many spiritual sects inhabiting this landscape. Even Oscar Niemeyer's sculptural government buildings have become symbolic participants. On the city's anniversary the sun is said to set directly between the towers of the congress building, backlighting the oversized national flag. Furthermore, in homage to flight, there is the famous resemblance of its urban plan to a soaring bird, a glowing vision when seen from an airplane at night. The purity of the plan's outline is preserved through Brasília's UNESCO designation as a World Cultural Site, prompting a moratorium on development in the surrounding open areas that could pollute its legibility.[5]

Oscar Niemeyer, National Congress in Brasília (1958-1960).

1 Andrea McDaniels, "For New Age Action, It's Hard to Beat Brasília," *The Dallas Morning News*, (May 22 1999).

2 Henry Chu, "Born of Prophecy, Haven for Cultists, Mystics," *Los Angeles Times*, (October 7, 2004).

3 Ibid.

4 See the first section that outlines the tactics and consequences of the passive colonial domination of the Portuguese in Brazil in what is now a classic, though controversial, 1946 study of Brazilian intellectual and sociological history. Gilberto Freyre, *Casa Grande e Senzala, The Masters and the Slaves*, second English edition, (New York: Alfred E. Knopf, 1956), 3-80.

5 Farés el-Dahdah, "Lucio Costa Preservatioinist," *Future Anterior*, vol. 2 no. 1, (Summer 2006), 65-66. Also see Costa's own justification for the preservation of the legibility of the monumental axis in Lucio Costa, "O Urbanista defende sua cidade," originally published in 1967, in Lucio Costa, *Registro de uma Vivença*. (São Paulo: Empresa des Artes, 1997), 301-305.

Brasília, aerial photograph (2006).

In Brasília, narrative, modern architecture, and flight are woven into the simultaneous building and writing of the modern capital. Oscar Niemeyer is known as the architect of Brasília's most important buildings and Lucio Costa as its urban designer. However, as Costa's competition entry for the city cultivates a myth about a place as much as it describes an urban proposition, it would be more accurate to label Costa as Brasília's author. Brasília was the culmination of a vibrant alliance between modern architecture and political patronage in Brazil, and Lucio Costa's entry for Brasília was perhaps the most heroic of his extraordinary body of writing that forged the link between architecture, modernism, and Brazilian national identity.[6] Although Costa did schematic sketches that outlined the city as a physical urban entity, his narrative presented a place where occupation could be understood, not through cognition but through imagination and flight.

While Brazil's best architects submitted thousands of pages of reports, reams of drawings, and collections of models to the jury, Costa's entry consisted of a series of fifteen freehand sketches and a ten-page, double-spaced, carbon-copy typewritten text. The unanimous selection of his proposal is especially curious when considering its introductory paragraph:

> In 1823, Jose Bonifacio suggested transferring the capital of Brazil to Goias and rechristening it Brasília.
>
> First of all, I should like to apologize to the directors of the development company and to the jury of the competition for the sketchy manner in which I am submitting the idea which I have

followed in my suggested outline plan for the Federal Capital; and at the same time, I must justify myself.

> It was not my intention to enter the competition —nor indeed, am I really so doing. I am merely liberating my mind from a possible solution, which sprang to it as a complete picture, but one which I had not sought. I therefore come forward, not as a properly equipped expert, since I do not even run an office of my own, but as a mere *maquisard* [guerrilla fighters of the French underground in World War II] of town planning who does not even mean to continue working out the idea offered in this report, save perhaps as a consultant.[7]

Costa began with an apology, a historical reference, and the description of a spontaneous vision from which he must "liberate" himself. Indeed, Costa humbly played down his agency and acted as a conduit, a "storyteller" of something divinely "sprung." Burdened with this vision generated from an out-of-body experience, Costa foregrounds his scheme as spiritually imbued rather than functionally efficient.

Costa actually had a precedent for envisioning Brasília's birth to which he implicitly refers. In 1883, Dom Bosco, an Italian saint whose story we will return to, dreamed of a city.

> Between parallels 15 and 20 there was a long and wide depression, in the vicinity of a lake. Thus spoke a voice, over and over again: "When they come to explore the riches buried in these mountains, here will rise the promised land of milk and honey, of unconceivable wealth . . . "[8]

This legend was widely known in Brazil, and it so happened that the site being considered for the capital was on the 15th parallel. Costa's vision was also further historicized and nationalized with his reference to Jose Bonifacio, who in the early nineteenth century articulated conditions by which Brazil could exist as a free nation separate from the Portuguese monarchy. This included proposing a geographically central capital known as Brasília, also at 15 degrees latitude, from which the nation's vast land mass could be better colonized and served. In referencing Jose Bonifacio and Dom Bosco, Costa was able to position his proposal as both the logical culmination of a long historical process and the manifestation of a spiritual vision that was beyond logic. The proposal articulated for Brasília a genealogy that preceded and a vision that exceeded President Juscelino Kubitschek's immediate political ambitions.

6 A collection of Costa's writings was recently compiled into a volume, Lucio Costa, *Registro de uma Vivença*. (São Paulo: Empresa des Artes, 1997). Pages 437-549 collect several essays that theorize historic work from the Baroque churches of Aleijadiho to eighteenth- and nineteenth-century colonial plantation houses. Concurrent writings gathered on pages 83-414 theorize his own works, the works of other modern Brazilian architects, and makes a case for modernism in Brazil.

7 Lucio Costa, "Plano Piloto," *Modulo* 18 (June 1960), rear insert, p. 1.

8 *Myths and Untruths about Brasília*, http://www.geocities.com/thetropics/3416/errors_and_myths_about_Brasília.htm#sonho cites Dom Bosco's entry for August 30, 1883, in his *Biographical Memories*.

In short, Costa was able to propose a creation myth for the city even as he proposed the city itself. Through connection to both history and divinity, this creation myth legitimized Costa's vision while denying the primacy of his authorship.

Legitimizing the modern through historical reclamations was an endeavor Costa undertook many times over during a prolific career that intermingled the making and writing of architecture to define a national architectural production as the modern Brazilian nation was defining itself. A quarter of a century before Brasília, Getulio Vargas formed Brazil's first non-oligarchic government, the Estado Novo (New State). He also began a tradition of political patronage for modern architecture. Based on the assumption that greatness was dependent on economic strength, the Vargas regime developed a nationalism that emphasized Brazil's future potential over its present condition and posited modernization as ideology. The government's positivist national rhetoric was disseminated through the Ministry of Education, Culture, and Health, which had the stated objective to "centralize, coordinate, orient, and guide the national image, internal and external."[9] The architectural projection of this "image" was unabashedly modern.

During this period, Costa operated in two seemingly oppositional capacities that in fact complimented each other in the development of a "Brazilian" architecture—as a modern architect and as an official in the Ministry of Education's Patrimony of History, which considered matters of preservation. Costa worked as architect of Brazil's most important building of the time, the headquarters for the Ministry of Education in Rio of 1936. Because of Costa's commitment to modernism, the minister Gustavo Capanema approached him to design the building. However, Costa deferred and agreed to work on the project only if others were included. The team included a young Oscar Niemeyer and Affonso Reidy, and, at Costa's insistence, Le Corbusier was invited to Brazil for a month to provide input. As in his Brasília proposal, Costa relieved himself of the agency of sole and principal designer and was able to "coordinate and orient," to articulate and position the work within a new Brazilian cultural narrative as it was designed.[10]

As a government official within the Patrimony of History, Costa oversaw the writing, or reframing, of much of Brazil's architectural history to integrate the written with the built and the historic with the modern. Defining what constituted "Brazilian" in the cultural history of this recently independent young nation involved doses of both historical research and mythology. In his writings, Costa selectively claimed certain aspects of historic production that were the result of colonization as

Portrait of Aleijadinho, mid-eighteenth century.

indigenous while dismissing others. Costa's research into colonial dwellings led to the neo-colonial movement, which foregrounded the formal simplicity and environmentally responsive elements of verandahs, sunshades, and materials to form links to modernism and articulate an argument of resistance to "imported" Beaux Arts academicism.[11] Costa supplemented this lineage with his studies of the Baroque, which he believed had transformed into something "Brazilian." Most interesting was his work on the leper mulatto architect/sculptor Aleijadinho, to whose withered limbs assistants would tie chisels to carve out architectural surfaces. Aleijadinho's work, too, was equal parts architectural history and mythology. As a character, Aleijadinho filled the requirements of a mythical cultural figure, while his work, often inseparable from his personage, tied architecture to mannerisms, exuberance, suffering, and inspiration. According to Costa, he transformed the Portuguese Baroque into architecture "truly Brazilian." In Aleijadinho, one could locate architectural origin in the biography of a mythical figure who could transcend the physical to create the divine. In his introduction to a 1950 Patrimony re-publishing of the original biography of Aleijadinho, Costa wrote, "Aleijadinho is both the key and enigma that intrigues and wins the utmost admiration of our modern architects."[12]

It is this utility of enigma that imbued Lucio Costa's narrative for Brasília with a transcendent quality that superseded urban function and design. Indeed, the sketches that Costa included were supplemental, meant to clarify the text of the proposal as opposed to every other competition proposal where the text was used to clarify drawings. In the first three of these sketches Costa established the primordial, the procedural, and the processional as the terms by which the city was to be understood. This interjected narrative time into the proposal at three levels: the narrative of historicizing the

9 Lippi, et al.; *O Estado Novo* (Rio de Janeiro: Zahar, 1982), 72.

10 Eduardo Costa Comas, "Monumento e Prototipo, um Ministerio, o Ministerio," *Projeto* 102, (1992) 155-160.

11 Lucio Costa, "Anotações ao Correr da Lembrança," in *Registro de uma Vivença.* (São Paulo: Empresa des Artes, 1997), 498-514.

12 Lucio Costa, *Arquitetura Brasileira* (Rio de Janeiro: Ministry of Culture, 1952), 34.

Lucio Costa, Affonso Reidy, Oscar Niemeyer, and others with Le Corbusier in advisory role, Ministry of Education, Rio de Janeiro (1936-1942)

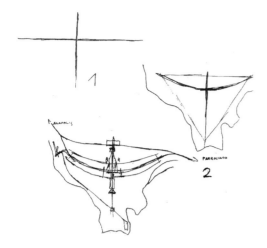

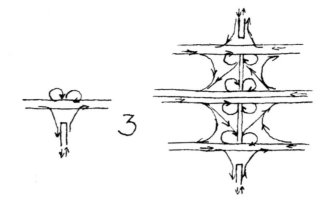

Lucio Costa, competition entry for urban design of Brasília, sketches 1 and 2 – Organizational diagram (1957).

Lucio Costa, competition entry for urban design of Brasília, sketch 3 – interchange diagram (1957).

city (the primordial), the narrative of making the city (the procedural), and the narrative of moving through and experiencing the city (the processional).

The primordial was exemplified in the first sketch, not as a design parti, but as the most basic act of marking, claiming, and, consequently, giving birth to a place.

> It was born of that initial gesture which anyone would make when pointing to a given place or taking possession of it: the drawing of two axes crossing each other at right angles, in the sign of the Cross.[13]

Both colonized and christened, the "place" was then given specificity as it merged with the physical place. Costa continues,

> This sign was then adapted to the topography. The extremities of one axial line were curved so as to make the sign fit into the equilateral triangle which outlines the area to be urbanized.[14]

In prefacing the city on the two elemental geometric ideals of the cross and the equilateral triangle, Costa seemed to be searching more for spiritual significance than order. As described later in the text, the triangle was replicated at the Place of the Three Powers: "The equilateral triangle—associated with the very earliest architecture in the world—is best suited to express the public buildings which house the fundamental powers."[15] The triangle that is the basis of the pyramid and the cross can be understood as a syncretic connection to the past and to the beyond. In these lines, Costa described the birth of the city as embedded in spiritual rituals that are as old as time. He also mined the ambiguity of the description as to whether these lines were being drawn in the sand or in his sketchpad.

Once the site had been marked, then shaped, and finally contained, it became transformed in an abrupt and rapid manner, as per the third sketch:

> Finally, it was decided to apply the free principles of highway engineering, together with the elimination of road junctions, to the technique of town planning. The curved axis, which corresponds to the natural approach road, was given the function of a through radial artery, with fast traffic lanes in the center and side lanes for local traffic. And the residential district of the city was largely located along this radial artery.[16]

The procedural logic of moving from a primitive marking to a highway system is posited as direct and foundational to the formation of a city. In continuing his description in the past tense, Costa historicizes his process and again suggests that he is describing the natural development of a city that already exists, at least in his dream.

After this point, however, the narrative shifts out of the past tense, and one is set in motion. The use of the past tense highlighted the procedure of the conception and design from birthing, marking, containing, and articulating a place. The scheme consequently attained its historical trajectory in its making, a history that in turn contained it own primordial references. Through weaving the historic with the projected, Costa legitimized the proposal as being something that was both grounded in a history and divine as a vision.

While the initial part of the narrative prefaced the city as having meaning beyond its objective comprehension, the specifics of the plan are described from the point of view of someone occupying the inevitable result of the city's initiation—the road system—in real time. One is immediately moving through the city, encountering it in moments and reconstituting the fragments into an imaginary entity. As the text shifts out of the past tense, Costa describes an action in process, in a place that already seems to exist.

> Slightly to one side of the central platform is the entrance hall of the interurban Transport Terminal with its ticket offices, bars, restaurants, etc. This is a low building connected by escalators [to] the lower departure hall, which, in its turn, is separated by glass

13 Lucio Costa, "Plano Piloto," *Modulo* 18, (June 1960), rear insert, 2.

14 Ibid., rear insert, 3.

15 Ibid., rear insert, 6.

16 Ibid., rear insert, 3.

partitions from the departure platform proper. One-way traffic forces the buses to make a detour, leaving the road under the platform; this gives the travelers their last view of the monumental radial artery before the bus enters the residential radial artery and is a psychologically satisfactory way of saying farewell to the national capital.[17]

Or again:

The city's cemeteries are sited at the ends of the radial arteries, so that funeral traffic does not have to cross the city center. They are planted with grass lawns and suitably wooded: the gravestones are the simple, flat slabs used in England, the idea being to avoid any sign of ostentation.[18]

In recounting an itinerary through narrative while diagramming with drawing, Costa foregrounded experience, and consequently occupation, through movement; inserted ritual, whether it be the daily act of acknowledging the capital or the periodic ceremony of acknowledging the dead, and shifted in scale from interchange to tombstone. The text constructed a place of disjunctive though fluidly related instances that could be envisioned and occupied at multiple scales through multiple moments. This illusory entity was given a semblance of unity in a narrative in which the city's primordial ties, procedural history, vibrancy of movement, and multiple moments of social exchange extended Brasília's identity beyond form.

The built city of Brasília is generally described as an overscaled and static organization of space that draws heavily from the mentor Le Corbusier.[19] However, the narrative city of Brasília that emphasizes moving or floating through space as the basis for the urban experience more closely resembles the Futurists' urban fantasy, particularly Antonio Sant'Elia's *La Città Nuova*. As Sanford Kwinter has written, *La Città Nuova* privileged field over monument, and the dissolution of the urban datum contributed to an "ungrounded" reading of architecture.[20] Drawings of urban conglomerates include a station for airplanes and ground transport taken from the point of view of a passenger in flight. In Costa's narrative it is implied that the urban subject is cruising through the city in the automobile, but the referenced sketches, like Sant'Elia's, show a raised vanishing point. Furthermore, both Sant'Elia and Costa focused on infrastructural transportation buildings, Sant'Elia in his drawings, Costa in his text.

Costa's narrative ends with the statement, "Brasília, capital of the aeroplane and the autostrada, city, and

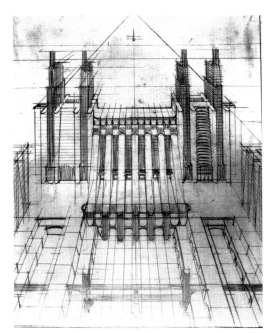

Antonio Sant'Elia, *La Città Nuova*, Station for Airplanes and Trains (1914).

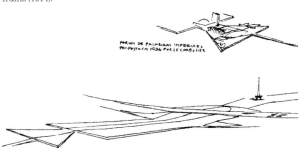

Lucio Costa, competition entry for urban design of Brasília, sketch – aerial view of monumental axis (1957).

park. The century-old dream of the Patriarch."[21] Jose Bonifacio did not likely anticipate movement and flying as being a conceptual basis for the capital, but Costa did not see a contradiction between his proposal and the patriarch's century-old wish—the word *modern* never appears in Costa's text. In Costa's Brasília, the "contemporary" was defined as the natural consequence of the national: presupposed, rooted in the primordial, but extending into the horizon.

This is the horizon of Master Yokaanam's flight, the hovering vessels above the Valley of the Dawn and the nearby "capital" Alto Paraíso (High Paradise). Alto Paraíso's distinction as a seat of power has no association with the state but purports to be the "Capital of the Third Millennium." Probably the best known of the area's spiritual destinations, Alto Paraíso blossomed about twenty-five years ago with the opening of an interstate highway, a result of the burgeoning economy in this area stimulated by Brasília. It sits at the edge of some of

17 Ibid., rear insert, 4.

18 Ibid., rear insert, 8.

19 Kenneth Frampton's description of Brasília in his *Modern Architecture: A Critical History* is emblematic of this point of view. While brief, his analysis has resonated outside of Brazil. See Kenneth Frampton, *Modern Architecture: A Critical History* (New York: Thames and Hudson, 1997, third edition), 256.

20 Sanford Kwinter, "La Città Nuova," *Zone 1/2* (New York: Urzone Inc., 1987), 104-106.

21 Lucio Costa, "Plano Piloto," rear insert, 8.

Alto Paraiso, Goias, Brazil.

the most dramatic landscape in the area, where strong geologic formations and abundant waterfalls emphasize the power of nature. As a result, its visitors include the frequently overlapping populations of eco-tourists and spiritual seekers.

In its urban form, Alto Paraíso shares little with Brasília. With a population of only seven thousand, it resembles a settlement more than a city, and there is no coordinated urban design, nor any aesthetic architectural guidelines. However, this does result in some eclectic moments that bear resemblance to Niemeyer's monuments. An elemental and welcoming limestone arch at the city's entrance and the Kaliandra, a small music hall designed to keep acoustic energy in while attracting heavenly energy from above, are particularly appropriate examples.

Architect unknown, Kaliandra Music Hall, Alto Paraíso, Goias, Brazil

Alto Paraíso's distinction as a capital lies in its own narrative. Though markedly different than Brasília's, it does further elucidate the legitimating utility of mythology. Alto Paraíso's "story" is most thoroughly recounted in Augusto de Franco's *O Segredo o Paraíso (The Secret of Paradise)*.[22] His book outlines both "past" and "future," skipping the present, and uses many of the same tropes of Costa's narrative. De Franco's claim of Alto Paraíso as the Capital of the Third Millennium results from a convergence of natural and primordial forces that make it "the heart of Earth." First, it is the "settlement of the 14th parallel," and while this falls outside the limits of Dom Bosco's vision, it is the same latitude of the Incan civilization of Machu Pichu. This, combined with locally recovered archeological relics of other indigenous populations, affirms the importance of the city's location in its spiritual connection to past cultures that were imagined to coexist more harmoniously with both earth and heaven. Second, the area has the highest concentration

of quartz crystal in the country, a resource mined by the military before the arrival of the most recent population. De Franco claims this abundance of crystal concentrates energy to the region and makes Alto Paraíso the most luminous point on the continent when viewed from space by NASA telescopes, a fact supported by geological surveys.[23] This view of the city from above connects Alto Paraíso to the cosmic and the magnetic forces that animate New Age discourse.

Narratives for Brasília and Alto Paraíso metaphysically distinguish and outline them as cities, centers, and capitals by transcending gravity and looking below. While Brasília's role as capital is in the context of the nation and Alto Paraíso's is articulated in more ephemeral terms, both employ the spiritual to similar ends. In Brasília this also plays out at the architectural scale where there is often a strange intermingling of monument and shrine that embraces and embeds both historic and cosmic time within the architectural objects of the state. While lesser known than the governmental buildings of the monumental axis, two shrines in particular entomb two dimensions of the city's creation myth— the narrative of transcendent flight and the illusion/allusion of history— that prepare the mythological ground for the capital: the Sanctuary of Dom Bosco and the Museum of the City of Brasília.

Alto Paraíso, Goias, Brazil, aerial photograph, (2006).

22 Augusto de Franco, *O Segredo o Paraíso* (Rio de Janeiro: Editora o Livro Aberto, 2006).

23 A. Crósta and C. de Souza, "Hyperspectral Remote Sensing for Mineral Mapping at Alto Paraíso de Goiás", *Revista Brasileira de Geociências* (September 2000), 551-54.

First, let's return to the Italian saint Dom Bosco's dream.

> Between parallels 15 and 20 there was a long and wide depression, in the vicinity of a lake. Thus spoke a voice, over and over again: "When they come to explore the riches buried in these mountains, here will rise the promised land of milk and honey, of unconceivable wealth . . . "

Dom Bosco founded an ascetic order of priests called the Salesean Order that had a relatively large presence in Brazil and the Americas in the late nineteenth century. Dom Bosco was actually very well known for his prophetic visions, including this one in 1883 where he was flying. The Brazilian government recovered this dream but reprinted it with a markedly different translation, "Between the 15th and 20th parallels, where a lake had formed, a great civilization will be born."[24] This brief statement omitted the metaphorical use of nature and plenty and replaced it with an urbanized version where the lake was formed rather than found. While the site of Brasília fell on the 15th parallel, the lake was missing. This was soon remedied when an existing river was dammed, forming the 80-kilometer-perimeter Lake Paranoa, and if not found, Dom Bosco's mythical land could be prepared, marked, and built.

Brasília's first building was sited along this lake, prior to any construction on the monumental axis of the capital. Designed by Oscar Niemeyer, the Oratory of Dom Bosco was inaugurated on New Year's Eve, 1956, honoring Dom Bosco as Brasília's patron saint, its founder in flight.[25] The structure is a flattened, stretched, and split pyramid that opens onto an expansive view of what would be the city. The viewpoint of the city was therefore conceived of and made manifest before the view, concretizing and replicating Dom Bosco's experience of flight. Eight years later his legacy graduated to the Sanctuary of Dom Bosco, which occupies a prominent place near the crossing of the monumental axis with the arced wing of the bird. This 25,000-square-foot, soaring, column-less space with blue stained-glass windows internalized the experience of flight. Unlike the oratory, there is no overt reference to the city, and while the gothic arches of the windows refer to earlier architectural tactics of uplift, the minimal reference to the heavens and abundant blue light projects a more abstract and spiritual experience of flight. Because the building is almost as prominent as the National Cathedral as a site of religious interest in the city, this simulated vertical transcendence has become embedded in Brasília's urban experience.

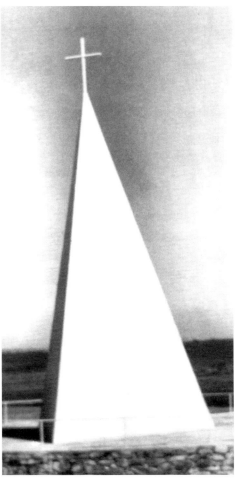

Oscar Niemeyer, Oratory of Dom Bosco, Brasília, (1956).

While the Dom Bosco building was the first shrine to Brasília's mythology, another small building adjacent to the congress building encased the reclaimed historical narratives that legitimized this endeavor. The city's first cultural building, the Museum of the City of Brasília, opened in 1960 on the equilateral Plaza of the Three Powers. It was the only "secondary," or nongovernmental, building along Brasília's monumental axis to be planned from the city's initiation.[26] Two seemingly monolithic beams asymmetrically cantilever from a seemingly monolithic base, providing a curious perceptual interplay against the optimistic vertical towers of the adjacent National Congress Building. Much of the rhetorical power of Brasília relies on its mastery of gravity: the power of the nation to rise above, to extend horizons, to embody unimagined possibility. While the two buildings for Dom Bosco projected the visitor up, the Museum of the City of Brasília formally plays with gravity to project an imaginary doubling of the towers, fallen but floating, prone but breathing. It is here that the various texts that are the basis for the city are enshrined, including Bonifacio's and Costa's. The documents encased in

24 Andrea da Costa Braga, *Guia de Urbanismo, Arquitetura e Arte de Brasília* (Ministry of Culture: Brasília, 2000) 90-91.

25 Ibid., 91.

26 David Underwood, *Oscar Niemeyer and the Architecture of Brazil*, (Rizzoli: New York, 1994) 114.

Oscar Niemeyer, Museum of the City of Brasília (1958-1960).

the Museum of the City of Brasília at the city's birth are not blueprints or instructions but rather a collection of legitimizing texts that prepared the capital and the nation for a history it had yet to create. The floating beams are actually hollow and house these documents tracing the impetus to build Brasília or, as Niemeyer wrote, "to preserve for posterity the projects connected with the building of the new capital."[27] The first tangible historic occasion of any life is birth, a moment that contains only boundless possibility. It is the preservation of this possibility, rather than the preservation of history, that is most important for the Museum of the City of Brasília.

The museum is unusual among Niemeyer's buildings on Brasília's monumental axis as it embodies both weight and float. The building's relationship to the ground is unambiguous, and the weight of the monolithic beams is emphasized by the space between them and the ground; this, however, is a weight not subject to laws of gravity. The legitimacy imbued by the tomb coexists with the possibility implied in its levitation. This strategy is not a grounding of history nor a burden of history but a balancing of the past where foundation is used to animate rather than solidify. Birth is entombed; possibility is preserved. The museum's aspirations as architecture were those of the city it symbolically encased at its inception. As Nietzsche wrote, "That which is decisive is produced in spite of everything."

The Museum of the City of Brasília preserves the making of Brasília, a monumental act of a people that transcends the seemingly impossible task of realizing the city, while the shrine for Dom Bosco recreates an act of transcendent consciousness connected to a higher spirit and thus a greater cause. Taken together, the buildings enshrine a narrative of transcendence: overcoming limits of body, mind, and self-interest to forge the commonality necessary to perpetuate both capital and nation. The buildings straddle and transcend the institutions of state and religion in pursuit of a more meaningful spiritual legitimacy. Both tectonically rely on Brasília's vast horizon to deny a reading of structural commitment to the earth: the Dom Bosco shrines project upward and outward, while the Museum of the City of Brasília floats above.

The rhetoric of transcendence that these buildings project is inextricably woven into national narratives. In his 1882 lecture "What Is a Nation?" the political philosopher Ernst Renan goes through a litany of conditions that bind people together (race, religion, institutions, etc.) in search of what defines and identifies nationality, only to conclude in the realm of the ephemeral. "A nation is a soul, a spiritual principle . . . . It presupposes a past; it is summarized, however, in the present by a

tangible fact, namely, consent, the clearly expressed desire to continue . . . . So long as this moral consciousness gives proof of its strength by the sacrifices which demand the abdication of the individual to the advantage of the community, it is legitimate and has the right to exist."[28] Like many of the surrounding cults, much of Brasília's spiritual foundation depends on narrative and nature. Narrative articulates a collective historical memory that Brasília's horizon propels into the future. Vision in flight was central to Master Yokaanam, Tia Neiva, and Lucio Costa in meshing communal consciousness. The most divine religious visions have often become unwitting conduits, a role Costa plays in his narrative technique of deference legitimizing Brasília's foundation and its existence. The myth of the city (and so the nation) formulates yet another sect floating on these plains with the monumental axis as its shrine.

27 Oscar Niemeyer, "Museu da Cidade," *Modulo* 14, (June 1959).

28 Ernst Renan, "What is A Nation?" lecture at the Sorbonne, March 11, 1882, translated and annotated by Martin Thom, from Homi K. Bhabha ed., *Nation and Narration* (London: Routledge, 1990), 19-20.

Brussels' Ideal Figures

Fremdkörper as Symbolic Forms of the Project of Liberalism

Alexander D'Hooghe and Neeraj Bhatia

Over the last decade, Brussels has redesigned substantial parts of its public space network: wider sidewalks, pseudo-nineteenth-century street furniture, traffic impediments, etc. This project harbors a deep-seated desire to re-create the city as a normalized bourgeois town—without proletariats, identity crises, or excessive bureaucracy, but with all the protection mechanisms invented by the welfare state. These mechanisms comprise all technological advances minus any visible signs of modern life. The underlying dream here erases matters of conflicts from the form of the city. It rewrites both history and the present to culminate in a timeless stasis—an endless re-living of Europe's nineteenth-century bourgeois city. Among the local bureaucracy and decision-makers, this project was welcome with considerable consensus. Still, a vocal minority of architects, artists, and intellectuals vociferously opposed this project, embracing instead a more recent version of the city: its mid-century modernism, a series of large, brutal and at times sublime projects scattered throughout the historical city. Platforms and towers in concrete and glass gleam in the skies as ruins of an optimism long gone. Each faction reviled the other's romantic ideals because they were mutually exclusive. Most important, each camp believed that theirs was the right solution, and the execution of their master plan had to amount to the suppression and effective destruction of the other's belief system.

The *Fremdkörper* of Brussels.

The notion of ideal form was banned from our discipline after the demise of modernism. The simplified equation between utopia and totalitarianism led us on a path to the celebration of the everyday and the common man. However, today's deep-seated discontent with globalization suggests that a deep sense of alienation has infiltrated everyday life. Therefore, a celebration of the everyday is no longer tenable as mass alienation leads to ever-wider calls for sectarianism and totalitarianism. The "everyday" and its "common man" have reversed their once critical role, sliding downward into an avalanche of mass anxiety. An increasing number of people are unable if not unwilling to read and internalize the signs of (Western) capitalism. How can an urban design project address this distrust and destructive mass energy without succumbing to either relativism or totalitarianism?

The urban structure of Brussels reads like a collection of *Fremdkörper* or "foreign bodies."[1] Freud used this term to denote a traumatic experience that was never incorporated into conscious memory because its contents were dangerous to the self-conception of the ego around which this memory exists. A *Fremdkörper* is by definition denied by its owner but nevertheless remains present as a strange, illegible form in the repository of memory. It presents itself in its absence: the painful recognition of its existence shatters the synthesis that the ego had constructed about itself. This paper examines Brussels as a series of *Fremdkörper* in order to extract a model we could call an assemblage of prefigurations that comprise a superimposition of conflicting microcosms, each of which contains, explains, and summarizes a total concept for the entirety of society and is fulfilled through its exhaustive execution. Simultaneously in Brussels, however, such ambition is stopped in its tracks by adjacent schemes. Importantly, this model has internally resolved the danger for a slide toward totalitarianism contained within each particular piece, while not surrendering the strength and clarity of form. This model, with its formalistic consequences, in fact demonstrates an uncanny analogy to the political utopia of liberalism.

Fremdkörper vs. the Imperial Principle of Urban Assimilation

Most European capitals operated until recently as the figureheads of imperialist national states, manifesting the Continent's continuous drive for unification under central command. Through integrating older and more deviant historical forms as well as new extensions within the capital's overarching logic, a synthesis was formed at each historical juncture—a myth of its own origins and

destiny. In fact, it is this constant utopian intention that has ultimately led to a totalitarian synthesis. Arguably, each city has un-adapted, atypical, and sizable elements that could never conform to the proper urban structure. Such forms contain a subversive ambition that threatens the self-conception of the surrounding city: they are its *Fremdkörper*. Cities with a strong self-conception are held together, such as in Paris, by a mikado of boulevards that suggest a unified urban fabric; or, as in Manhattan, organized by a grid wherein each citizen can locate his or her own place in an open system of exchange; or, as in Moscow's 1935 General Plan, often digest and integrate what otherwise might have become *Fremdkörper* into their urban structure. Exactly such a synthesis is lacking in Brussels, the *Fremdkörper* of which were never assimilated into a comprehensive master plan, as the city itself was never continually subjected to a powerful national center of command. Instead, we have a series of foreign bodies, each a recording of the ambitions and belief systems at the time of its origination without a totalizing integration. Therein lies its promise. The absence of a strong national state allows us to see the presence of the utopian intent, recorded in a symbolic urban form but liberated from its totalitarian association.

Brussels' *Fremdkörper*: an Aesthetic

Although individual *Fremdkörper* posit their own specific myth through their formal structure, there are elements within this structure that are shared independently of their utopias. These can be summarized as follows: having a legible boundary, differing scale, clear internal organization (form, paths, or space), recognizable form (iconic), and, finally, strict separation from the surrounding fabric. The presence of such characteristics reveals the underlying tension between the *Fremdkörper* and the surrounding urban structure. Each project asserts a myth about society, whether through religion, economics, politics, or aristocracy, but most often these myths are disliked or despised by a considerable amount of its citizens. However, it is these myths that mold the general characteristics of the *Fremdkörper* into specific schemes. Brussels in the early 1990s is saturated with such bodies. Let us for a moment examine four different *Fremdkörper* in Brussels that are rooted in differing myths: religion, democracy, capitalism, and political unity.

The **Koekelberg Basilica** is one of the largest churches in the world. King Leopold II first commissioned the complex in the late nineteenth century with the intent of creating the

largest neo-gothic cathedral in Europe. The project was only completed after World War II due to slow construction and massive budget increases. By that time what had started as a neo-gothic footprint had transformed into a neo-Byzantine monstrosity erected out of armed concrete and brick. Ornamentation had become incredibly austere, reduced to a series of prefabricated molds with highly repetitive and abstract patterns. Intriguingly, although architecture was assimilated into a differing myth, urbanistically, the overall project still sits as a *Fremdkörper* within Brussels. How can we be so sure that the basilica is in fact a *Fremdkörper*? Let us quickly examine the characteristics of the urban project. The basilica is situated at the peripheral end of the city's majestic north-south green axis, monumentalizing its position at the city's then edge. The basilica stands amid an island of lush greenery that digs into the city fabric like a dagger. A boundary clearly marks this form and is further clarified with tree-lined edges. The sizable volume could easily consume eight of the surrounding blocks. Furthermore, the basilica, taking the form of the Roman cross and stepping up through the layering of domes, completely overshadows the scale of the surrounding fabric. The importance of the basilica is emphasized through a radial set of paths and the framing of trees along the axis that mark it as the center, a notion which culminates on the interior in the massive dome. A long public corridor is concentrated in front of the basilica, allowing for pilgrimage and gathering while placing particular import on the iconic front façade. Ultimately, the basilica stands as the symbolic marker for the myth of elevation through religion. But as myths go, this one had vanished by the time the monument approached completion: For today, the basilica offers few religious services, rendering its scale completely alien to the society in which its sits. Catholicism is but a memory of an abandoned myth in Brussels, yet its *Fremdkörper* formally persists within the current city.

The **Palace of Justice** was also commissioned by King Leopold II and financed through the pillaging of the Congo, a Belgium colony which funded many of the king's outlandish projects. The king's vision for Brussels—to find seven hills in its topography and have each topped by a vast monumental power center of the supposed Belgian Empire (church, justice, executive branch, king, parliament, etc.)—never fully transpired, but the plan did leave behind two projects that occupied strategic places in the urban structure. The bigger irony is the dissolution of any remaining sentiments for Belgian national-

1 Sigmund Freud, *Beyond the Pleasure Principle*, trans. James Strachey (New York: Norton, 1961); *Moses and Monotheism*, trans. Katherine Jones (New York: Vintage, 1958).

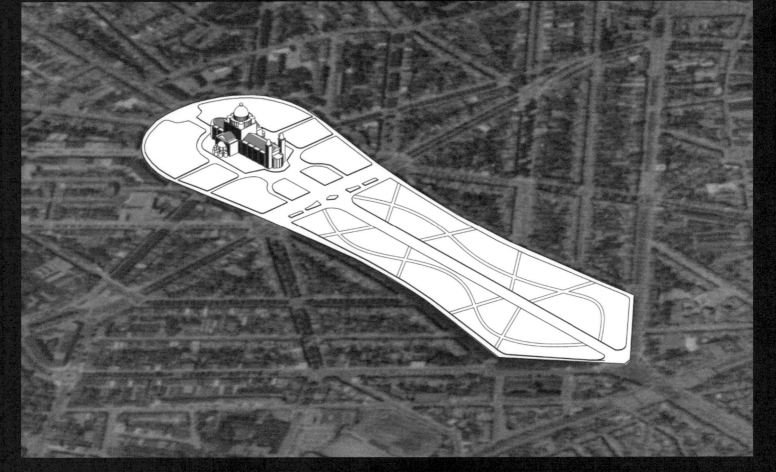

Koekelberg Basilica

ism. What results is another myth that never reached fruition but left traces of its intention. Just such a trace, the *Fremdkörper* of the Justice Palace is a massive, impenetrable block enveloped in open space. Similar to the basilica, the project marks a center around the idea of justice. The internal organization comprises linear buildings that symmetrically interlock to form the boundary edge and cross to denote the center. In section, the Justice Palace steps up like a ziggurat at this crossing and is topped with a dome. Again, the towering building becomes an unavoidable symbol in the Brussels skyline. The building's internal structure functions in and of itself without providing any concessions to the surrounding fabric. Three of the four entrances do not align with surrounding streets, nor does the building correspond in scale or material to the city's fabric. The largest public gathering space is dedicated to the front entry, further monumentalizing the central axis. What results is an independent island positing the supremacy of the law over the common folk. This supremacy is embedded in its origination wherein the palace had been purposely constructed overtop a popular neighborhood, erasing its fabric and instilling a myth of order. Today, although many sentiments of this supremacy have faded, the

Justice Palace still towers over the remnants of the neighborhood fabric.

A more contemporary example of a *Fremdkörper* is the **Administration City**, headquarters for the national administration of the Belgian government. Built during the 1960s, Administration City consists of a massive concrete platform with elegant slabs and towers, built on top of the medieval city. The oversized platform provides a legible boundary, marking the limits of the project just as the surrounding fabric marks the limits of their blocks. Five towers rest on this slab, anchoring the project while shadowing the surrounding city. In fact, the largest of the towers is an elegant modernist sliver containing the elevating myths of modernism. The complex acts as an instrument for elevation. The modernist buildings do not conform in scale or material to the surroundings, making themselves legible through their difference. The internal structure of the project does not operate through marking the center as the previous two but rather through framing and producing interstitial space on the platform. Thus, public space is not precisely positioned in front of the building to enhance its hierarchy; instead, it emerges between the buildings. It is here, ultimately, that the

myth of modernism rests: the emancipation of the individual on the free space of the platform, enabling freedom through the openness of choice. Beneath, an oversized parking garage separates the project from the urban grid, save for an exit ramp from an adjacent urban highway. Today, the national administration has sold the complex to a private developer who is tearing down segments and re-cladding the project with postmodernist lingo. Despite privatization and the re-cladding and removal of fringe elements, the clarity of the initial myth and the large amounts of concrete required for its materialization have prevailed within this *Fremdkörper*.

The last project of particular interest is the **European Parliament.** Designed during the 1980s by a group of local architecture firms for a consortium of local banking and insurance offices, the project was pushed through with the aid of the Belgian government. This support by the government was in a bid to strengthen Brussels' status as the capital of Europe. For this utopia to transpire, it effectively required the destruction of half a neighborhood. Instead of incorporating the eighteenth-century block structure into the scheme, megastructures were formed and

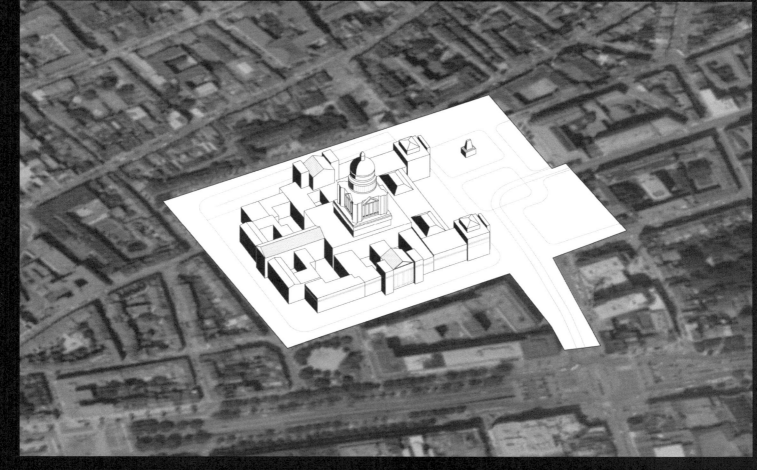

Palace of Justice

surrounded by remnants of the old, which were later fragmented by muscular urban highways. The project, rich in po-mo ornament, has already become for both elite and popular audiences an emblem for all that was wrong about Belgium and Europe. Situated on two oversized blocks, the parliament comprises a massive oval structure and, alongside it, an even larger linear complex of buildings. An interiorized public street structures the latter, creating a private, miniature city within Brussels that is fed by the railway station below. The central axis of the oval perpendicularly intersects the midpoint of the linear megastructure, linking the two buildings into an overall complex. Intriguingly, although the myth of this new *Fremdkörper* has quickly vanished—as a parliament it is only ten years old—it is still impregnated onto the urban structure, revealing the ideals at the time of its conception.

These are but four of thirty or so examples of a *Fremdkörper* in Brussels. Curiously, the foreign bodies are so abundant and in such close proximity in the city that the remaining interstitial tissue itself also falls apart into a series of isolated bodies. The density of the *Fremdkörper* destroys the very notion of a "normalized" city to which they are supposed

to be the exception. The historical city fabric, which in London or Paris forms an urban background, in Brussels is reduced to a mere accident between other disrupted fragments. This theoretical framework turns upside down: the *Fremdkörper* become the norm. Instead of figures marked on a background of an integrated city fabric, a multitude of such contradictory figures *is* the background. Each of these projects now presents, through its own form, its own wishful dream, a differing final ambition for the totality of the city. The map of Brussels looks like a montage of contradicting pieces: a series of closely packed, self-enclosed statements, bumping, rubbing, pushing, and shearing against each other on the underlying flow of myths touted throughout the city's history. These projects are conscious of the totalitarian streak contained within their utopian statement. They originate from a completely exaggerated vision about cultural dominance, a ruthless victory of the commissioner's vantage point over all others: the installment of his utopia is the hegemonic one. Their ambition is not realized by a complete reconfiguration of the entire city, for we are simply witness to their first phase, but this phase is already a microcosm of a total plan. In essence, a total project is prefigured in a limited and discretely cir-

cumscribed zone. Each such pre-figuration is actively contradicted by the adjacent ones. In fact, each successive one was erected in order to contradict other existing figures and prove its own supremacy. With such an interpretation, these *Fremdkörper* come awfully close to the definition of the symbol in the nineteenth-century aesthetics of German Romanticism. From Schelling to Robert Vischer and Wilhelm Worringer, the symbol is defined as an ideal aesthetic category, one that contains its meaning within its own complete structure—the content and the form are completely identical; the meaning is embedded within the form, and that is why the symbol operates as an almost pre-linguistic diagram or schema. In them, a myth materializes and becomes recognizable as an ideogram that captures, describes, and summarizes its entire narrative within its own formal structure. Importantly, German symbol theory was not meant to be a science of linguistics; it was fundamentally a normative aesthetic theory of the sublime, for which the yet-to-be-realized category of the symbol was defined as the closest approximation. Brussels' *Fremdkörper* approximate this romantic ideal. Thus, each figure accesses in its own way the sublime. Each of them has an ideogrammatic order that, while radically different for each,

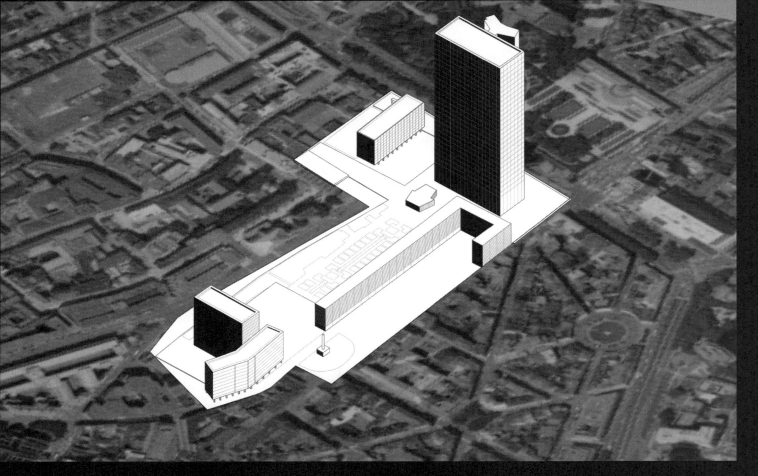

Administration City

also contains a statement about an ideal future and a desired destiny for the entire city. These bodies do not want to obscure, include, or compromise in any way; rather, they are extremely clear about the worldview embedded in them. They are that worldview.

A Symbolic Form of Liberalism

Projects with utopian overtones have traditionally channeled distrust and destructive mass energy. Nevertheless, Adorno and Horkheimer's[2] basic critique of the utopian still stands: upon its execution, utopia inexorably regresses into its opposites, totalitarianism and myth. Dramatically speaking, since every urban design project is based on a particular belief system, (an ideal) that is rolled out over a segment of society, every urban design project carries a totalitarian seed. Moreover, that seed is the essence of its existence. Without an ideal, a design project would be identical to the perceived status quo and cease to exist as a recognizable entity. The victory of any single ideal—for instance, in a master plan for the city—ultimately implies the erasure of opposing belief systems and therefore realizes the totalitarian intent contained within urban designs. Brussels offers us insight into how a society aspiring to be open and pluralist need not

step into the pitfalls of relativism and still formulate powerful and antagonizing utopian figures. Its symbolic form is the assemblage of conflicting pre-figurations. What are the principles, then, of the assemblage of pre-figurations? First, these bodies have boundaries; they are consciously finite rather than totalizing. Precisely because of their (inadvertently) exclusionary nature, they are legible as symbols. Their failure to achieve hegemony across the territory is what guarantees their strength as a symbolic form. Without a boundary, they would not even be legible as entities. Second, each *Fremdkörper* is, in its essence, a civic complex, comprising a piece of infrastructure, public space, and one or several buildings. The project is never an object but a combination of elements, creating what J. L. Sert referred to as the "civic complex." As such, each composition proclaims its own vision for the entire city, yet is complete within itself. Third, as a finite figure, each of them leaves plenty of room for others—in fact, it calls for differing and conflicting ideals. The large urban structure becomes that of an assemblage of civic complexes. Fourth, formalism, the representation of a complete worldview through a single and concise urban design project, is of the essence. In

the end, the *Fremdkörper* do not effectively realize or install a different socio-political regime, but they do in fact speak of a promise, a pre-figuration of such a model. This promise remains caught, locked up in everything from the overall plan to the architectural details. This changes the deployment of utopia in architectural urbanism from realization to homage.

Formalisms of the Liberal Project

This surreal city of Brussels presents us with Isaiah Berlin's "agonized pluralism." This model could be to the ideals of liberal democracy what Boris Iofan's Soviet Palace was to Stalinism. Berlin's last mention in architecture and urban theory came through Colin Rowe and Fred Koetter's Collage City, a thinly veiled argument against modernism. His deployment in the current context, however, is in fact based on a redeployment of the idealistic lineage in modernism. Berlin's liberal philosophy is often summarized with the following quotation:

> It may be that the ideal of freedom to choose ends without claiming eternal validity for them, and the pluralism of values connected with this, is only the late fruit of our declining capital-

2 Theodor Adorno & Max Horkheimer, *Dialectic of Enlightenment*, trans. John Cumming (New York: Herder and Herder 1972).

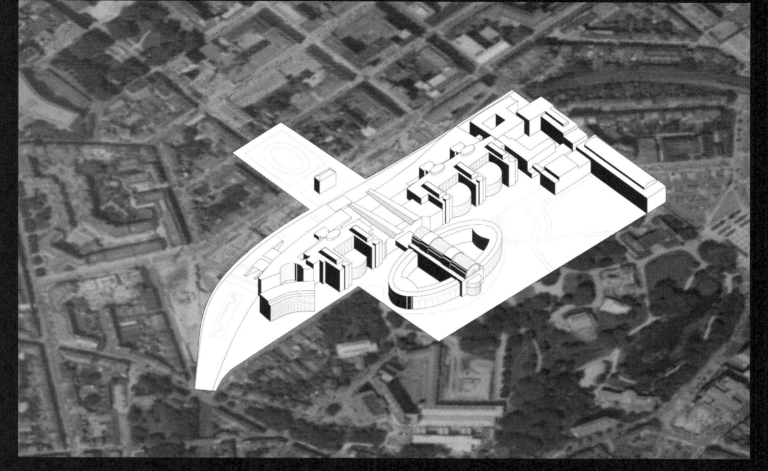

European Parliament

ist civilization: an ideal which remote ages and primitive societies have not recognized, and one which posterity will regard with curiosity, even sympathy, but little comprehension . . . . "To realize the relative validity of one's convictions," said an admirable writer of our time [Schumpeter], "and yet to stand for them unflinchingly is what distinguishes a civilized man from a barbarian." [3]

Berlin's model is that of a pluralism of absolute convictions. This is exactly the model of Brussels' *Fremdkörper*. Without absolute conviction within the constituent bodies, there is no project. But the analogy goes further. A liberal political philosophy distrusts pure, direct democracy, and so did Berlin. Direct democracy leads to the legitimacy of majority rule, or *Majoritarianism*.[4] This is, in fact, nothing less than the tyranny of the majority of the urban fabric. Against this tyranny, liberalism posits a plurality of power centers, and in order to achieve this it effectively institutionalizes *and formalizes* this plurality. In this argument, democracy is replaced by representation. By formalizing democracy and staging a representation of the *demos*,

rather than actually letting it achieve its tyrannical status, liberalism saves the idea of democracy. Progressive examples include rules of affirmative action, strengthening the representation of women and minorities; conservative ones include the British Upper House as a chamber of Parliament where historical upper classes are represented above their numerical weight. Representation thus supersedes democracy itself as the foundational principle of a liberal concept of the public sphere. The parliament serves as a figure that crystallizes a liberal vision of the entire body of the public and indeed of society as a layered cake of different interests. For that reason, the liberal figure of the parliament reduces democracy to a mere ritual, but this reduction is necessary to save the idea of democracy, by protecting it against its own authoritarian impulse. The fundamental consistency between representation as a political concept of liberalism and representation as an aesthetic project in the arts is to be found in the underlying notion of formalism. Politically speaking, formalism is associated with the representation of citizens and community in institutions, while informality is associated with grass-roots democracy, direct democracy, and the elevation of everyday

culture to the norm against which other expressions become deviant. Aesthetically speaking, formalism is related to a reading of form as its own content, independent of outside references, as in German symbol theory, Russian formalism, or American architectural modernism.[5] In a sense, both formalisms treat the form as its own ideal content, irrespective of the degree to which it actually represents the world of phenomena; the form (or representation) of the public is independent from its actual statistical composition. This crystallization of a vast, sprawling culture into a single symbolic form requires the introduction of a high degree of formalism. The form of the public that is crafted here is its own content, namely the ideal of liberalism itself.

What makes Brussels an intriguing template is the assemblage of *Fremdkörper* representing absolute convictions of differing constituencies throughout the city's history. As an assemblage, it conveys its utopian intent without reaching totalitarian synthesis. The continual tension in the urban structure is something to be embraced as an ideal of a liberal political aesthetic. As this precious invention of the Enlightenment is increasingly endangered, it is of crucial importance to stand up for it.

3 Isaiah Berlin, *Two Concepts of Liberty,* (1958).

4 Trevor Pateman in *Majoritarianism: An Argument from Rousseau and Condorcet,* In *Cogito,* vol. 2, no. 3 (1988), 29 - 31.

5 Similarly, the rise of the informal society in the Sixties in opposition to society's formal structure corresponds to a similar evolution in architectural urbanism, eloquently expressed by Bernard Rudofsky in his 1964 *Architecture without Architects.*

Invisible
Urbanism
in Africa

Vyjayanthi Rao
in conversation with
Filip De Boeck and
AbdouMaliq Simone

In *Kinshasa: Tales of the Invisible City*, Filip De Boeck writes:

"In spite of the fact that an analysis of the different physical sites through which the city exists and invents itself helps us to better understand the specific ways in which the materiality of the infrastructure generates particular sets of relations in the city, I would submit that in the end, in a city like Kinshasa, it is not, or not primarily, the material infrastructure or the built form that makes the city a city. The city, in a way, exists beyond its architecture . . . the infrastructure and architecture that function best in Kinshasa are almost totally invisible on a material level."[1]

Selling furniture in the street. Commune of Masina, Kinshasa.

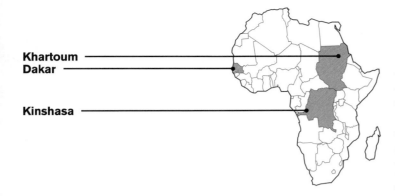

Khartoum

Dakar

Kinshasa

This understanding of the city, expressed so succinctly by De Boeck, is shared by all three of us. But as anthropologists speaking to architects, we are also concerned with exploring the relation between visibility and invisibility and with the "networks of concrete becoming," as AbdouMaliq Simone puts it, at once engaging and going beyond the artifice of material infrastructure and physical site.[2] Built form may be, as De Boeck states, "produced randomly in human sites as *living space*."[3] As urban studies have taken a "southern turn,"[4] with an increasing number of works in mainstream urban studies focusing on cities of the Global South, this contrast between built form and living space is indeed critical. But equally central, it seems, are questions of global scale and the possible political and spatial de-scriptions of particular cities, especially these cities of the South, at the global scale.

For this conversation, we take as our point of departure the multiple uses deriving from the latin root *capitalis* (chief, principal, in the sense of sovereign power) which is both the root of capital as well as of *capitellum*, meaning "small head," or the "top of the column" in the architectural sense.[5] By juxtaposing these multiple uses, we enter into a contradiction: we are speaking both about the sense of fixing, of the vanguard, of that which tops off and shows off the solidity of the architecture as well as that which circulates and controls the expression of sovereign power in the political sense, insofar as it is able to circulate.

We are especially concerned with where we can situate "networks of concrete becoming," both in terms of forms of accumulation and in terms of the possibilities for articulating political power in a continent that is increasingly held hostage to global flows of finance capital, resource extraction, and migration. We found that the best place to begin was with the transformations of the physical environment of African cities. While Simone unpacks the developments in and around Dakar and their political effects on other Senegalese cities, speculating on the causes of such massive investments in construction, De Boeck reflects on the intensification of *urbanity* without architecture throughout Congo, partly also as a result of the diamond trade. The relationship between what De Boeck calls the "ejaculation" of wealth and the accentuation of non-investment in the physical space of Kinshasa is contrasted, for example, with the imaginary "urban planning" encouraged by the various churches that have gained enormous popular appeal in the Congo. Can a conventional understanding of architecture sustain the weight of this imaginary planning? Can one think of the city outside of material forms of representation and aspiration such as those of architecture? These questions also motivate De Boeck's explorations of Kinshasa at the 2004 Venice Architecture Biennale and his more recent exhibition, *Kinshasa: The Imaginary City,* in Johannesburg (2006).

Non-investment in material terms might also be linked to a return of the colonial *comptoir* economy, the economy of the trading post and the generativity of certain kinds of urban performance. These performances are centered around the "hunter's landscape," in which capital works only

through its incessant circulation rather than through a logic of accumulation and maximization of profit. It works, in other words, through the creation of social networks that make investments work for the urban hunter. In this landscape, colonial histories seem to endure inasmuch as the city continues to be seen as a site of exclusion by the vast majority of the people who developed Kinshasa outside its colonial boundaries. It is therefore a place where everything that comes from elsewhere, from outside the ludic spaces of social networks in formation, is thought of as being there to be "ripped off."

Thus, the concentration of political power in the realm of the capital city is challenged by its circulation in and through diverse spaces and among those networks that constitute the invisible architecture of connections of the contemporary African city. The physical aspect of the city, especially as the signal of a growing densification and convergence of trajectories, has, however, also become crucial. A history of Dakar, from its origins in the *comptoir* economy and its territorial incorporation into France that defined its relations with the other cities in the Senegalese metropolitan system, reveals these new trajectories. These trajectories are at once global in their reach—controlled by actors from the Senegalese Murid diaspora as well as the Lebanese diaspora—while also having effects at the level of the nation, expressed in the investments that new actors from the hinterland are making into the landscape of Dakar, gaining new visibility for their activities.

We explore here these dispersals of capital (financial and human) and their relation to these capital cities (Dakar, Kinshasa, and Khartoum) and in the peculiar relations that cities like Lagos have to "capital" in both senses, economic and political. In other words, we try to open the question of the location of "capital" in this conversation. In so doing, we attend to other forms of invisibility as well. For what happens in the course of the circulation of capital across Africa is the generation of capital and of urbanity outside of known forms, outside of the structuring contexts of architecture and the planned insertion of material infrastructure. "These cities are often invisible to the outside world," De Boeck says, because "they function in ways that we are not used to seeing and therefore go unnoticed." Thus we face the question, where should capital/the capital city be located by asking, what is the scene/site of urban action? We face the question of what conduits of access are being developed vin order to facilitate investment, expansion, accumulation or "ejaculation" of capital by asking, what forms of social complexity are being explored in the development of these conduits? What sort of etiquette is being developed by residents of these cities in their drive to becoming visible in order to enable social being? We turn to situations of boundary maintenance in Abidjan and in Khartoum, and we also turn to the emergent play of aspirations that reach for undercoded territories. Recent Malaysian investments in Senegalese social housing in the name of an ethical Islamic practice as well as Chinese investment in a transcontinental railway system represent gestures of a new kind of global play. In this conversation, we think these contradictions between the material and the non-material and the visible and the invisible articulates the relationship between political power and capital and reveals aligned and accumulated stashes of wealth in its multiple forms.

Vyjayanthi Rao

1 Filip De Boeck, *Kinshasa: Tales of the Invisible City* (Ghent: Ludion, 2004), 233-235.

2 AbdouMaliq Simone, "The Visible and Invisible: Remaking Cities in Africa," in *Under Siege: Four African Cities: Freetown, Johannesburg, Kinshasa, Lagos: Documenta11_Platform4*, 24.

3 De Boeck, 233.

4 Vyjayanthi Rao, "Slum as Theory," *International Journal of Urban and Regional Research*, vol. 30 (1).

5 Webster Dictionary online.

Followers of Etienne Tshisikedi, calling for a boycott of the elections, burn a Kabila election billboard, central Kinshasa, July 2006.

Capital/City: Imaginary Urban Plans

Vyjayanthi Rao: What are the spatial expressions of capital in contemporary Africa? How do these expressions relate to expressions of political and subjective power?

AbdouMaliq Simone: Currently in Dakar, you have the rather recent and still opaque project of building a new capital, for the moment designated as "Dubai sur Atlantique," some sixty kilometers to the north. Partly this reflects the generalization of the reinvented logic of the *entrepôt* associated with Dubai; partly it emerges from the fact that there exists a kind of conurbation that leaves Dakar and then begins to link what were some major small cities like Thies and M'bour. In some ways you have this residue of a kind of colonial bifurcation. Fifty years ago, Dakar started to become too overcrowded, becoming too much of a threat to certain kinds of order and processes. Dense quarters were displaced to Pikine and Guediwaye, and that in some ways, culturally, became the real Dakar. Outside of colonial specifications, these areas reflected many of the tensions of urban spaces attempting to articulate temporal and spatial divergence. The same for Freetown, the same for Conakry, the same for Dakar and to a limited extent for Abidjan—you have coastal capitals where, geo-morphically, it's quite limited in how they can grow. You have this kind of concentration in these very limited physical spaces. It becomes impossible to navigate. This kind of trajectory of expansion then makes it quite physically difficult to access the centers of power and centers of commerce. So, in terms of President Abdoulaye Wade saying we can no longer have the airport where we have it, we can no longer have ministries where we have them, we have to relocate, we have to bring them out to make them more accessible, to recenter, to reconstitute somehow the gravitational field of the capital means in one sense this old reiteration of new, grand works. Still, the former center, Plateau, continues to be a huge building site. I mean, you still see these immense kinds of constructions taking place.

Filip De Boeck: It's incredible. I just drove through it a couple of weeks ago. Whose money is driving this?

AMS: In some sense the appearance of continuous development signals a certain availability of this area to investment of all kind, and this plurality itself can constitute a platform for real occupation. Whatever is put up will in the end be used in some way. So residents in Dakar don't usually have the sense that this is something that's being inflated. Spaces are being bought. There's a market. People are buying these things: office space, apartment space . . .

VR: It's not virtual.

AMS: I can't say for sure, but there's a kind of popular understanding that there are real buyers for these things, real occupancy.

FDB: I think that is the difference with a place like Congo. Clearly in Senegal or in Dakar, you have a middle class or upper middle class of people, merchants with financial means who are doing their own trade and commerce and investing in their own city. In Congo, such a local middle class is absent, and there are, of course, historical reasons for that. For a long time the whole country was run by a small group, a power elite around Mobutu. There was no middle ground between the very poor and the very rich.

Mobutu's downfall created a void in that respect. Those with money left. In Kinshasa, as a result, the housing market just collapsed. Those who remained in the city could afford to buy housing. Today, real estate is booming again as never before, but the boom is not caused primarily by Congolese. The capital flowing into the city comes through ex-pats and foreigners (the latter often Lebanese)—people from outside who start to redevelop the city but only to a certain and very minimal extent.

VR: What about the diamond trade in the early 1990s and the kind of wealth it generated? Was it at all reflected in what was happening to the physical space of Kinshasa?

FDB: Well, on the one hand, it just accentuated the level of non-investment in physical space because all of that money would leave. Very little of it would be invested in infrastructure. On the other hand, it did have a huge impact in other ways because the informal diamond economy allowed for local actors to all of a sudden gain access to a lot of money. People, often youngsters, would go to Angola to dig diamonds, and often they would come back with a $1,000, $10,000, or even $100,000.

VR: And they didn't know what to do with it?

FDB: Well, most of the time it was very quickly ejected and spent—kind of ejaculated, really, all over the place. Few were those who invested it in building, in houses, in plots of land. But some areas of certain neighborhoods in Kinshasa did witness a modest construction boom thanks to that kind of money. But already, when you talk about the capital of Kinshasa, the question immediately is, The capital for whom, or who defined what the capital is, and who has access to it. In Dakar, it was merely a discussion of *where should it be*. In Congo, the colonial city really emerged as a non-place. It was defined as a "centre extra-coutumier," that is, the city placed itself right from the start outside of all locally existing cultural, social, and political frameworks. In the postcolonial period, Kinshasa became a major political center. But in recent years, even that role has slightly changed. In the late 1990s we saw how regional players (Rwanda, among others) tried hard to make the capital move eastward, away from a Francophone sphere of influence. In the end that hasn't worked, if only because of the sheer size and weight of Kinshasa as a cultural center. And it has, of course, also remained an important political center, but contrary to an earlier period, it is perhaps no longer exclusively the only political center. There are other centers of power as well. With the Kabila dynasty, Lumumbashi, for example, has once again become more important.

And, second, the capital, already when the city was founded or when it grew out of really a *comptoir* economy, it was a trading post originally and then transformed into a huge labor camp. The city that the Belgian colonial administration developed was a deeply segregated one, certainly in terms of race but also in terms of gender, for example. Basically, it was a depot of cheap labor force. Access to the city was strictly controlled. The city itself was dual: there was "la Ville," the exclusively white, colonial heart of the city, and then there was "la Cité," the vast, indigenous peripheral city, inhabited by Congolese. The city in itself has always maintained a state of exclusion, even today. For example, where the colonial borders of the city end today, the real city starts, much like Pikine. But in Kinshasa, you have a colonial city with a very small heart, which stopped growing in 1960, when Kinshasa's population did not exceed 400,000. Afterward, 4 million to 6 million people have been added onto that, but in areas that have not been urbanized along formal lines.

Today, one of the access points into the old colonial Ville is marked by a statue, which Father Kabila erected in memory of Lumumba, Congo's first prime minister after independence. The statue itself is of a Lumumba who stands with one hand raised. And there are all kinds of popular interpretations of that statue. First of all, in Congo, there is no real culture of statuary in public places, so its sudden appearance generated all kinds of comments. Painted in gold, the huge and heavy statue reminds one of the former Soviet Union's aesthetics. The first remarks people made were, "This is going to be heavy to move and steal when another wave of looting sweeps through the city." And second, "Why is he standing there with his hand like this?" He's basically saying, "Stop, you can't get into the city." To all of the multitudes who live in the peripheral city that has become the real city, the statue says, "You're not allowed to come in." It's basically perceived as the government denying access to all these people who want to get into the city but who are not allowed to, who can't afford to, who can't make use of it, who are blocked and excluded.

The areas and neighborhoods that extend beyond the statue are referred to as "La Chine populaire," or the Peoples Republic of China, because they are so populous. They are called "Bana terre rouge," or the children of the red earth, in reference to the dusty and unasphalted sand roads in those areas. The people living there have never had a real sense of the colonial city as their own. Very often, I think, they don't feel as if the city belongs to them. It's not their city.

Father Kabila, I believe, understood that very well and tried to decentralize the urban space, much like Wade. As an alternative to the Central Market in the colonial center, Kabila ordered another market to be built in the city's newer periphery. But even then that market picks up only very slowly because people do not really consider it their own: it is a top-down government initiative. It has been there now for almost ten years, and the feeling about that market is not good. People start working and functioning around the market, but the market itself as a constructed space by the government has never really been fully adopted.

So that other city, that peripheral city that is the real city, has developed according to its own notion of what capital might mean, or what forms of accumulation might mean. In order to exist socially in a city like Kinshasa, expenditure, circulation, and conspicuous consumption are far more important than accumulation or maximalization of profit. Accumulation requires a directionality, a teleology, a specific temporality that is not the temporality of the city today. The city, on the contrary, is a space of the sudden, the unforeseen, the unexpected and fleeting moment.

In order to survive in it, one has to know how to capture that moment. It is this praxis of capture and seizure that determines life and survival in the city, which itself is often compared to the space of the forest. As such, the city does not function according to a standard capitalist logic as we know it. The city, essentially, is a hunter's landscape. In order to survive in this forest-city, one has to be a good hunter, that is, know how to seize an opportunity and know how to make that known. The new figures of success within the city, whether it be preachers, politicians, or musicians, are, in a very real sense, the city's best hunters: those who know how to capture wealth, inject it again in social networks, and gain social weight through it.

That also means that the urbanscape is not so much shaped by the dynamics of modernity but rather that it is constantly infused with all kinds of other notions and moralities that often have longstanding, rural roots.

The practices of seizure and immediate expenditure make for the fact that there is no buildup of any surplus; the notion of accumulation is absent. Everything you have or everything that is sold in the market is everything that can be contained by one's belly, everything that can be eaten and digested immediately in the moment. There is no use in buying ten cans of something because you don't know whether on the tenth day you will still be there to drink it. So you buy what you need in the moment. You don't buy a whole bar of soap, but you buy just a third of it, enough to wash yourself with this one time. You don't buy a whole pack of cigarettes; you buy just one or even half of one cigarette. And so all the heaps of foodstuffs that you see at the market are measured by the quantity of the belly, the quantity of the stomach. Capital in that sense starts to mean something else; it becomes something else, away from standard notions of accumulation.

VR: So there's a different sense or understanding of investment also?

FDB: Well, there is a lot of investment in social relations and in one's self-realization through these relations, but far less investment in material infrastructure. Not in buildings, not in a city that is still perceived as something that is not fully ours after all those decades. And since it is not fully ours, it means there isn't a sense of responsibility about it: the material infrastructure and everything that comes from above and from outside is there to be ripped off, to be captured and taken advantage of, whether legally or illegally. The term now is *kisanola*, or (combing your hair.) "Combing" in the sense people now give to it means "stealing," looting, ripping off. If I, as a white person, walk through the street, people will make the *kisanola* sign, by which they indicate "You are there to be ripped off," basically because I don't belong there and can therefore be taken advantage of without any moral objections or feelings of guilt or wrongdoing. Similarly, a money changer in the street might advertise "double *kisanola*," meaning, "Here you will be ripped off twice." It indicates that the money-changer you are dealing with knows what he is doing, that he is shrewd and street-wise. Paradoxically, the fact that he is not to be trusted is a sign you can trust that guy. Another image people use is that of an injection. In order to socially exist and survive in this urban environment, one has to know how to stick a needle into someone and suck the victim's blood. So that's the way in which capital moves in the city, that's what it is about. It's not about accumulating, it's not about maximalizing. It is not about having but about being, not about possessing but about consuming, about singularizing oneself by immediately putting capital in constant circulation.

VR: So it doesn't have this capitalistic notion of investment, which is directed toward some distant future, directed toward something that might materialize at some other point in time.

FDB: Such a sense is emerging today but in the religious sphere, where money has come to mean something very specific. Within Pentecostalism and other "prosperity churches," you see how the switch toward a capitalist notion of money and of accumulation is made. There you also witness the introduction of new notions of individualization. These churches turn away from older collective identities based on kinship or ethnic belonging. Within that new religious public sphere these former group identities are disfavored. On the contrary, one becomes an authentic Christian as an individual and through one's own work and effort. And that's the constant message of these churches. Here one witnesses the introduction of a new subject formation, the introduction also of a new work ethos and of new notions of accumulation. In these churches accumulation is no longer something that is socially negative. It is, on the contrary, something that is favored, even though the fruits of that labor and accumulation are often not harvested instantly in this life. When people give money and goods to the church and to their preacher, they do so because they believe that God will multiply these gifts and return it to them. During Masses and prayer meetings the believers often listen to testimonies by people who died and were resuscitated through the force of prayer. Often they report back to the church community about what they witnessed in paradise: "Every-

thing that we give to the church, everything that we give to the preacher, is being invested for you in heaven," they would say. "And with the money you give they are already building your house and your villa in paradise. When you die, your house will be there, a house that you were never able to afford here on earth." So giving in this religious context has become an investment in real estate, even though that real estate is located in heaven. In this sense, the churches do contribute to a new form of urban planning, but it is an imaginary urban planning in the hereafter.

In those churches, within these new forms of Christian fundamentalism, you clearly see how the switch is made from the notion of the gift toward a notion of capital, with all of the fallout that it produces too—because it means that stress is put on individual success and not on group solidarity. And it means that the notion of the group, of what "family" is, for example, is being redefined at the moment away from the reality of the extended family toward the new and more restrictive notion of the nuclear family. In the process, people whom one would have defined as kin before are now being labelled as outsiders, strangers, or even witches. These are radically new geographies of inclusion and exclusion that emerge within the urban locale and redefine the boundaries between inside and outside, kin and stranger, endogamous and exogamous.

A city like Kinshasa has really become the fault line where these two different logics—the logic of gift- and kin-based reciprocity and the logic of money—meet, so far without really merging, and that produces huge upheavals—

VR: In the book, you talked about the idea of the jungle and how it's becoming part of the landscape of the city. The growth of the city is premised upon this encompassing of the forest.

FDB: Well, as I said, it's again about the hunter. In the forest, in order to survive, you have to know how to hunt. In the city, in order to survive, you have to know how to hunt. Well, that means, what does the hunter do when he goes hunting? He comes back with meat and then distributes it according to specific roles and rules that indicate what one should give to one's maternal uncle, first wife, the owner of the gun, the owner of the land where you shot the animal on, and so on and so forth. And that's how he makes that capital gain, in this case, work for him. He gains in social prestige by investing in social capital.

In order to survive in the city, you have to do the same thing. You have to constantly make sure that you create and invest in certain networks, which are no longer the network of the household, maybe, or of your ethnic group or your village, but different kinds of associations, different kinds of groups of cooperation—maybe a gang, maybe all kinds of groups. But you constantly have to invest, you constantly have to be present, constantly have to exchange, constantly be "in touch" with others. In order to survive in the city you have to know how to do that.

When people speak of the city as a forest, they refer to a specific kind of forest. It's a forest in which you can become modern, where you can attain and access a certain modernity, even if it's only in imaginary or oneiric form. I gave the example the church, but the bar is another concrete example of a space where you can do that, and the church and the bar overlap to a certain extent. They are basically the same ludic spaces.

VR: I was also interested when you talked about the hollowing out of political power in Kinshasa—the colonial Kinshasa, not the

A statue of Patrice Lumumba erected by Laurent Kabila, and an unfinished tower built during the Mobutu years look down on Jean-Pierre Bemba supporters as they make their way to a rally, Kinshasa, July 2006.

other Kinshasa which has developed later on—and the concentration of that power in other cities, like Lumumbashi. What is the relationship between these various concentrations and expressions of power? What is the kind of impact they have on the landscape of the capital city?

AMS: Looking at some of the overlaps and divergences of Dakar may be somewhat interesting. Because one has to keep in mind that Dakar and other Senegalese towns were actually—

FDB: Those were *comptoirs*.

AMS: They were *comptoirs* and also part of France at one point. Dakar was literally integrated into French territory and done so in a way to mark the strong divide between the city, the urban and the hinterland. The hinterland was the province of the *Marabout*, a kind of religious power that had to be contained, that had to be marked. I don't know a lot about that history, but it is a clear history with ramifications to this day. In some ways, outside of Kinshasa is a hinterland that is teeming with certain possibilities. It teems with both an excess of life and death.

Whereas outside of Dakar is increasingly a hinterland that is over. It's wasted.

But what's interesting, too, is the fact that you have Touba. It was a religious city and was at one time exempt from taxation and had no kind of local municipal structures. The buying and selling all was concentrated as a kind of terrain of the Murid structure and also exempt from certain kinds of applications of customs law.

Touba really grew a lot through trade, so it was a kind of *entrepôt* masked as sacred city. Then, when people began to realize that it was a sort of booming commercial center on the basis of illegal trade, there was the attempt to domesticate it in some way. The domestication, the complex negotiations to bring its urban economy, which was not just an economy of Touba, but a transnational economy—

VR: Of the Murids?[6]

AMS: That somehow symbolically and administratively was administered from Touba. The complicated negotiations to try to bring it into the ambit of the state meant that certain deals had to be worked out. And an important deal was that Plateau, the commercial, administrative, colonial center of Dakar, became—through many different policies, many different deals—increasingly availed to the Murids. So, the Murids began to take over. They began to take over certain Lebanese commercial interests, particularly that kind of intermediary between wholesaling and retailing. What was interesting is that the Dakar urban economy in some ways became an extension of Touba. But you have then a kind of indigenous entrepreneurship that really is within an urban economy and is really strong, unlike in many other places.

FDB: That's really different than Congo. I mean, in terms of indigenous entrepreneurship, what has worked well in the past decades are those parts of the country that knew how to evade Kinshasa. A very good example are the Nande cultivators and traders of coffee in a secondary city such as Butembo, in eastern Congo, who through their own networks managed to really inscribe themselves in transnational commercial movements that link them to Dubai and Asia. Very wealthy, a whole new form of urbanization, a kind of very provincial urbanism, all of it because they are not under the control of the capital city and know how to evade the state. Otherwise, it would never have happened. The real urban growth and the notion itself of urbanity often develops, I would say, outside of Kinshasa, as long as it's not controlled by the capital.

The same is true of the diamond trade. Even though materially they do not represent much, little diamond towns that spring up along the border with Angola, for example, or the gold-mining towns in the east, those are the places where the idea of capitalism and urbanity is most fully generated. But again, materially, these cities and towns do not correspond to the form of what we think of as a city. And yet it is much more urban in a way in its dynamics than what goes on in the "real" city.

AMS: In Senegal, in some ways, the predominant mode of urban accumulation can be attributed to what goes on outside of Senegal. There's nothing within the nation of Senegal itself that could account for the kind of—

FDB: No, but within Senegal, there are local authochthonous groups that have the capacity and strength to impose themselves and become key players and control that game. In Congo, you often don't have these, in that sense. Whether small trade and commerce or industrial activities in the fields of mining or wood-logging today, these activities often were and still are not in Congolese hands but are controlled by the Lebanese, for example, or the Chinese, for that matter. Even in the early years of Kinshasa's existence, the trade was not in Congolese hands but was often controlled by what were called the "coastmen": people coming from Freetown or Dakar, or later the Greeks and the Portuguese and now the Lebanese and the Pakistanis and so on.

When it comes to the broader geopolitical game, I mean, why is Uganda there? Why is Rwanda there? It seems to be Congo's fate to always be exploited by and profited from outsiders. Congolese, even the Congolese government, tries to get its hands on some of the crumbs that fall off the table, but it never fully controls the game, it seems to me. Whereas these Murid are in control of what they're doing, to some extent.

AMS: And increasingly so.

FDB: And increasingly so, yes, increasingly taking over the state.

AMS: So that sort of division, of keeping the state separate from capital, Dakar separate from Touba—

VR: In practical terms, it's blurring. This relation between the capital city as the expression of political power and capital as economic field of operation—

AMS: It's not there. For example, during the periods of intense religious ceremony in Touba, you can walk down the main street of Dakar and have almost no traffic. Otherwise, streets in Dakar, where I used to live not far from Plateau, which used to be a 10-minute taxi ride, today takes an hour and a half.

FDB: Absolutely. Or even longer now, because of the road works.

AMS: But also because there are limited feeder roads, because of the increased densification. In some ways, what accounts for that kind of densification? All right, many of the Lebanese have gone away, have been displaced. So they go, but many of the Lebanese also continue to have important kinds of economic circuits. As they're displaced from certain kinds of economic activities because of the ways that many of those Lebanese networks were implicated within the socialist party, they simply take another form of accumulation, which is through extending their real estate. So, you have these big Lebanese investments in building.

Now, the Murid are also capable of doing that. I mean, it's not that the particular form of economic activity is anything different from a kind of corporate structure. They do that as well. But there is something important about the market. There is something important about the logic of the way in which the market operates as an intensely mutable form. There's something very material about the way that this market operates: small traders who are more than small traders, of shifting alliances that are made visible, of a form of visibility where people can watch, observe, see what's going on, who's dealing with whom. But that has to be serviced, so you have big trucks coming in and traffic.

---

6 The Murids are part of a Senegalese Sufi movement centered on the life and teachings of a local saint named Sheik Amadou Bamba—also known by the honorific "Serigne Touba"—who lived from 1853 to 1927.

It becomes a densification by virtue of multiplying these trajectories in a way that's partly symbolic, partly a kind of nerve center. The antecedents want to reproduce themselves spatially, yet veer off and transform into a sort of Murid version of corporate headquarters—big buildings, because they're investing in that as well—and also the way in which Dakar is increasingly implicated in other economies elsewhere. For example, the political crises of Abidjan during the past several years has meant key corporations, multilaterals, move from Abidjan to Dakar.

But what's also interesting is the attempt to host the Organization of the Islamic Conference in Dakar, something that was supposed to have already taken place. It has been postponed now three times, so now it's to take place at the end of 2007. Wade always says the reason for this delay is because Dakar needs adequate infrastructure in order to sufficiently host the meeting. For him, that means the construction of eight new five-star hotels on the Corniche.

In some ways the infrastructure of hosting this meeting already exists. It already exists in tourist areas outside the city. But in some ways, that's too much a kind of budget tourism, bordering on some sleazy activities that can't really be the site to host an Islamic meeting. Maybe any other meeting could take place there. But because this is the Organization of Islamic Confere and as the basis of accumulation of the Murids has always in some sense been marginal to the rest of the Islamic world, there is some perceived need to use this gathering as a way of normalizing Senegal's relationships with the Muslim world.

Not that Senegal itself hasn't always been seen as part of the Muslim world. But increasingly, as the Murids assume increased political and economic power and then become available as an expression of a certain kind of national cohesion, the distinctiveness of Senegal as a nation but also its integration into a larger theater of operations. "We're Muslims, we're clearly Muslims, we take Islam seriously," but the role of Senegal being in some sense, "We're Muslims, but we're also a different kind of Muslims." Singularity is very much wrapped up historically into a sense of national identity, a sense of national cohesion.

In some ways, the hosting of the Organization of the Islamic Conference signals almost the normalization of Senegal's position within the Islamic world, so it has to be done right. But to be done right means that you have to make this big intervention into the built environment. The money is coming from Dubai, from Kuwait. These hotels basically belong to them, and what is their interest? What is the interest of the Emirates in the Gulf? The financially ambiguous role of Dubai World and its real estate arm, Limitless, in the proposed construction of the new capital simply accentuates the impression that the country is being brought into a particular field of orbit that is being elaborated through major urban and financial engineering projects managed by Gulf companies across the Maghreb.

Somehow there's something about locating what will be Gulf-owned pieces of real estate on the Corniche, facing the Atlantic in the western-most Islamic country. A six-hour flight from New York—there's something about that.

FDB: Are you saying this or is this way this has been perceived?
AMS: On the street in Dakar, there's this kind of talk, you know?
FDB: Like we're in the middle of—
AMS: All I'm saying is that when you look at the relationship between capital and the capital city, the kind of project of centralizing, the kind of expression of the capital, of the national cohesion—

VR: The way I'm hearing it is that there's some relationship between being aligned to these other sorts of flows—from Dubai or elsewhere—on the one hand, and on the other hand, to the regeneration of the city, of the nation, but which gets expressed in this particular way, which can't be expressed without this alignment, right? Without this movement toward bringing those elements into the space of the city—in a very concrete expression, the buildings almost become that medium as it were, where—

AMS: Yes, but combined with a very old story too. Wade is a very old guy. He's in his early 80s. He's just begun his last term in office at what may be a high political price for the country. He knows that time is running out, and he's waited to be in power for a long, long time, and somehow the notion of the *grands travaux*, the big works—
FDB: Very French. Like a French president.
AMS: To make the mark, to leave the trace, with also very old ideas about making Senegal really a modern nation—that's reflected in this. It's an old story.

Invisible Infrastructure

VR: Turning to a related but different question, I want you both to elaborate why the notion of "invisibility" seems so analytically central to thinking about the contemporary African city?

FDB: The question seems to be the things that Maliq was talking about: urban networks and how people move through the city, make use of the city, and create the city and generate the city while doing so. How can you capture that? How can you start to understand, capture, contain, and represent urban life? How do you represent an urban reality like that? You cannot. All the means that we have at our disposal to do so, whether it's writing or whether it's photography, seem to be in a way not sufficient.

VR: So the question is also about epistemology having to do with the object itself. It seems like writing about invisibility is a productive way of describing what's happening in African cities. And part of the interest is also to understand whether those forms of description are particular only to Africa or if they can travel to other urban conditions.

FDB: Well, invisibility can mean many things. There is invisibility on many levels, of course. There is the fact that these cities are invisible to the outside world because people don't know much about African cities. There is the fact that these cities function in ways we're not used to, and that we therefore do not see, that go unnoticed. There is the fact that forms of urban planning and so on continue in very much literally invisible ways, like the urbanization that I was talking about, urbanizing in Paradise rather than the real life. Invisibility might mean a number of things.

AMS: I agree. As part of this New School grant, there has been this project in Douala for the past eighteen months. One piece of that was to have a working group of young, middle-class kids in a middle-class area of Douala, Bonamoussadi. They meet once every two weeks for eighteen months. This notion of invisibility was something that was on their minds as well. It was a word that was used, it was a concern that they had, it was a very particular kind of concern because these are middle-class kids. They come from families that are civil servants or lawyers or teachers, professors, business people, and live in a quarter of Douala that has maybe 300,000 people. It's not small; it's a significant chunk of the city.

When they talk about the changes that they have seen taking place over the past couple of years, the discussion started on the level of something very visible. That is, the changes in the built environment and the way in which there was this popularity of a certain kind of tile that was being put on the houses. Old houses were being torn down, and on the façades of these new ones that were being built was a particular kind of tile—white tile. They started to talk about the way in which this was a kind of uneasy thing, an unsettling thing, for them because it had these connotations of the cemetery, the mortuary, of death—the kind of the white that you would put on graves.

They would talk about the façade as some kind of death. In many of the new constructions, people would spend so much money putting the tile on the façade that they didn't have enough money left over to furnish the house inside. You'd have these beautiful, nice façades but inside something that—

FDB: Emptiness.

AMS: Emptiness. So, again, sort of intensifying this kind of connotation of death. They would see their neighbours, but the concern was, "Okay, this is the built environment, it's a nice house, but who is inside?" This thing about being visible in the built environment was also a kind of concern about with whom do we live? The sense about living with people you don't quite know.

And then, of course, the notion of the living dead—those who are able to operate in the city without being interrupted, whose operations cannot be made visible, rendered visible. We don't know how someone's gotten their money. All of a sudden they have a lot of money, or all of a sudden someone loses a lot of money. Or all of a sudden, people move from a house without anyone knowing.

In some ways, their concern was "Okay, we're all sort of middle class in this boat. We all have sort of narratives about how we got here. My mother, my father, they went to university . . ." But they would talk about going to shop at a new mall, a new supermarket. They would talk about the anxiety of with whom would you be shopping, because you never know who it is that these people are. So the concern was always to make that which is invisible visible—to interrupt it, to trip it up, to find ways of trying to slow down possible neighbors who could operate with such speed through the city that they wouldn't be visible. How do you make them visible? How do you trip them up? How do you set up roadblocks?

They then went on to talk about what people they knew were actually doing to try to trip them up. The stories get quite complicated and quite political and involve other territories and people in the city that they would never deal with. The notion sometimes of visibility and invisibility is a concern that people themselves raise. It's a kind of language that they themselves bring, so it's not an analytical thing necessarily imposed. It can be that, but . . .

FDB: It's a natural thing that comes out of the reality that people inhabit. In Kinshasa, the same. The relationship between visibility and invisibility is a very weird one, in a way, because on the one hand, in order to exist socially in the city is all about being as visible as possible. It's about appearance. That's why you have that whole popular urban culture of *sape* and elegance, about the clothes you wear. It's about knowing how to put yourself on stage, and it's the only way to acquire social weight and impose yourself in public space. All of a sudden there is this person emerging, this preacher, politician, musician, or businessman, very theatrical and very physically present, although you never see how he got there. The modes in which visibility was achieved remained rather invisible.

Performing Urbanity

VR: So are there particular forms of etiquette associated with becoming visible?

AMS: I am thinking about the work I did in Lagos, which was some time ago. It was in a particular neighborhood in Lagos, which was very peculiar to Lagos, very particular to Lagos. There, the questions of visibility and invisibility were largely about witnessing. How do you turn yourself into a receiver of the kinds of information that might be useful to you in order to know how to insert yourself into a some kind of emerging deal or scenario? Because all that this neighborhood had was its deals: the deals that didn't take place inside but always outside. There was always this kind of incessant process of visiting each other, showing up, visiting, making oneself visible, to go to a store where other people are showing up. But then as other people are showing up, how do you not insist upon your agenda? How don't you dominate this space, this scene, but how do you become visible and almost disappear in the face of others who are also there, in some sense, for the same agenda? Because this was largely a Hausa neighborhood within a Yoruba city—or a Muslim place, West African Muslim place—it wasn't that there weren't visible associations and visible rules and visible representatives of the emir and his business interests. Somehow, in order to make the thing work, people had to put together new crews with new kinds of skills, with different kinds of experiences and trades than in the past, because you're trying to take on something new. You're trying to configure new kinds of deals now, you're trying to go to new cities, you're trying to buy new commodities, you're trying to relate to other kinds of syndicates.

So, I want to put together a new crew, but how do I do that? But also, how do I *not* enter? It's complicated because this is a spatial arena that knew it had to survive in some way because Babandiga and the military wanted to seize itbecause it's an interlocked, an interstitial zone between Lagos island and Victoria. It was ceded by the British to the Hausa as a kind of space of operation, so there are very visible solidarities that had to be maintained. You can't include everyone, but you can't be seen excluding people in particular. How do you create the sense that your new crews are in some sense self-selected, that you're not the one who's excluding?

So it's just a complicated kind of elaboration of a social etiquette in a way, a kind of business practice that had to keep channels of information open, had to not keep secrets, but had to have an informational economy where you minimized competition. It was all done through these quotidian practices of having sites that apparently didn't sell much of anything but were places of reception. There's a way of managing an economy of visibility and invisibility, where the two had to be brought together in some kind of functional calibration and recalibrated all of the time.

Within the larger scope of Lagos, given the fact that there are usually eight people to a room, always in very dense quarters, how can you keep something to yourself? How can you keep something away? Is there, in any sense, privacy?

Privacy doesn't really exist spatially. It has to be a calibration of not seeing what you see, and also seeing what you don't see, because you have to be able to see.

Even in the everyday cognition of this kind of density, visibility and invisibility are day-to-day matters.

FDB: But you also need to be invisible or to know how to disappear and reappear at a good time.

A traditional dancer and crowd salute Jean-Pierre Bemba as he walks to a rally from the airport, Kinshasa, July 2006.

AMS: Timeliness.

FDB: Time is very important.

AMS: The calculations of acting in a timely matter . . .

FDB: That's why everybody also seems to be waiting all of the time, I think.

AMS: Given the sort of big-man or big-woman syndrome, particularly in a place like Lagos, you need a protector, you need a patron, you need someone you can have recourse to, you can appeal to, who can arbitrate, who can make a decision so that you don't have to: "Okay, I know the one that I appeal to, that I regard, that I owe, that I depend on . . ." This person has a lot of other people around. What happens if we all show up at the same time? How do we know how not to all show up at the same time?

VR: To crowd the space?

AMS: To crowd, yes.

FDB: In this one area I lived in when I was living in Khartoum, people from Darfur were living with people from the south in a complicated relationship with lots of tension but lots of complementarities. As the area was growing, so were demands for space and services. But it was always interesting because the households from Darfur were saying, "Implement Sharia. We want Sharia, we want to live in terms of Islamic law. We want this to apply to ourselves."

And so these people working in the area—local NGOs, activists—were always concerned that in some way this would create a legalistic divide with people from the south, who would not fall under Sharia law. The people from Darfur were saying, "No, you don't have to apply it. But we want to live under it. Please make it applicable for us; we want it." There was always the concern that this would polarize relationships more and really intensify conflict.

But because people from the west would then say, "No, this is not the point. We want Sharia for us. We want to mark the difference with our neighbors even more, because it will allow us to deal with them in a much easier way When I then do all these other things, it's not that I'm doing it as part of my zone of operation, but I'm becoming part of their zone of operation. So I'm then exempt; I don't have to implicate myself. I can retain my sense of being a good Muslim, because that's my operation in their zone."

In some ways, the desire for the legalistic divide wasn't a desire to cut off contact but, quite on the contrary, to maintain a sense of a certain kind of integrity.

VR: It seems that there is an interesting contradiction here with laws in the municipal, urban planning sense, and these other understandings of law, which don't quite territorialize in the same way; in other words, not quite cutting off or zoning behavior and restricting it to a particular sphere of operation. Instead, allow universalization, based on that which is mobile, which can be carried around, through the person, through their ability to act and be governed by a set of invisible structures, rather than visible barriers of the ways in which cities are normally understood:

barriers of neighborhoods or barriers of access or transportation, infrastructure of various kinds, and so on.

FDB: But at the same time do exist.

AMS: This is the claim that's made by my friend Ousman Dembele, who is an urban geographer in Abidjan. If you're in Kumasi [a quarter of Abidjan largely populated by Ivorians from the north of the country] the kids are stuck in Kumasi for the most part because surrounding them, if you go to Marcory, it's dangerous territory. You could be killed, you could be beaten up. These territories of operation depend on where you're from, your religion, your region, and your political affiliation. The territorialization is really strong.

But what Dembele describes is that in some ways it's impossible for this kind of strict territorialization to be maintained. Somehow there's a sense of boundaries, and the boundaries are dividing lines but also works-in-progress in some ways. They become spaces of revision, trying to come up with new terms of connection. But, of course, this is somewhat invisible work. He claims that at these boundaries, there's a lot of boundary maintenance work taking place. The maintenance is not to keep the division in place necessarily, but to work out what are the terms through which there is interchange. It's impossible for people to stay put necessarily.

We know that there's a lot about urban life that increasingly enables the capacity to stay within segregated spaces but, we know, also risks atrophy overall. It risks the kind of urbanizing trajectories that an urban system needs in order to be able to function.

We also know that these kinds of spaces of segregation are dysfunctional in some ways. In some way, the boundary becomes a kind of place where it's transgressed, not just about transgression, but about trying to come up with something that you don't necessarily commit yourself to, which is continuously revised, worked out—a language, a terrain of transaction itself.

Dembele claims that the relationship between contiguous areas with very different histories of inhabitation, where everyone is an enemy to each other, when you look at it as a kind of system, it can't function just simply by being. There are these points of intersection at boundaries, but you can't make them too visible because you know that people might be looking; you could be killed. There's something else that does take place.

From Colonial to Global: The Capacity for Networking

VR: If we were to return to our original point of departure and think about the problem of the visible again, we have to also confront these various global trajectories of investment in Africa that are also increasingly visible.

AMS: The Chinese will probably end up putting in one billion dollars to Lagos, and much of that will go to the cultivation of a kind of Chinese *entrepôt*. I'm not sure if this is still the case, but at one point this was to be the site of Chinese personnel, of services, businesses and residents—of those that are responsible for managing West Africa.

It's almost like a large, gated community, but it's also more than just a kind of residential facility. So what happens? Always the thing is that unlike colonial relationships of the past, where the ability to operate was predicated on all of these other, ancillary activities like civilizing missions and destructive—

VR: The display of excessive power—

AMS: Yes, but this is: "We'll leave you alone if you leave us alone." It's a kind of capacitation of a kind of parallel play, of a quid pro quo. You allow us to bring our engineering teams, our staff, our personnel; you allow us to evacuate particular kinds of resources, again using our infrastructure, then we will pay you for the right to have done that. Part of that payment is, once again, investment in infrastructure. This is a kind of connection that will have really massive implications.

VR: Yes, that's something that I want to hear more about, especially in the light of our discussion about the operation of very low-end Chinese merchants or retailers in places like Douala and smaller towns in Africa—the ways in which they integrate themselves into local networks, markets, economic flows, and so on. How do you think this massive infrastructural investment and capacitation that arises from that is different? Or maybe it's not different. What is it going to do to the shape of the city or the future of the city?

For example, I'm thinking of the way that Khartoum is being transformed, not from the West but from India, from China, and not in the traditional forms of trade that are historic. You have had Indian merchants wandering around Africa for centuries, coming in through the Indian Ocean trade, and similarly the Chinese as well. But this is something new. This is Capital, with a big "C," coming in from the East. That's not so much built of these human networks but built of something more inhuman, a creation of an inhuman platform. It probably has great ethical implications for the way that architecture particularly inserts itself into the city.

AMS: Yes. The Malaysians, for example, wanted to make this deal with Wade where they would build 30,000 units of social housing, but they had to be built within one year, and it had to be done under particular kinds of conditions. And in some ways, it was. It was a Malaysian company that specializes in quick housing construction for lower-end consumption, from which they think they can profit. It has antecedents in a particular kind of Malaysian aspiration, which is that Malaysia can embody a kind of progressive, Islamic capitalism that is able to take certain kinds of risks yet has an interaction with other fields of possibility.

It's still a playing field. In Cabo Verde, Irish investors want to build 15,000 units of retirement housing for European investment. In some ways, there is this sense that there is no place that can't be inhabited, there is no place that can't be potentially occupied, there is no place that is in some ways off-limits. Because you still have these kinds of under-coded territories, they also can become playgrounds for the ideas and the aspirations and of a variety of different external actors.

The Chinese juggernaut is the most dominant, the most visible kind of actor in this, but there are others.

<u>VR</u>: It's perhaps appropriate to end here with this gesture toward these singular projects that have great potential for generating urbanism beyond the city in ways that are perhaps different from those projects for renovating the capital city that we began with. Thanks very much to both of you for your time and energy.

Acknowledgements: Vyjayanthi Rao would like to thank Kanu Agrawal for inviting her to conceive this conversation and AbdouMaliq Simone and Filip De Boeck for making it possible. Special thanks to Filip De Boeck for his hospitality in Brussels and to Jesse Willard for assistance with the transcription of the entire conversation.

The Walled City and the White City: The Construction of the Tel Aviv/ Jerusalem Dichotomy

Alona Nitzan-Shiftan

HINEH ANI BA	HERE I COME
Hineh ani ba...	Here I come...
Yerushalaim, ir shavah pitzutz	Jerusalem, a city worth an explosion
Holech bamidrechov mar'gish k'mo kibutz galuyot	Walking in the street feels like in gathering of the exiles
Elef tarbuyot, lechol echad yesh ach veteisha achayot	A thousand cultures, everyone has a brother and 9 sisters
Aravim beseder charedim becheder	Arabs in order, ultraorthodox in the study-room
Vekulam po kol'tim et Elohim - beteder	And all are receiving God here—at a frequency
Ach'rei tedi Yerushalaim da'achah maher	After Jerusalem's Teddy stadium burnt out fast
Miyom leyom Tel Aviv natzetzah yoter	From day to day Tel Aviv sparkled more
Chaverim azvu o hitkarvu lebore shamaim	Friends left or got closer to the creator of the heavens
Afor, mesha'amem, ein yam	Gray, boring, there's no sea
Mach'shavot al azivah	Thoughts about leaving
Shalosh shanim lakach li lekabel t'ahachlatah	Three years it took me to get the decision
Orez t'achafatzim letoch hamizvadah	I pack my belongings into the suitcase
Mehakfar la'ir bekivun hayeridah	From the village to the city in the direction of descending
Tel Aviv - hineh ani ba	Tel Aviv – here I come
Ani megi'a - hineh ani ba	I'm arriving – here I come
Bati lehazi'a - hineh ani ba	I came to sweat – here I come
Ki at hayechidah ani nishba	Because you're the only one, I swear
Yatz'ati lekivun mishur hachof	I went in the direction of the shore's plain
Eizeh shok ani omed lachatof	What a shock I'm standing to steal
Ve'achshav kshe'ani beTel Aviv sof sof	And now that I'm in Tel Aviv finally
Mish'talev im hanof hakol tari vezeh tov	I mix in with the scenery all is fresh and it's good
Wai, kamah shadaim, nis'refu li ha'einaim	Whoa, how many breasts, my eyes got burnt
Ach'rei sh'nataim shel s'dom ve'amorah	After two years of Sodom and Gomorrah
Lo mezaheh et atzmi bamar'ah	I don't recognize myself in the mirror
Makir, mitarev, mitmazeg, mitchabek im	I know, I mix, I fuse, I embrace with
Kol habe'alim shel hadiskotekim	All the owners of the clubs
Achshav kshe'ani in, mevin, zeh lo notzetz	Now that I'm in, I know that it doesn't sparkle
Kamah ra'ash, kamah piach, ten li deshe ten li etz	How much noise, how much soot, give me grass give me a tree
Kol hayom mitbazbez al shalom, shalom	The whole day is wasted on "shalom" – "shalom"
Hash'kirut hon halechut veshiga'on	The rent wealth dampness and craziness
Ve'az nafal ha'asimon,	And then the token fell,
Gan eden hayah li bayadaim	I had paradise in my hands
Mach'shavot al azivah	Thoughts about leaving
Shalosh shanim lakach li lekabel t'ahachlatah	Three years it took me to get the decision
Orez t'achafatzim letoch hamizvadah	I pack my belongings into the suitcase
Meha'ir lakfar lekivun	From the city to the village in the direction
Yerushalaim - hineh ani ba	Jerusalem – here I come
Chozer elaich - hineh ani ba	I'm returning to you – here I come
El chomotaich - hineh ani ba	To your walls – here I come
Ki at hayechidah ani nishba	Because you're the only one I swear
Chazarti liy'rushalaim, po hachumus tov zeh baduk	I returned to Jerusalem, here the chumu is good that's known
Ten li roge'a, ten li sheket, lo yazik eizeh pihuk,	Give me calm, quiet, so no yawn will do damage,
Matai pa'am ach'ronah samti eizeh petek bakotel,	When was the last time I put a note in The Wall,
Hishk'ati ba'ochel,	Invested in some food,
Asiti chaverim chadashim,	Made new friends,
Ha'ir hazot tach'zir li t'ashlitah bachaim	This city gives me back the control over life
Nitarbev im atzmi bim'kom le'arbev mayim	We'll mix with ourselves instead of mixing water
Nin'shom k'tzat avir harim tzalul kayayin	We'll breathe some moutain air clear as wine
Yalla beita''r, yalla chaim bak'far!	Let's go betar, let's go life in the village!
Ha'ikar lihyot me'ushar	The main thing is to be happy
Hineh ani ba...	Here I come...
Tel Aviv - hineh ani ba	Tel Aviv – here I come
Ani megi'a - hineh ani ba	I'm arriving – here I come
Bati lehazi'a - hineh ani ba	I came to sweat – here I come
Ki at hayechidah ani nishba	Because you're the only one I swear

Hebrew and English lyrics for "Hineh Ani Ba (Here I Come)" from the album *Be'ezrat Hajam (With Help of the Jam)* by Hadag Nachash; lyrics reprinted from www.hebrewsongs.com, words transliterated and translated to English by George Jakubovits of Toronto, Canada (georgejakubovits@hotmail.com). A special thanks to Liat Muller for her input on the English translation.

Aerial view of Tel Aviv, 1947.

Bird's-eye view of the Temple Mount with the Dome of the Rock in the foreground and the Western Wall in the background.

The Walled City of Jerusalem and the White City of Tel Aviv are both inscribed in the UNESCO World Heritage List as sites "considered to be of outstanding value to humanity."[1] Three thousand years of sacred history and religious monuments holy to the three major monotheistic religions won the first its place. In contrast, the second won a similar status for its modernity: the stark newness of a twentieth-century city, with generic nonmonuments and modern houses dressed in white. Hence, one was chosen for its indisputable uniqueness, its gravitating aura of faith embodied in stone, while the other was chosen for its explicit sameness, a specimen of the International Style drifting to particular places. UNESCO's list reasserts and fortifies entrenched stereotypes of Israeli Jews, who distinguish their official capital of stone, religion, and beauty from their alternative agnostic capital of cement, finance, and entertainment.[2]

As Israel is caught in a bitter national conflict with Palestine, controversial politics continuously provoke and inform its cultural production. In this inflammatory context, the dichotomy between the two alternative capitals assumes political and moral dimensions. The Right summons the symbolic possessions of Jerusalem, located at the heart of the Israeli-Palestinian conflict, to incite nationalist sentiments, while the Left's aversion to the occupation finds comfort in Tel Aviv as a symbol of an agnostic European past, not contaminated by the conflict. Both depictions amplify the small yet fundamental distance of the sixty kilometers that separate the mountainous and shore-hugging Israeli capitals; one is the capital of the Jewish *Nation* and the other of the Hebrew *State*.[3]

Scholars of globalization use a similar set of polarities to describe the way world cities participate in the new global infrastructure—globalization that, on one hand, undermines the unity of the nation-state by introducing transnational economies, and on the other hand particularized identity politics.[4] The old dichotomized stereotypes of Tel Aviv and Jerusalem fall neatly into this new mold, which subordinates the cities as a whole to a perpetuating mechanism, securing each at its assigned polar end. Whereas the conflict with Palestine keeps Jerusalem captive by the state and halted by national politics, Tel Aviv's privatization undermines government controls in order to participate in the global game of world cities.[5]

Accordingly, the global McWorld fits the image of a dynamic, transient, and daring Tel Aviv, replete with lush residential and commercial skyscrapers and economizing its white modernist past for real estate and tourism attractions. By contrast, the local jihad comes close to the image of the religious, stagnant, and essentialist Jerusalem, of traditional and neo-Orientalist stone-clad buildings and multiple walls cutting through its urban fabric and constraining its multiethnic population.[6] Architectural criticism of Jerusalem's and Tel Aviv's prime public spaces complies with the same duality. Comparing the architecture of the Western Wall Plaza to that of Tel Aviv's municipal square (the Kings of Israel Square that was dedicated to Yitzhak Rabin after his assassination there), the biographer of the latter's architect concludes "while people come to the Western Wall in order to feel *Jewish*, they come to the Kings of Israel Square in order to feel *Israeli*."[7] Recent media reports further challenge this dichotomy. This year, the awe-inspiring and armed official Memorial Day ceremony by Western Wall lost prestige to the alternative ceremony in Tel Aviv's municipal square. Replete with TV celebrities and pop stars, the alternative ceremony won higher TV ratings. In the context of a growing tension between global cities and the nation-state in which they are located,[8] the old dichotomies between Tel Aviv and Jerusalem no longer describe dependent, complementary halves, as the ancient and modern silhouettes of the national body. Rather, they function as antagonistic weights that pull this body apart—one stretches modernity to its most radical ends, the other retreats into a reactionary fundamentalism that halts life with irreducible essentialist truths.[9]

Depictions of this nature are strongly rooted in the menacing reality

1 See http://portal.unesco.org.

2 For this cultural dichotomy see, for example, Nurit Govrin, "Jerusalem and Tel Aviv as Metaphors in Hebrew Literature: The Development of an image," in Lavsky, *Jerusalem in Zionist Consciousness and Action* (Hebrew) (Jerusalem: The Zalman Shazar Center for Jewish History, 1989), 434-450; Dan Meron, *If There Is No Jerusalem: Essays on Hebrew Writing in a Cultural-Political Context* (Hebrew) (Tel-Aviv: Hakibutz Hameuchad Publishing House, 1987); Ziva Sternhall, "The Distance between Rehavia and The White City" (Hebrew), *Ha'aretz* (July 19, 2002); Mordechai Omer, "Upon one of the Mountains': Jerusalem in Israeli Art," "The Wave and the Tower: Tel-Aviv in Israeli Art", both in Mordechai Omer, *Contemporary Israeli Art* (Hebrew) (Tel-Aviv: Am-Oved, forthcoming). For a recent critical collection about Tel Aviv, see Sigal Barnir and Yael Moria, *Back to the Sea: Catalogue of the Israeli Pavilion in the Venice Biennale of Architecture* (2004).

3 Vered Vinitzky-Sarussi, "The Commemoration of Izhak Rabin and the discussion about National Identity in Israel: Between Jerusalem and Tel-Aviv", in Lev Grinberg, ed., *Contested Memory: Myth, Nation and Democracy: Thoughts after Rabin's Assassination* (Hebrew) (Beer Sheva: Ben Gurion University, 2000), 19-37.

4 Saskia Sassen, *Territory, Authority, Right: From Mediaval to Global Assemblage* (Princeton N.J.: Princeton University Press, 2006); *Globalization and Its Discontent: Essay on the New Mobility of People and Money* (New York: New Press, 1998); Cities in a World Economy (Thousand Oaks, California: Pine Forge Press, 1994). Manuel Castells, *The Power of Identity* (Malden, Mass: Blackwell Publishers, 1997); *The Rise of the Network Society* (Malden, Mass: Blackwell Publishers, 1996).

5 Nurit Alfasi and Tovi Fenster, "The National City and the International City: Jerusalem and Tel-Aviv" in *Israeli Sociology: A Journal for the Study of Israeli Society* (Hebrew) vol. 6 no. 2, (2005): 265-294; Tovi Fenster, *The Global City and the Holy City: Narratives on Planning, Knowledge, and Diversity* (Harlow, Essex, England: Pearson/Prentice Hall, 2004).

6 See Uri Ram, *The Globalization of Israel: McWorld in Tel Aviv, Jihad in Jerusalem* (New York: Routledge, 2007).

7 Sharon Rotbard, Avraham Yaski, *Concrete Architecture* (Hebrew) (Tel Aviv: Bavel 2007), 132, italics added.

8 James Holston, ed., *Cities and Citizenship* (Durham: Duke University Press, 1999); Arjun Appadurai, "Deep Democracy: Urban Govermentality and the Horizon Polities," in *Public Culture* 14, 21-47.

9 Uri Ram, *The Globalization of Israel*.

of the Israeli-Palestinian conflict and describe current trends no less than a national state of anxiety; as such, they occupy a position in the dichotomy they describe. This paper aims to explore the dichotomization mechanism in which they participate. To that end it suggests shifting the discussion of these estranged cities to the cultural registers, where constructed heritage and urban magnificence participate in a symbolic economy that casts a different light on global processes. In this cultural arena, it is possible that the global and the local are not located at the two polarized ends of Jerusalem and Tel Aviv but rather play in a complex web of simultaneous temporalities and overlapping national and postnational structures in each city.

The recent policy of UNESCO nominations exemplifies these overlaps: the "capital of the Jewish nation" was nominated to the world heritage list actually by Jordan, and in 1982 its Old City was declared an endangered site due to Israeli development.[10] By contrast, Israel nominated the "capital of the Israeli state" to the same list in 2004, following a passionate national campaign that instilled pride in Tel Aviv's International Style as a "truer" and "cleaner" national heritage.[11] This notion is in stark contrast to the widely perceived image of Jerusalem as national and thus "local" and of Tel Aviv as cosmopolitan and thus "global," raising unsettling doubts regarding the polarized depiction of Israeli "glocalization."[12]

Thus, the task of this paper is neither to describe the differences and oppositions between Israel's two capitals, nor to analyze how their dichotomized images reflect Israeli reality. It offers instead a recent history of the politicized urban dichotomy in which they are caught. This predicament is examined by exploring the cultural mechanisms that polarize urban images, endowing them with moral values and mobilizing their efficacy for political ends. What are the powers that are implicated in such depictions? How are they mobilized in both local and global arenas? How do they impact the cities under consideration?

Since the polarized legacies of both cities in question are increasingly contingent on international legitimization of their cultural resources, the paper explores such involvement, particularly that of the international Jerusalem Committee and that of UNESCO, in institutionalizing their built heritage. Looking at the dichotomy between Jerusalem and Tel Aviv through such cultural politics, seemingly disparate issues are tied together: built heritage and urban beauty, the tension between cities and their governing nation-state, and the politics of the Israeli-Palestinian conflict. The interplay between these domains is dynamic and sensitive to the political barometer, and its account necessitates a historical perspective.

Zionism and the Two Cities

As a matter of fact, neither Jerusalem nor Tel Aviv adequately expressed the Zionist aspiration for a national Jewish revival on an ancient land, a quest that culminated with the founding of the state of Israel. Quite the opposite, the Labor Zionists who saw themselves as the founding fathers of the young Israeli state negated the idea of a city wholeheartedly, preferring the promise presented by agricultural settlements: scientifically planned projects, bespeaking not only progress and development but, more important, a utopia, a new beginning, a departure from the diaspora's bourgeois lifestyle.[13]

Tel Aviv, however, despite its embarrassingly bourgeois culture, could boast ample notions of the new. Founded on the coastal sand dunes in 1909, it hosted the first institutions of the renewed, or reinvented, Hebrew culture in the "land of Israel"—a Hebrew school, theater, and

10 See http://whc.unesco.org/en/list/148.

11 See http://whc.unesco.org/en/list/1096.

12 For an early formulation of the term "glocalization" that demonstrates the tension between the global and the local in contemporary societies, see Robertson Ronald, "Glocalization: Time, Space Homogeniety-Hetrogenity," in M. Featherstone, et al., eds., *Global Modernities* (London: Sage, 1995), 25-44.

13 Michael and Bracha Chyutin, *Architecture and Utopia: The Israeli Experiment* (Burlington, VT: Ashgate Pub., 2007); Jeannine Fiedler, *Social Utopias of the Twenties: Bauhaus, Kibbutz and the Dream of The New Man* (Wuppertal: Muller+ Bussman, 1995).

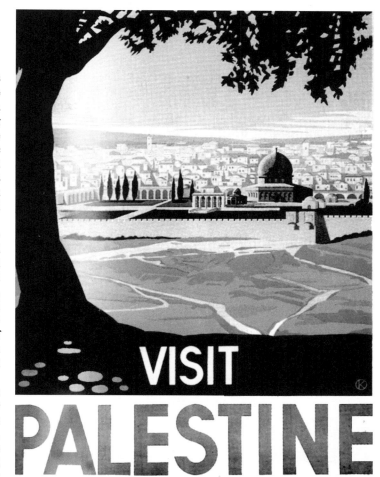

Franz Krauss, "Visit Palestine" (1936), poster issued by the Tourist Development Association of Mandate Palestine.

Arieh El-Hanani, "Tel Aviv: The Jewish Town," an illustration for Keren Hayesod booklet cover, Jerusalem (1932).

newspaper. By the 1930s it was already established as the cultural and political center of the *Yishuv*, the Jewish population in Mandate Palestine. Shining under the Mediterranean light and energized by waves of immigrants, Tel Aviv was reputed for its ethnic "purity"—a Jewish city under a European mandate, a pacifying alternative to the competing mixed cities that the British chose to develop: Jerusalem and Haifa. Initially, Tel Aviv was founded as a new suburb to the ancient port city of Jaffa and as an alternative to what it represents. However, it grew into a city that consumed Jaffa within its municipal domain.

The concepts of the Jewish city and the new architecture went hand in hand; both were modern and pregnant with newness. Patrick Geddes, the famous Scottish planner, prepared Tel Aviv's urban blueprint according to the tenets of *Garden Cities*, delineating a grid bisected by wide boulevards.[14] The city was divided into lots that Ram Karmi would later describe as a systematic series of green frames encircling white cubical houses.[15] Once becoming a part of the urban mythology associated with the legacy of the famous school, these buildings won the oxymoron combination: Bauhaus-style architecture.

The combination of Geddes' urban planning and the modern architecture that developed into Tel Aviv created a unique urban center that is not similar to any other in Israel or throughout the world in its size and quality . . . The [1925] plan included an area of approximately 3,000 dunams [740 acres]. Geddes imagined Tel Aviv as a special kind of city of gardens. He developed the characteristics of the green residential neighborhoods built in southern Tel Aviv since 1909 according to the following principles: The buildings will be constructed on plots of at least 560 square meters and each will be surrounded by a garden. The building area will be no larger than a third of the plot area. The distance between the buildings on each plot will be at least three meters and four meters from the street and five meters from the plot in the back of the building. There will also be a green boulevard from the south to the southeast surrounding the residential neighborhoods. The plan created a hierarchy of city streets clearly distinguished by main streets serving as main traffic lanes and central routes in the city and narrow, short residential streets. In this way, Geddes created a network of traffic arteries and main streets bordering quiet blocks of residential areas of less than 500 meters in length. Geddes planned that in the center of each block there would be a public building to serve the residents of that block. An urban cultural center was planned to be built at the highest point and later the Mann Auditorium and Habimah were built (Geddes nicknamed them the "Acropolis"). A square surrounded by architecturally uniform buildings was planned and at a later date Diezengoff Square was built. The combination of modern architecture in Geddes' planned urban blocks created a mosaic of white cubes surrounded by gardens. Modern building spread uniformly in all the planned areas created a free and intimate urban fabric. The relationship between gardens, commercial, and quiet residential areas create a pleasant balance between the green city, the needs of the residents, and commercial and cultural activities which grant Tel Aviv a quality of life among the highest in the world.

—http://www.white-city.co.il/english/index.htm

"With us in 90 minutes," advertisement of Egged Buses Cooperative for its Tel-Aviv Jerusalem line.

Tel Aviv was quick to be built and quick to deteriorate. Its growing reputation as a cultural hub coexisted with its counter depiction of neglect and ugliness. In its lack of care, poets read down-to-earth secularism, and artists celebrated material poverty[16]— a liberating, nonimposing, let-live urban presence. Despite the state's nation-building ideology of population dispersal, Tel Aviv continued to grow into a metropolitan center, the heart of Israeli culture and commerce. It was where a sense of Israeliness took shape and where the Israeli locus was clearly located until 1967.[17]

The leading figures of the first generation of Israeli-born architects grew up in Tel Aviv. Daring idealists, fully secular, and yet totally committed to the national cause, they poured the Israeli *hutzpa* into coarse concrete frames. They found in Le Corbusier's béton brut, in New Brutalists such as Peter and Alison Smithson, and in Americans such as Paul Rudolph and Marcel Breuer powerful sources of inspiration.[18] The resultant gray architecture of Tel Aviv developed particularly around the city's public spaces and civic monuments. Tel Aviv's university, courthouses, numerous cultural institutions, and commercial buildings display their method of construction. Modest and bare, yet powerful and masculine, the coarse and textured concrete went hand in hand with the contemporary art scene of material poverty. While their fellow artists followed the path paved by American and European contemporaries—Robert Rauschenberg, Jean Dubuffet,

14 For Tel Aviv Geddes Plan, see Rachel Kallus, "Patrick Geddes and the Evolution of Housing Type in Tel-Aviv," in *Planning Perspectives* vol. 12 no. 3 (1997): 281-320. For revisions of the Geddes Myth, see N. I. Payton, "The Machine in the Garden City: Patrick Geddes' Plan for Tel Aviv," *Planning Perspectives* vol. 10 no. 4 (1995): 359-382; Arindam Dutta, "Organicism: Inter-Disciplinarity and Para-Architectures," *JSAH* vol. 64 no. 4 (December 2005).

15 Ram Karmi, *Lyric Architecture* (Hebrew) (Israel: Ministry of Defence, 2001).

16 Sarah Britberg Semel, *The Want of matter: Quality in Israeli Art* [exhibition catalogue] (Hebrew) (Tel-Aviv: Tel-Aviv Museum of Art, 1988).

17 Dan Meron, *If There Is No Jerusalem*; Maoz Azariahu, *Tel-Aviv, the Real City* (Hebrew) (Beer-Sheva, University Press of Ben-Gurion University of the Negev, 2005); Barbara Mann, *A Place in History: Modernism, Tel-Aviv, and the Creation of Jewish Urban Space* (Stanford, Calif.: Stanford University Press, 2006).

18 For postwar architecture see Joan Ockman, ed., *Architecture Culture, 1943-1968: A Documentary Anthology* (New York: Rizzoli, 1993); Sarah Williams Goldhagen and Rejean Legault, eds., *Anxious Modernisms: Experimentation in Postwar Architectural Culture* (Cambridge, Mass. and London: MIT Press, 2000); for the Israeli context, see Zvi Efrat ed., The Israeli Project: Building and Architecture, 1948-1973 (Hebrew) (Tel Aviv: Tel Aviv Museum of Art, 2004); Gilad Duvshani and Hari Frank, *Build Ye Cities: An Exhibition of Israeli Architecture* (Institute of Architects and Town Planners in Israel A.E.A.I., 1985); Miriam Tuvyah

In the context of a growing tension between global cities and the nation-state in which they are located, the old dichotomies between Tel Aviv and Jerusalem no longer describe dependent, complementary halves, as the ancient and modern silhouettes of the national body. Rather, they function as antagonistic weights that pull this body apart—one stretches modernity to its most radical ends, the other retreats into a reactionary fundamentalism that halts life with irreducible essentialist truths.

the CoBrA Group, Arte Povera—Israeli architects constructed the profane, down-to-earth Tel Aviv.

Unlike Tel Aviv, Jerusalem had always provoked ambivalence among Zionist ideologists and diplomacy.[19] Its sacredness to the three monotheistic religions intimidated the labor Zionists. Moreover, the senior Jewish inhabitants of the Old City belonged to the Old *Yishuv*, an Orthodox Jewish community that preceded the waves of Zionist immigration and the antithesis of everything that is Labor. Until 1948 it was the seat of the British government, whose Orientalist celebration of Jerusalem's antiquity contradicted the revolutionary spirit of socialist Zionism.[20] After Jerusalem's partition during the 1948 war, Jerusalem became a frontier, a dead-end city surrounded by Jordanian territories. Until 1967 it was the stronghold of intellectuals and politicians but remained at the margins of the new and bubbly Israeli culture.

Zali Gurevitz and Gidon Aran argue that Jerusalem was unsettling in a deeper sense: from the Jewish religion Zionism inherited the notion of Zion, that is, Jerusalem, as an idea, a text, a longing. Jerusalem always existed as an abstract entity out of reach, as a subject of yearning, of essential distance. The possibility of reaching Jerusalem, of concretizing the idea in an actual tangible territory, presented itself as an inner contradiction. In Jerusalem, "Zionism was fearing its own fulfillment."[21] It might not come as a surprise, then, that during the 1967 war the defense minister, Moshe Dayan, while standing on Mount Scopus gazing at the Old City asked, "What do we need all this Vatican for?"[22]

Dayan's was a foretelling remark. Following Israel's occupation of east Jerusalem and the Old City during that war, Jerusalem's Jewish population was immediately swept up in messianic feelings of redemption. At large, Israelis felt that their national project had reached its climax. The biblical landscapes, from which they believed to have been separated for two thousand years of exile, were now within reach. Jerusalem became the top national priority for Israel and consequently for Palestinians, whose national demands were not yet recognized by the Israeli Labor government.

Moreover, the 1967 watershed date was critical in shaping Jerusalem's urban landscape. Since Israeli independence, the urban and architectural imagery of Jerusalem was subjected—like that of any other city or settlement in Israel—to the ideology of modernist planning institutions. Its housing estates as well as its governmental edifices were built under a strict modernist code of plain cubical volumes, separated from each other by ample open green spaces.

Jerusalem's 1959 master plan followed the guidelines of the British, yet created governmental, educational, and memorial precincts, stretched toward the western end of its municipal boundaries. The Old City stood at the center of the city, yet behind the Jordanian border. Its enigmatic presence placed the essence of the city very *near*, yet certainly not *here*. It brought to light a yearning for something out of reach.

For Israelis, the walls of the Old City symbolized the boundaries of the inaccessible, the Jewish quarter and the sacred sites. A poster from that period, combining socialist imagery with the ancient surfaces of the city wall, strikingly reveals the incapacity to stage the symbol of yearning with daily living on the former's symbolic terms.

The situation changed abruptly with the conquest of east Jerusalem. According to renowned literary critic Dam Meron:

After 1967, with the simultaneous change of the map and the national consciousness, Jerusalem started demanding its rights not only from its phraseology but also from the sincere national sentiment. To be precise: what was hitherto a form of poetic convention (such as the song "Jerusalem of Gold" that was written prior to 1967) was suddenly invested with concrete content. The beaten metaphors became literal truths. The large cultural and political shift has begun.[23]

The Beautification of Jerusalem

The ecstatic postwar celebrations of Jerusalem's tangible beauty forcefully demonstrated the gap created during the nation's building years, between the state's social-democratic ideology and its ethno-religious symbolism. The modernist practices of Israel's planning agencies were evidently incompatible with the national narrative that celebrated the return to Jerusalem as the winding up of two thousand years of Jewish exile. The state's modernist building apparatuses fell short of expressing the symbolism of the moment. Jerusalem's schism, between its present form and the just fulfilled national sentiments, attracted different forms of civic and professional protest.

Consider the forceful rise of the Council for a Beautiful Israel in 1968 as a civic movement that passionately condemned the longstanding Zionist embrace of high modernism.[24] The charismatic head of the council's Jerusalem branch, journalist Yehuda Haezrahi, explicated the dilemma.

and Michael Boneh, eds., *Building the Country: Public Housing in the 1950s* (Hebrew) (Tel-Aviv: The Israel Museums forum: Hakibbutz Hameuhad, 1999).

19 For the location of Jerusalem in Zionist thought, see Hagit Lavsky, *Jerusalem in Zionist Consciousness and Action*.

20 Cultural Zionism, which was the trend developed by Ahad Ha'am, favored Jerusalem as a center because it was the place from which an aura of the Jewish Renaissance should emanate onto the world.

21 Zali Gurevitch and Gideon Aran, "Al Ha-makom" *Alpayim* 4 (Hebrew) (Tel-Aviv, Am Oved Publishers, 1991), 9-44; reprinted in Zali Gurevitch, *On Israeli and Jewish Place* (Hebrew) (Tel-Aviv, Am Oved Publishers, 2007) 22-73.

22 See Nadav Shragai, *Temple Mount Conflict: Jews and Muslims, Religion and Politics since 1967* (Hebrew) (Jerusalem: Keter, 1995), 18. During the conference, "Six Days – Thirty Years" (Tel Aviv: Rabin Center for Israeli Studies, May 26-28, 1997), Amnon Rubinstein mentioned that in the Cabinet the Zionist religious party was the most reluctant to venture into the Old City. The papers in this conference were published in Asher Susser, ed., *Six Days – Thirty Years: A New Look at the Six-Day War* (Tel-Aviv: Am Oved, 1999).

23 Meron, *If There Is No Jerusalem*, 229.

24 "The Council for a Beautiful Israel, founded in 1968 by decree of the Committee, functions as a public non-profit organization in cooperations well as public bodies. It is a unique association of volunteers and together to safeguard, develop, and beautify the environment and enhance the people of Israel." See http://www.israel-yafa.org.il.

The architectural style that took shape in Israel during the last thirty years—if it is at all possible to call it a style—is absolutely unsuitable for the building of New Jerusalem. Should we indeed agree that Jerusalem would be cut into two, as with the strike of an axe: one part ancient, interesting, beautiful— and the other part new and ugly?[25]

What was strikingly novel in Haezrahi's argument is the identification of the "new" with the "ugly." In contrast, Israel's long-established slogan of "progress and development" took the new to be the bearer of moral as well as aesthetic merits. However, building a modernist New Jerusalem would have perpetuated the rift between west Jerusalem and the hitherto Jordanian orientalist city to the east. Since the symbolic resources resided in the east, Israelis suspected modernist practices would pose a severe obstacle to their desire to "reunify Jerusalem."[26]

This criticism touched the open nerve of post-World War II architectural culture. At the time, critics of high modernism gained growing attention worldwide. The younger generation of Israeli-born architects closely followed Jane Jacob's 1961 rebuttal of urban renewal.[27] Admirers of architects Peter and Alison Smithson, Aldo van Eyck, Jaap Bakema, and other members of Team X since the mid-1950s, they adopted the group's 1968 *Primer* as the second bible to Le Corbusier's *Oeuvre complète*.[28] Israeli "Brutalists" started to win architectural competitions, while regionalists, tuned to architects such as Giancarlo de Carlo and Geoffrey Bawa, joined the generational celebration of Rudofsky's *Architecture without Architects* of 1964.[29] Louis Kahn was looming already in the local sky since the 1950s, when he helped designing a new Israeli town, *Ir Habsor*.[30] His respect for history stirred the criticism of the highly modernist tabula-rasa ideology. At the time that international organizations such as ICOMOS were founded, the renovation of Old Jaffa as an artist colony, for example, was well under way.[31]

The young Israeli generation pointed this criticism toward the state's modernist establishment, asking to replace the state's "housing solutions" with a new focus on the Israeli place, community, and local roots. Ironically, the search for a local, rooted place led architects to the Palestinian vernacular, which provided them with clues in their search for a "native" Israeli architecture.[32] These critics were not posing postmodern challenges to the grand modernist/Zionist narratives; rather, they identified themselves as critical members of the modernist

"This is what we are fighting for—insuring a normal living for the nation and peace for the country."

The archeological park at the foot of Al-Aqsa Mosque, 2006.

club, following post-World War II architectural trends that were compatible with the welfare state and its centralized building market. The 1967 conquest of east Jerusalem caused a boom in the building market exactly in the middle of this generation shift, turning the city into a huge testing ground for postwar urbanism.

Despite the new criticism of high modernism, the urban 1968 master plan for Jerusalem made by an acclaimed team of architects and planners promoted Jerusalem as a modern capital.[33] Preferring efficiency to spirituality, it bounded the city limits and prescribed modern infrastructures.[34] The master plan protected Jerusalem's sacred sites by composing a preservation list, most items of which were located in the city's ancient core. Jerusalem, according to this vision, was an ordinary modern city and a capital, keeping the "Oriental aura" for tourists and pilgrims. A wide national boulevard threaded its national institutions, conceptually distinct from its sacred core. Being closely scrutinized by the international community, the propositions made by Jerusalem planners required authoritative arbiters.

In 1969 and 1970 the consultants arrived. Louis Kahn, Buckminster Fuller, Philip Johnson, Bruno Zevi, Isamu Noguchi, and Jaap Bakema, among a group of thirty members of the Jerusalem Committee, landed in Israel to review the 1968 master and adjunct plans. Teddy Kollek, Jerusalem's legendary mayor, attracted his guests to advise on the "beautification and restoration" of Jerusalem by appealing, he hoped, to the universal values of urban beauty. To Kollek's disappointment, the Jerusalem Committee, which he himself had formed, "tore to shreds" the highly modernist 1968 city plan.[35] The committee, on behalf of "world cultures," took upon itself the mandate of protecting Jerusalem from the hungry teeth of modernization, a city perceived to be even more in danger due to its political importance.[36] Raw, authentic, and spiritual, Jerusalem offered the foreigners the necessary ingredients to combat "the crisis of the modernist city."[37]

Responding to these concerns, Kollek and local architects did their best to create for Jerusalem a physical image that would cater to the threefold pressures: one of post-1967 national sentiment, the second of

25 Yehuda Ha'ezrahi in Michael Avi-Yona, et al., "A Symposium on the Adrichalut" *Architecture* 6 (October-December 1968): 38.

26 Arthur Kutcher, *The New Jerusalem* (London: Thames and Hudson, 1973).

27 Jane Jacobs, *The Death and Life of Great American Cities* (Harmondsworth, Penguin, 1972).

28 Alison Smithson, ed., *Team X Primer*, (Cambridge: MIT Press, 1968).

29 Bernard Rudofsky, *Architecture without Architects: An Introduction To Nonpedigreed Architecture* (New York, Museum of Modern Art 1964).

30 The city was never built but was an important landmark in Israeli planning. For the corpus of Louis Kahn's work see David B. Brownlee and David G. De Long, *Louis L. Kahn: In the Realm of Architecture* (New York, Rizzoli, 1992). For his speech in Jerusalem see Louis Kahn, "Words in the Third Conference of Architect and Engineers in Jerusalem," *Alef Alef* 5 (1974): 8-14.

31 For the work of this generation in Israel see Ram Karmi, *Lyric Architecture* (2001); Osnat Rechter, *Yaakov Rechter: Architect* (Israel, Ha Kibbutz Hameuchad, 2003); Sophia Dekel-Kaspi, *David Reznik: Retrospective* (Tel-Aviv: University of Tel-Aviv, 2005); Orly Robinzon, *Saadia Mendel: Architect* (Or Yehuda: Kinneret, Zmora-Bitan, Dvir Publishing House, 2006); Sharon Rotbard, *Avraham Yaski: Concrete Architecture* (Tel-Aviv: Bavel, 2007).

32 Alona Nitzan-Shiftan, "Seizing Locality in Jerusalem" in Nezar AlSayyad, ed., *The End of Tradition* (New York and London: Routledge, 2004).

33 The interim report of the plan, which outlined its major tenets after the city's unification, was submitted in 1968. The final reports were published consequently in 1970 and 1972. See A. Hashimshoni, et al., *1968 Jerusalem Master Plan* (Jerusalem: Jerusalem Municipality, 1972 and 1974). 34 Alona Nitzan-Shiftan. "Capital City or Spiritual Center? The Politics of Architecture in Post-1967 Jerusalem," *Cities*, vol. 22 no. 3, (2005): 229- 240.

35 Wolf Von Eckardt, "Jerusalem the Golden," *Planning* (February 1987): 25-26.

36 Ari Avrahami, "Planning for Change" in Avrahami, "Jerusalem's Not So Golden Plan" (Hebrew), *Architectural Design* XLI (1971): 215.

37 Amos Elon, "Jerusalem—Not of Gold: Echoes to the Crisis of the Modern City in Deliberation on Planning the Capital," *Ha'aretz* (December 25, 1970): 17.

the Western imagination of Jerusalem, and last the post-World War II criticism of modernism and search for locality. Expressing these demands and motivations, the architectural styles of the reconstructed Jewish Quarter of the Old City and the new housing estates on Jerusalem's outskirts were inspired by east Jerusalem's vernacular, devising an architecture of stone and alleys, broken masses, arches, and domes.[38] Bearing no resemblance to the proposed master plan, the air of the Old City finally emanated onto the new construction.[39]

Jerusalem's beautifying architecture, tuned to preservation, contributed greatly to the city's dichotomization with Tel Aviv. During the 1970s, the act of contrasting Jerusalem's urban beauty to the ugliness of Tel Aviv's peeled-plaster modernist buildings became a commonplace event. Jerusalem's beauty stood for universalism, while highly modernist housing was viewed as the outcome of a financially constrained early statehood. At stake were the politics of a compelling yet confusing definition of urban beauty. In Kollek's words:

> The physical beauty of Jerusalem embodies the universal spiritual truths basic to all faiths and people. To enhance the natural charm of Jerusalem is to make manifest a belief in the love of beauty and the desire for peace inherent in all mankind.[40]

The notion of eternal beauty, conjoined with history and spirituality, was hitherto foreign to the modernist Zionist discourse. Its appearance on the national stage raises intriguing questions: what is urban beauty? Who defines it and for what purpose? The euphoric post-1967 majority favored the Oriental beauty of Jerusalem, attaching to it virtues ranging from "cultural-aesthetic values, rich in history and sacredness"

to the inducement of "better citizenship and healthier social life."[41, 42] In contrast, the modern architecture of western Jerusalem was viewed as a recipe for an ugly city lacking identity as well as historical and spiritual values.[43]

Along these lines, Yehuda Ha'ezrahi, of the Council for a Beautiful Israel, suggested judging Jerusalem's Israelization by international standards. Illustrating the explicit relation of aesthetics and politics, he reasoned that turning Jerusalem into "an ugly, secular city" of conglomerated "unsightly blocks" was politically inadvisable. Alternatively, he argued, "If we are able to preserve Jerusalem's beauty and even enhance it, we will be judged favorably."[44] This was exactly the aesthetic strategy that Mayor Kollek enacted. Kollek confronted the following dilemma: if a "reunited Jerusalem" continued to manifest the modernist legacy of western Jerusalem rather than the allegedly universal idea of the city, it would lose the moral ground for controlling this internationally resonant treasure. On the other hand, by protecting and nourishing the idea of Jerusalem, Israel might then assume the role that Britain once had: the caretaker of Jerusalem, protector of "a sacred trust."[45] Opening the planning apparatus to international scrutiny, Kollek reassured his guests that Jerusalem "belongs, in a sense, to the entire world, to all those people who are Jerusalemites in their hearts and minds."[46] Thus, while aiming at gaining the international community's legitimization, Kollek was relying on Western mythology, yielding its sentiments toward Jerusalem.

1967 and Both Cities

A strong Israel equipped with a "united capital" emerged out of the 1967 war, swept with euphoria and self-righteousness. As a result, the window of opportunity for negotiating with neighboring Arab countries

Cohen Fritz, Malhei Israel Square in Tel Aviv with illuminated Municipality Building crowded with celebrating Tel Avivians on the eve of Independence Day, July 22, 1969.

Ben Gershom Amos, "Tisha Be'av" prayers near the Western Wall in the Old City, Jerusalem, August 9, 2000.

38 Alona Nitzan-Shiftan, "Seizing locality in Jerusalem"; Alona Nitzan-Shiftan, *Israelizing Jerusalem: the Encounter between Architectural and National Ideologies, 1967-77* (dissertation, MIT, 2002); Amiram Harlap, ed., *Israel Builds 1967 / 1973 / 1977* (Tel-Aviv: Ministry of Housing Division of Physical Planning, 1967, 1973, 1977).

39 The architectural history of modern Jerusalem was written primarily by David Kroyanker. For English, see David Kroyanker, *Jerusalem Architecture* (New York: Vendome Press in association with the Jerusalem Institute for Israel Studies, 1994).

40 First letter of invitation from Teddy Kollek to Lewis Mumford, March 26, 1969, Mumford Archive, University of Pennsylvania. Similar letters were sent to all members of the Jerusalem Committee.

41 Yehuda Haezrahi, "Policy, Aesthetics" in Ha'ezrahi, ed., *The Entire Jerusalem, The Story of a Public Struggle* (Jerusalem: the Council for Beautiful Land of Israel, 1971), 17.

42 Letter from Kollek to Israeli cartoonist Dosh, the Jerusalem Archive. This was the reasoning marshaled by the City Beautiful Movement in the U.S., which was also led by a journalist.

43 Ha'ezrahi, "Policy, Aesthetics," 17.

44 Ibid.

45 Kendall, *Jerusalem—The City Plan, Preservation and Development during the British Mandate 1918-1948* (London: H. M. Stationery Off, 1948), foreword by the high commissioner.

46 Kollek, *The Jerusalem Committee, Proceedings of the First Meeting*, 13.

Moshe Safdie, slide comparing an Arab village (Sillwan) to Israeli modernist housing (Kiryat Yovel).

overdeveloping the city within its extended municipal boundaries.[49] In 1980, the Likud broke the political status quo by declaring "United Jerusalem" the Israeli capital and implementing Israeli law on east Jerusalem. International protest was quick and fierce: all foreign embassies left Jerusalem, the official capital, mostly going to Tel Aviv.[50]

Jordan was quick to take advantage of this political atmosphere, turning to the cultural domain of preservation. In 1981, Jordan succeeded in bending UNESCO's rules by nominating the most symbolic part of east Jerusalem, the Walled City, as a World Heritage Site, unique in being listed under no specific nation-state. In 1982, UNESCO declared this "orphan" city "endangered" by post-1967 Israeli development. This was a severe blow to the cultural politics of Kollek. Apparently, the Jordanians were quick to implement the politics that he had hitherto perfected: they turned to the international community in order to score points in the moral race to rule Jerusalem.

Jerusalem quickly became identified with the political right, which accelerated the political dispute over its sovereignty. This predicament encouraged the Left's embrace of Tel Aviv as symbolizing sanity, secularism, and entrepreneurship, an urban response to the aversion the left developed toward the politics of holiness in Jerusalem. In an influential article, Dan Meron explicated his choice between the cities, dichotomizing them toward new frontiers of ethical distance:

> [The] Jerusalem of today lives in its entirety, in all its
> stones and thrones, the real Israeli existence, the meaning
> of which is occupation or struggle over an area not yours,
> dispossessing the other, realizing your rights as if they were
> the only ones, eternity of transcendental credo, imposing your
> lifestyle as if it is the only style of life worth living. Tel Aviv of
> today, in contrast to Jerusalem, is a soft and forgiving city, a
> Riviera-like beach city. All that continues here is an eternal
> struggle over property, status, success, and benefits. This
> is a traditional competition, its teeth are blunt, and there is
> no blood or madness in its eyes. Meanness is regular, banal
> meanness, devoid of the charm of radical meanness. Here,
> one people do not fight the other, and the population, despite
> all its contrast in terms of status and origin, is at the bottom
> line homogeneous. There is no tangible hatred in the streets.
> Today's Tel Aviv is the city of the old Yishuv in the actual
> meaning of the concept.[51]

The soft, banal, homogeneous, and forgiving capitalism of Tel Aviv now stood in stark opposition to the dispossessing bloody and mad transcendental fundamentalism of Jerusalem. Speaking for many of his generation, Meron exemplified the momentous post-1967 transition in Israeli society from the "classical" political Left and Right, that debated social priorities, to Left and Right that differentiate themselves by their attitude toward the occupied territories. Thus, the "banal meanness" of Tel Aviv's capitalism can enjoy the appearance of benevolence and justice that is traditionally associated with the Left.

The Modernization of Tel Aviv
In light of this ambivalence about Jerusalem and the escalating political conflict, Tel Aviv came to be a center for calm and nostalgic recollections. Growing out of the dunes according to a tabula-rasa modernist ideology, it was purely "modern" and thus disentangled ethnically from Palestine and historically from the remainders of the

was missed, leading to the 1973 war. The war's devastating death toll and the ensuing social and economic crisis greatly weakened the Labor Party, which up until then had been the exclusive ruling party in Israel. Later that year, the right-wing Likud Party came into power, with Menahem Begin eventually hosting the Egyptian president, Anwar Saadat, during his historic visit to Israel in November 1977. The great wars and the new hope for peace thus framed a decade that transformed every possible aspect of the Israeli society.[47]

This decade had shaken the relationship between the two cities. From the time of the British Mandate, the set of diametric oppositions that was used to describe both cities had been disseminated through literature, press, and popular conventions. In this fashion, dichotomies such as old/new, close/open, conservative/daring, static/dynamic, as well as beautiful/mundane landscapes of rock/sand, enabled both to emerge as stereotypical entities, the tension between which was complementary.[48] During the rocky events that followed the 1973 war, the competition culminated between the two cities over a sense of "Israeliness." Since 1967, Jerusalem was at the center of the national interest, and its centrality enjoyed a tentative consensus so long as the Labor Party stayed in power. The rise of the Likud, however, changed this delicate balance both locally and internationally.

When the Likud took power in 1977, it launched a new policy that prioritized settling the periphery of Jerusalem, Judea, and Samaria,

[47] See: Uri Ram, "A Decade of Turmoil: Israeli Society and Politics in the Seventies," in Ellen Ginton, ed., *The Eyes of the State: Visual Art in a Borderless State* (Tel Aviv: Tel-Aviv Museum of Art, 1998).

[48] Ziva Sternhall, "The Distance between Rehavia and the White City"; Nurit Govrin, "Jerusalem and Tel Aviv as Metaphors in Hebrew Literature."

[49] Menachem Klein, "Jerusalem as an Israeli Problem," in Amirav Moshe, ed., *Mr. Prime Minister: Jerusalem—Problems and Solutions* (Hebrew) (Jerusalem: Carmel, 2005), 75; Menachem Klein, *Jerusalem: The Contested City* (London: Hurst & Company, 2001).

[50] For the legal status of Jerusalem see: Shmuel Berkovitz, *The Temple Mount and the Western Wall in Israeli Law* (Jerusalem: Jerusalem Institute for Israel Studies, 2001); Bernard Wasserstein, *Divided Jerusalem: The Struggle for the Holy City* (New Haven and London: Yale University Press, 2001); Ruth Lapidoth, *Israel and the Palestinians: Some Legal Issues* (Jerusalem: Jerusalem Institute for Israel Studies, 2003).

[51] Meron, *If There Is No Jerusalem*, 231.

The "nothingness" on which Tel Aviv was founded underpinned the ultimate white utopia: it had no prehistory and hence was indisputably and authentically Zionist. Paradoxically, in the search to redefine a secure Israeli past distinct from the Jewish past that became the domain of Jerusalem, the longing for the architectural roots of "Israeliness" was focused on the modernist channel, ahistorical by definition.

conflict and the Orient. The modern as a past as well as the nostalgia for the new turned into a heritage that allowed one to dispense with the menacing immediacy of contemporary Israeli life. On the occasion of the "Bauhaus in Tel Aviv" national celebration in 1994, for example, Michael Levin wrote in the city's major newspaper *Ha'ir* (The City):

> In the realm of architecture, Le Corbusier proclaimed this as the birth of a new architecture, which was more or less creating something out of nothing. In the realm of society, politics and even personal life, the leaders of the Zionist movement and the Jewish Yishuv proclaimed this moment the birth of a new society and a new man. This too was the creation of something out of nothing.[52]

Louis Kahn and Buckminster Fuller touring Jerusalem with the Jerusalem Committee.

Salo Harshman, Cluster 11, Gilo, Jerusalem (c. 1970s).

The "nothingness" on which Tel Aviv was founded underpinned the ultimate white utopia: it had no prehistory and hence was indisputably and authentically Zionist. Paradoxically, in the search to redefine a secure Israeli past distinct from the Jewish past that became the domain of Jerusalem, the longing for the architectural roots of "Israeliness" was focused on the modernist channel, ahistorical by definition.

In 1984, a year before Meron wrote his painful disdain from Jerusalem, Levin curated the pivotal exhibition, *White City: International Style Architecture in Israel, a Portrait of an Era*.[53] The success of the exhibition's new emphasis on the formal properties of the country's existing modernist buildings was linked to two arenas. For architects in Israel and abroad, it was a timely relief from the already exhausted experiments with postmodern architecture, conceived as flat and corporate. Judy Turner, who photographed the white houses of the New York 5, joined forces with Levin to produce the second catalogue that salvaged modernism while giving it a blessed local twist. Shortly before DOCOMOMO was established and at a time of a growing interest in "other modernisms," the only city constructed almost entirely in the International Style already in the 1930s had great appeal.

To the bourgeois Israeli of the 1980s and 1990s, the exhibition, as well as the 1994 Bauhaus or International Style celebrations, presented a tangible past of physical objects rather than an ideology no longer in vogue. This modernist vernacular was repoliticized as a visual emblem of "the modest" Zionist spirit that produced it.[54] The "portrait of an era" thus confirmed the hegemonic ideology that had formed the state of Israel. Moreover, it suggested alternative Israeli architectural roots in Tel Aviv and a comforting architectural heritage. The 1994 celebrations followed six years of Palestinian intifada as well as growing internal conflicts between secular, religious, and ethnic factions while provided the secular bourgeoisie with an encouraging sense of legitimized legacy.

Tel Aviv's efforts to offer Israelis a secure secular past accelerated since the 2000 onset of the second intifada, culminating in UNESCO's recognition of its White City as a World Heritage Site, the only modernist urban site besides Brasília. The UNESCO declaration was celebrated in Israel's largest theater, where a sizable audience of invitees stood up to inaugurate an event of architectural significance by singing the national anthem. The stage set included four white, modernist buildings, scaled representations of the Bauhaus style. On the screen the audience could watch the president of Israel, the minister of education, and other dignitaries from the U.N. preservation agencies. The "whiteness" of Tel Aviv[55] during this event represented not only socialist values of modesty and equality but, more poignantly, democracy and pluralism, which we have been led to believe, or want to believe, are enabled by the newness of Tel Aviv.

The popularity of the Bauhaus style in Israeli consciousness echoes an active agreement among a leading architectural trend, a national ideology, and the historiography that binds the two.[56] A similar current architectural effort wishes to resurrect the gray period of Tel Aviv's public buildings. It reads in the ample neo-Brutalist, exposed-concrete architecture of the Fifties and Sixties a truly honest and modest

52 Michael Levine, "In Praise of the White City" (Hebrew), *Ha'ir* (May 20, 1994): 31-33, 37.

53 Michael Levine's landmark exhibition had two catalogues: Michael Levin, *White City: International Style Architecture in Israel, A Portrait of an Era* (Tel Aviv, 1984), and *White City: International Style Architecture in Israel, Judith Turner: Photographs* (Tel Aviv, 1984).

54 Leaders from the Left and the Right endorsed the style, but promoted it differently. For Shimon Peres, for example, who was the foreign affairs minister in the Labor government at the time of the 1994 celebrations, the style was the heritage of the Labor Zionism that founded the state. His opening speech at the 1994 conference is partially quoted in Daniel Monk, "Autonomy Agreements: Zionism, Modernism and The Myth of a 'Bauhaus' Vernacular", in *AA Files* vol. 28 (1994), 94-99. Roni Milo, Tel Aviv's right-wing Mayor, found in the International Style architectural heritage a foundation for tourism and a springboard for future economic

development of a city with a strong tradition. See Milo's introduction to the celebrations of 'Bauhaus in Tel Aviv' in the accompanying brochure.

55 For recent studies of "whiteness" in the context of Tel Aviv see Alona Nitzan-Shiftan "Whitened Houses" (Hebrew), *Theory and Criticism* no.16 , (2000): 227-232; Sharon Rotbard, *White City, Black City* (Hebrew) (Tel Aviv: Bavel Publishers, 2005).

56 Recent scholarship confirms this bond. See Jeannine Fiedler, *Social Utopias of the Twenties: Bauhaus, Kibbutz, and the Dream of the New Man*; Richard Ingersoll, "Munio Gitai Weintraub: Bauhaus Architect" in *Eretz Israel*, (Milano, Electra Press, 1994); Gilbert Herbert argued that the greatest influence on 1930s modernism in Palestine was that of Gropius, the Bauhaus, and the various Siedlungen projects. See Gilbert Herbert, "On the Fringes of the International Style," *Architecture SA* (September-October 1987): 36-43.

A celebration after UNESCO's declaration of the White City of Tel Aviv as a World Heritage Site, at Mann Auditorium, Tel Aviv, June 2004.

Israeli expression. The reminders of "these wonderful gray years"[57] intermingle, as do the architectural practices that produced them, with the new glass towers that decorate Tel Aviv's skyline. Israel's laboratory of global architecture spreads primarily along the inter-city highway, boasting among others Philippe Starck's Yoo Towers that scrape the skies of residential cost per square meter. While an Israeli financial elite holds up to the challenge of new standards, it does not eclipse the thriving real estate market of Jerusalem. In yet another paradoxical inversion, the international community of French and American Jews, searching for authenticity and charm during the high holidays, "ascend" to Jerusalem in great numbers in order to be near its spiritual skies. One wonders which is more transnational, Moshe Safdie's David Village, a horizontal gated community located next to the Jaffa Gate of the Old City, or the vertical local community of Starck's Yoo Towers?

A commentator recently said that three thousand years ago, after King Solomon's death, much strife had arisen within the Israeli community. The result was the separation between Judea and Israel. Why not, asked Eli Zvuluni, separate Israel once more and establish a new state around greater Tel Aviv, to be known as the Dan Block? Citizens of the state of Dan would enjoy complete civil freedom and no ethnic tensions. Relieved from the financial burden brought on by the settlements in the occupied territories and the huge security budget, they would enjoy economic prosperity and would stress secular education, welfare, and culture. "It may sound like a hallucination, maybe," the writer admits, "but what a pleasure it would be to hear the sentence, "This is Rubi Rivlin from (re)built and glorious Jerusalem, which is bound together firmly" and know that it is some minister in a different, faraway country."[58]

According to recent architectural criticism, the ground for this separation was already apparent in the new era of post-1967 architecture: "the imperial architecture in the 'Israel' style was made of concrete and was built primarily within the Green Line [otherwise referred to as the 1949 Armstice Line]; the imperial architecture in the "Judea" style was made of stone and was built in the occupied territories in the West Bank around Jerusalem." The commentary's "hallucination" bluntly exposes Tel Aviv's detestation for the city of Jerusalem, raising the question, where are the boundaries of the Israeli collectivity, centered in the white utopist city, actually located?

The Two Cities and Zionism

Tel Aviv is an amazing city. Even in August, it is effervescent, vibrant, steaming with desire, flush with cash. From morning to morning, from beach to beach, Tel Aviv celebrates itself—a city with no precedent, a city with no inhibitions, a suntanned, hipster-pants, sleeveless city. A city whose hedonistic trip is so intense that it leads her to believe there is no Israel apart from it, no Judaism and no Islam around it, no real people outside its circle of revelers.

—Ari Shavit, *Ha'aretz,* August 5, 2004

Tel Aviv's past, some would argue, was no less national or colonial. Socialist Mapai established the settlement project, Jerusalem included, and the first Hebrew city of Tel Aviv shares a municipal territory with Jaffa, a Palestinian city turned into an artists' colony.[59] Such contradictions motivated this essay's attempt to reveal the false "inevitability" in the current, dichotomic depictions of both cities.

A. Yasky - J. Sivan Architects + Architect Rachel Feller Associates, a computer illustration of Yoo Towers and Tzameret Park.

Moshe Safdie, David Village, Mamila, Jerusalem.

57 Ester Zandberg, "Those Wonderful Gray Days" (Hebrew), *Ha'aretz* (April, 8, 2007).

58 Eli Zvuluni, "Medinat Gush Dan," (The State of the Dan Block) (Hebrew), *Ha'aretz*, June 25, 2002.

59 For the emergence of Tel Aviv-Jaffa see: Michael LeVine, *Overthrowing Geography, Re-Imagining Identities: A History of Jaffa and Tel Aviv, 1880 to the Present* (New York: New York University, 1999).

Jerusalem became a precedent of the American/European search for salvation from its own modernity and perhaps from its *own* secularity.

"The Spirit of Israel," *Life Magazine,* 1973.

Jerusalem's reluctance to take on the characteristics of a modernist city, as well as Tel Aviv's denial of its Palestinian past (and present) from its urban heritage, do not follow a destined path but rather betray the politics that shaped their urban images.

Scholars currently judge both cities according to the financial infrastructural measuring rod of world cities. Globalization studies help deepen an already entrenched dichotomy, distancing its opposite poles toward the local and global ends, thereby weakening the nation-state. By suggesting a cultural lens for viewing and analyzing current urban processes, the discussion of preservation, heritage, and urban beautification shifts from finance to symbolic economy.[60] In so doing it reveals how cultural politics mobilize cultural symbols through a complex net of national and postnational, local and global forces that act simultaneously. Such examination requires a retrospective analysis, so the politics of the dichotomy between the two cities must be historicized, not simply described, asking what forces are at work in this process, by whom are they mobilized, and how do they impact the cities under consideration.

Had the 1968 master plan been implemented, Jerusalem might have turned, like Tel Aviv, into a modernist city, with its Old City left as a reservoir of religiosity for tourists and pilgrims. However, the international community refused to relinquish its shares in the spirituality of Jerusalem, and Jerusalem became a precedent of the American/European search for salvation from its *own* modernity

and perhaps from its own secularity. Moreover, the Jerusalem Committee's mission of preserving Jerusalem relied heavily on the idea of the city as it was nurtured in the Western imagination. The implementation of this idea carried distinct Orientalist and imperialist undertones. At the same time, as the politics of the Council for a Beautiful Israel demonstrate, Israelis were busily searching for an alternative authoritative program for the national architecture, one that would agree with the Israeli narrative of a modern return to the biblical homeland and to Jerusalem. In searching for their own roots, they orientalized Israeli architecture, wrapping Jerusalem with a Mediterranean garb. The result was a regionalist, localist "architecture of the place" inspired by the Palestinian vernacular and by contemporary post-World War II architectural culture.

But even those architectures that prevailed through the 1970s and the early 1980s could hardly survive the conflicting pressures brought on by the settlement policy and the conflict's politics. Traumatized by the aftermath of the Lebanon War, which broke the Israeli consensus, architectural attention shifted its focus to Tel Aviv in the mid-1980s. Jerusalem was already identified then with the Likud, the leading right-wing party at that point. For many members of the Zionist Labor elite that founded the state, under these circumstances Jerusalem became "the core of the truth of Israel, the open abscess that exposes the illness that runs in the entire body."[61] A decade later, the vehement demonstrations against Prime Minister Rabin that took place in

60 Sharon Zukin, *The Culture of Cities* (Cambridge Mass, Blackwell, 1996).

61 Meron, *If There Is No Jerusalem,* 234.

An image from "Women Cross Boundaries," the 2004 catalogue of the *Comme Il Faut* fashion line.

Jerusalem's Zion Square further aligned the city with the extreme right. As a result, the old Yishuv, now settled in Tel Aviv, attempted to outline new borders, borders that would define its secular, modernist culture. In physical terms it meant consolidating a modernist architectural frontier, composed of the White City and the "gray years," which ran through Israeli society and separated Tel Aviv from both the Palestinian other and Jewish nationalism. By extracting Jerusalem from Tel Aviv and cleansing everything it stands for, the citizens of Tel Aviv would keep the "illness" behind the boundaries of their city-state.

Alas, albeit the "partition plan" of *Israeli* Tel Aviv and *Jewish* Jerusalem, these cities remain Siamese twins who share the problematic Zionist history of a settler society, liberating one people while disposing the other. Modern Tel Aviv is still united with Jaffa, and west Jerusalem is still united with east Jerusalem—ancient cities once populated by Palestinians.

The story of Tel Aviv's beautification/whitening reveals the strong national sentiments that coexist with the globalizing drift. The descendants of Tel Aviv's bourgeois socialists promote the recognition of the White City, and in doing so they fight for the old values of the Labor Party. This is apparent, for example, in the current struggle to save Tel Aviv's symphony hall, a monument of Israeli 1950s modernism that was once portrayed as the secular temple of the Israeli-European high culture. On the other hand, Jerusalem's beautification project is an international arena in which Israelis and Palestinians are competing for better scores, and the international community is strongly invested in every step through political and diplomatic power and territorial interests.

In this light, the continuing dichotomization between the two cites is yet another aspect of the Israeli political inversion, where a neo-liberal Left covers its capitalist practices with a fig leaf of peace seekers, and a neo-fundamentalist Right aims to expel Palestinians from "the foundation stone of Jewish existence."[62] Can Tel Aviv's confluence of global trends and local history of white/Hebrew purity help its residents escape the aftermath of the Zionist settler project by which it was built? And can the beautification of Jerusalem by means of animating its "local" vernacular hide the dispossessing practices of the occupation? Can Jewish Jerusalem survive without Israeli Tel Aviv?

Epilogue
As these words are written, the separation wall between "Western Israel" and "occupied Judea" is being unilaterally erected as a barrier through which Israelis want to separate from Palestinians and the settlers that crave for the Judea mountains. Intended to separate Palestinians from Israelis and to protect the latter from suicide bombers, in Jerusalem it separates mostly Palestinians from Palestinians, intentionally dividing their beloved capital. The wall seemingly follows, yet grossly distorts, the Green Line that divided Jerusalem from 1948 to 1967. Despite the mutual post-intifada desire to divide lands and peoples from each other, the unilaterally built wall reflects Israeli interests, violates Palestinian rights, and is the subject of numerous legal appeals.

From the point of view of Tel Aviv, the wall is a Jerusalem phenomenon. It creates yet another division in a city already split and torn by a conflict from which Tel Avivians want to disentangle. The international community often protests against the wall's physical features, yet enjoys it as a tourist spectacle; buses loaded with curious visitors from around the world stop in Abu Dis to authenticate their media-generated knowledge. In the theoretical and critical domain, architects verify and exemplify through the wall the potency of built form.[63] While condemning its oppression, they simultaneously celebrate the evident capacity of a simple, linear, vertical, evenly divided, and topography-driven element to produce instant political reality. The wall thus proves architectural simplicity to be effective, powerful, and, if judged by the media, extremely photogenic.

The merits of the wall perfectly suited the Tel Aviv-based fashion house *comme il faut* as a backdrop for its 2004 catalogue. Following the Benetton precedent, their campaign wedded political provocation with financial benefit, while exploiting the aesthetic qualities of the criticized object. The slim, tall, bare concrete modules of the wall dictate the choreography of the models, while soldiers and Palestinians complete the composition of the exquisitely produced catalogue. A sophisticated wink exposes to the viewer the real "workers" on the site—the photographers who labor to compose the multiple players on the scene in an exact and minimalist fashion. This exposure of the catalogue's production adds a twist that matches the refined yet crude aesthetics characterizing *comme il faut* ("as it should be" in French).

Politically progressive, prosperous Tel Aviv came to Jerusalem to draw attention to its menacing new wall. The clean and aesthetic exposition of the wall as a stage set for fashion rather than for intifada kids reveals the extent to which Tel Aviv is complacent. The anorexic models from Tel Aviv march by the great bare architecture that stands for Israel, while the soldiers and Palestinians of Judea guard their steps. The *hutzpa* of the Brutalists, who built Tel Aviv's nonmonuments in order to touch the raw nerve of Israeli culture, splendidly runs along the Judean hills. Instead of polarizing the two cities, the resultant concrete spectacle bespeaks the cities' shared history, culture, and militancy. Can Tel Aviv escape Jerusalem? Does it really want to? Jerusalem surely can't survive without Tel Aviv.

62 This is an expression Bibi Netanyahoo used to justify his decision as prime minister to open the exit from the Western Wall tunnels onto the Via Dolorosa, a decision that triggered severe violence.

63 This was evident, for example, in Hal Foster's keynote talk at the "Critical Architecture" conference, The Bartlett School of Architecture, fall 2004, when he referred to the work of Eyal Weizman and Rafi Segal on the politics of settlement in Israel.

On March 16, 2007, the editors of *Perspecta 39* interviewed **Nader Tehrani,** a principal with Office dA, via phone to discuss the firm's winning 2006 competition entry for the Villa Moda Competition in Kuwait City, Kuwait.[1]

Office dA: Proposal for the Kuwait City Villa Moda

Perspecta 39: What kind of strategy is involved when building in a capital city? Are there certain kinds of protocols that you must go through in order to build in capitals as opposed to other places or any other city? What kinds of forces, national and regional, determine design decisions in such sites?

Nader Tehrani: In this case, it's probably important to note that Kuwait, as in all countries but maybe more than others, is a real artifice. Kuwait City was formed in the late eighteenth century, but the real expansion occurred in the twentieth century, in the 1950s and onward. Therefore, it did not develop organically over a protracted amount of time.

1 Thanks to Mohammad al-Asad for his input and fact checking.

Background: Study of coffering geometry.

Aerial photograph of site.

The public ground of the project is covered with a singular and extended canopy resembling the canopy of this tree.

So, regionally, you're looking at what was primarily nomadic land, and it doesn't have a substantial presence outside of modern politics. In that respect, it is based on, for the most part, postwar politics and the distribution of power to a small elite, now ruled by the Al Sabah family. What we're witnessing now is the expansion of the capital; effectively, Kuwait is the country's only city. So, there isn't the traditional distribution of power or wealth between a capital city, its provinces, towns, and requisite villages as in other countries. Instead, it's important to understand Kuwait City within the larger geo-political context of the Middle East, its emergence through oil, and the wealth of a very thin crust of the elite that oversees the work of the rest of its population, mostly composed of migrant labor: for instance, a technocracy of Palestinians, a working class of Bangladeshi, Indians, Filipino child care, and a range of other stratifications—Egyptians among other Arab nations—each aligned with their own labor. So, I think, in that sense, the notion of a capital city is slightly different than if you were going to compare it to India, Chile, or other places you may be discussing.

In talking about Kuwait City proper, its formal order and urban morphology are equally important: originally a port city organized around the bay and waterfront, it later expanded around its historic core in concentric rings. There is a first ring, a second ring, a third ring, and so forth, each corresponding to different spurts of development, and our site occurs on the sixth-ring road, which vaguely corresponds to the asymmetrical beltways we have seen in the U.S.

Not significantly far from downtown Kuwait City, the site is a substantial plot of land, about 100,000 square meters, or about one million square feet, with a projected program of 400,000 square meters. What is maybe more significant about the site is that the sixth-ring road is the very highway that connects Kuwait City to both Saudi Arabia and Iraq, the two forces that have had the most significant impact on the recent urban development, both direct and indirect. The reason that this portion of the capital city is developing now is essentially the war in Iraq, the sites on the sixth-ring road serving as the real estate for warehousing, infrastructure, services, and logistical headquarters for the ongoing U.S.-influenced operations in Iraq. So, the asymmetry of the city's evolution may be compared, metaphorically, to the tennis player's forearm, where one portion of the body develops disproportionately in comparison to others—this portion of the sixth-ring road playing a more critical role than its eastern edge. I think the competition, of which we were a part, tapped into this potential of the site quite self-consciously, while also foreseeing a future in the site, anticipating a life after the war.

P39: It is fascinating to think about a Middle East network of infrastructure where transport becomes a way of integrating different regions.

NT: Well, when I say infrastructure, I do mean transportation, but beyond that I refer to the amount of warehouses, structures, and housing required for the effort. Imagine how much space it takes to store the goods to feed 100,000 soldiers, for instance. This competition was actually made up of three sites, and each site was dedicated to different programmatic aims. The one featured in this publication is the mixed-use facility, but the second site, on a neighboring plot, was dedicated entirely to warehouses, but not of any significant architectural or urbanistic value. As you well know, the buildup of the war took months—as will the retreat—but it requires a good deal of real estate to house the goods of the war: food, clothing, spare parts, and the very people that support it indirectly. This is not a question of weeks of organization.

It is anticipated also that when the war is over that some of these warehouses, and their requisite technologies—telephone systems, wiring, roadways, and so on—and other such infrastructural elements will be transferred back to the city for other purposes. Accordingly, the structure of development within the capital city is based on the Build-Operate-Transfer system. Are you familiar with the BOT system? It is basically a public/private joint-venture operation. They have organized competitions where developers get the land for free or for nominal fees. The developers then set up a development package with a pro forma, and they manage and operate the site for twenty-some years, making their profit and then transferring it back to governmental agencies down the road. As we speak, though, this system is being reformed due to its abuse, but it has been a dominant development model in recent years.

P39: And so that's the case as well with the Villa Moda competition?

NT: Yes, the competition was one of the BOT affairs. But I think the project's interest emerges more from its place within the larger context as much connected to the region—the Persian Gulf, Iraq, and U.S. politics—as to the site proper.

P39: Projects like yours in Kuwait are echoes of the developments in capital building of the 1970s. Riyadh and Abuja, among other cities, were planned capitals built—or fueled—with oil money. How do you see the current building boom, evident in the widely publicized development of Abu Dhabi and Astana,

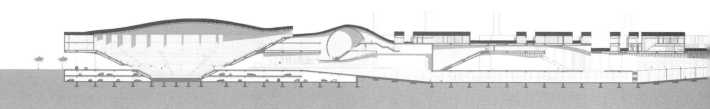

Longitudinal Section displaying the "green" canopy that extends throughout the length of the site in the form of courtyards that give shade and protection to the residential component of the project.

View of the theater-plex.

Exterior of the rifle club hotel with its iconic towers distinguishing the various suite functions.

Kazakhstan, as differing from the projects of thirty years ago?

NT: I think they're comparable from the perspective of massive acceleration, but the scale and their underlying techniques often differ significantly than that of the 1970s. If the techniques of the earlier developments were rooted in more dry or disciplinary considerations of urban systems, consider what has been happening in Dubai as they learned certain lessons from Shanghai and the Far East. I am referring as much to the spectacularization of form via Disney or Las Vegas as to the hyper-accelerated speed of production. In these lessons is also the realization that the Middle East and Gulf states can envision themselves as destinations and compete in the world market of real estate speculation, tourism, and the kind of escape that other sectors of the Islamic world cannot provide.

Imagine the "playground" role that Beirut used to play thirty years ago, before their war. That role can now be played in places like Dubai and Qatar. Others are joining in this competition now, too. Generally, the connection between the repressive regime and its escapist "other" is also a fascinating question from the perspective of urbanism: here, imagining the connection between Saudi Arabia and Beirut, Solidere, land ownership, development, and ultimately the negotiation of power in Lebanon. I am not suggesting that Kuwait is going this route—its Islamic foundations forbidding the kind of escape I am referring to—however, it has found alternative paths to substitute its otherwise stern repressions: shopping, form, architectural surplus, and a bit more shopping.

The more immediate scenario in Kuwait is still linked to its oil, on the one hand, but also, I think, it's linked to their connection to the U.S., the infrastructural support they provide for, the war, and the way they are delicately negotiating their regional politics with neighboring countries. Part of the larger plan, on which we can only speculate, is the containment of Iran. I am imagining that the more money that goes south of the border, the more Iran feels pressured to make concessions, join the game of the U.S., or be completely eclipsed in the emerging Sunni-Shiite divide. So, one can only speculate to see how is it that the Americans plan to evaluate their presence in the Middle East—in Iraq, in the Persian Gulf, and in the region in general—or if at this point, it is even within their control.

P39: Western spatial practice has long been exported to other cultures and more recently it has appeared as a sort of "gated globalization." This can be read as a desire on the part of the clients to use Western spatial and aesthetic tactics to appeal to an upwardly mobile transnational clientele. You can look for examples in advertisements for the housing for upper-middle-class people in India that depict Westerners inhabiting them, lounging in Jacuzzis in water-scarce regions. When catering to the desires of the upwardly mobile, the anxiety of the flattening effect of globalization has been replaced by the imbalance of market forces—capitalist development in socialist systems—and resources: high-energy use in limited-energy zones.

NT: First, a personal answer and then a more disciplinary answer. Are you calling our practice a Western practice?

P39: That's a very interesting question. How do you define your practice?

NT: Myself, coming from Iran—and Monica from Venezuela—I wouldn't call us a traditional, Western practice, but also I would not want to dismember our connection to our own education here in the West. I'd say we're both walking with our feet planted in diverse ends of the globe already, and we can't escape that. I grew up in Pakistan, South Africa, Iran, England, and the United States, so ideologically one would say that I am the materialization of a certain composite. Monica grew up in Venezuela—her family is Spanish—and she moved to Miami and eventually to Boston. So yes, she is from a different profile but no less global. For this reason, whether natural or ideological, I would say that we don't approach practice with the certainty of a singular model, be it Western or otherwise. If anything, we tap into heterogeneous sources and certain speculative uncertainties as a platform for transformation.

So this is one way of diffusing a simplistic notion of the idea of exportation, the other being that we are always already participating in some notion of exportation. How is it possible to develop any sort of architectural, urbanistic, or morphological transformation without some notion of projection from the outside? Isn't the architectural act, local or global, always guilty of some sort of exportation?

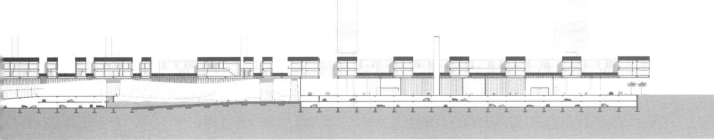

Background: Study of hexagonal coffering geometry.

Coffering geometry for the arena form.　Coffering geometry for the arena form.　Coffering geometry of lower-stair core.　Coffering geometry of upper-stair core.

This being said, there is a considerable difference in what Kahn or Wright did in the Middle East forty years ago and what our generation is up against. The Middle East is no longer merely the Middle East as much as we are no longer merely Western.

P39: It may be helpful to refer back to the project at hand and the urban question in Kuwait.

NT: Kuwaiti developments of the past two decades have basically imported a brand of American urbanism in parallel to business models. There are gated residential communities, office parks, malls, and recreational centers—all somehow linked together by way of highways, feeder roads, and subdivisions. It is a rare occasion that you will get any kind of urban density where you can get some sense of heterogeneity or layering that you could call the city: conventional, modern, unprecedented, or otherwise. For the Villa Moda competition, we were given some leverage in determining the program. Working with the client, there were certain assumptions about retail and commercial real estate they had, but they were also interested in developing a broader conception of the public realm, supporting programs, and the life of the development in a twenty-four-hour cycle.

Our first goal was to counter the prevailing tendencies to divide program in separate subdivisions and develop a strategy to layer and overlap various uses, as a way of fostering some kind of urban experience. Second and maybe most critically, while the clients saw the project as primarily commercial- and retail-oriented, we sought to introduce a residential component to the development, offering the project other cycles of life beyond the nine-to-five business hours. Therefore, in addition to the supporting programs—hotel, spa, convention hall, cineplex, and arena—we introduced a thick, inhabitable canopy above the entire scheme: a two-story layer of housing, which coincidentally and strategically reinforces the environmental argument of the proposal.

The typology of housing, which we adopt, responds to certain market forces in terms of program, square footage, and layout but varies considerably from the housing types in the marketplace today, especially in terms of its urbanism. In many ways, the mat organization reintroduces a historic idea about density, proximity, and community but updates its specifications with respect to lighting, air circulation, privacy, outdoor area, parking, and a variety of amenities that are so central to the current expectations. There is good reason why a conventional urbanism may not work in Kuwait City as the temperatures get upward of 120 degrees. So let's not try to romanticize an idea of the city as a place that you can walk the streets with storefronts, plazas, etc.—this is not about that. In fact, this is more trying to speculate about an urbanism for which there isn't any precedence in the nineteenth and twentieth centuries, nor in the segregated and stratified contemporary city. The idea of environmental control was critical in producing a mat building that could foster a kind of shade and air circulation that expands its urbanistic role as part of a community that it sustains … this, by extending the inhabitable outdoor months by a few months in each direction, in the cooler ends of the spring and fall.

While the canopy gives shade, the towers that you see extending out above it are filled with hanging concrete "chandeliers" generating heat from the sun, then drawing up the hot air from below to expel it out of the top. This strategy is a collaboration with ARUP, obviously, and only one of the various working points that they helped us with in configuring a tighter relationship between the broader spatial concept and the structural/environmental layout.

The other thing that may be different about this project is the ambiguity it sets up between the disciplines of architecture and urbanism. A million square feet is large enough to require the kind of hierarchies, scalar shifts, and public/private demarcations that are part and parcel of urban projects, while at the same time the phasing and speed of construction is and will be so fast that it will require the kind of efficiencies that are demanded by architectural systems, means, and methods of fabrication and techniques of deployment.

In the beginning, we had totally misunderstood what they meant by "phasing," assuming that they were shooting to develop the master plan in traditional phasing stages. We thought, "Ah, this is like Kendall Square in Cambridge. You will build a building, and then you will build the next one in five to ten years, and in twenty-five years it will be built out." In fact, their plan is quite the opposite. It was always anticipated that this will all be built in less that three years, but they will build the mall as a way of subsidizing the other areas within the program that cannot generate the same kind of revenue. So when you're talking about phasing, they're literally talking about a fast-track process of construction that gets the mall built, and then the following phases are built immediately after that, as the mall has a life of its own. The economic environment within which this is happening is closer to a Chinese market, where there is twenty-four-hour construction, cheap labor, and a kind of network of managerial and administrative assistants that can help foster the motors of this kind of development.

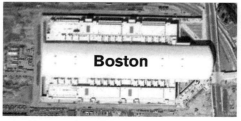

Boston

New York

Seoul

With a length of 2/3 km, the site is a bit longer than two New York City blocks, the new Convention Center in Boston, or the COEX center in Seoul.

View of the theater-plex.

Coffering geometry supporting the theater-plex and the convention hall.

Geometry of coffering supporting housing elements above and the souk below.

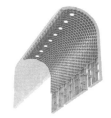

View of the theater-plex.

But getting back to your question, the substitute for the Jacuzzi in this scheme is the investment in a civic monumentality as conceived through the formal and figural surpluses of both the ground plane and the structural canopy; basically, an investment in urban and public space. In actuality, within the context of the program, it's pretty sober as compared to the frivolities of private amenities... that is, there's a distinct difference between the public and private profile of the building, so we basically diverted the cost per square foot from the private to invest in the public realm, altering the conventional net-to-gross relationship and giving the surplus to public amenities. But one can also still market the units as high-end or market-rate units, but they don't thrive on a projection of Westernization. They construct a new identity based on a different set of market indicators, rooted somewhere in between cultural assumptions and projections. Now, if you look at this not from the Office dA perspective but from the developer's perspective or the Kuwaiti public consciousness of today, there is little doubt that their own identity is very much marked by a transnational and global set of circumstances. I have met few clients in Kuwait City that were not educated in the West or whose annual itineraries do not include such places like London, Zermatt, and Cape Cod. You're not talking about a traditional notion of national identity within the public consciousness of the people you're working for, either.

To search for a national identity would be to attempt to essentialize something that is not there or, even worse, to reduce them to certain clichés. Who knows, maybe the jet-set crowd is the new cliché? But their identity is not rooted in some reductive notion about their culture, their site, their desert, or genius loci.

P39: Perhaps we can move to your use of ornament and your citation of what could be described as traditional Arab or Islamic forms. Given that Kuwait lacks a long history as a nation, what was your intention when citing traditional *souks,* arches, *muqarnas,* or other regional precedents?

NT: As you know, we don't have *muqarnas,* and there's hardly anything traditional about the coffering system we've adopted here. However, when you write texts for clients, they're different from what you do in an academic context. By way of introduction, I would say that as an architect you speak various languages and adopt different discourses. For the cli-

ent, you have to appeal to some notion of convention, of recognizability, or communicability of an idea, and more often that not you do that through some cultural context to which they can relate. If you have read something within the text that we wrote that refers to some notion about the architectural heritage of the region, it probably has a more rhetorical function. If you look at the structural system, its relationship to the coffering and the patterning of the ceiling, it is a placeholder for a certain kind of potential, both structural and semantic.

We didn't make any particular investment in the specific typologies that you see at the public level or the private, for that matter—the arena, the auditoria, the garden, the souks, and so forth—all of those are vestiges of recognizable types that one could somehow decipher from the manuals of history purely as a repository for form. There is no critical transformation of those things, at least not in any significant way. They come from graphic standards, Neufert, or they come from known typologies without substantial alterations, although they've been adapted to the site.

The important aspect of this project is the coordination between the contradictions of these types through a unitized coffering technique that offers a continuous system—a singular system that gives a strong civic identity to the project on the one hand but also imagines a construction system that can unify a great range of differences. The patterning serves to topologically negotiate the varying conditions underneath and reconcile the geometries of the program types with the geometry of the smaller grain of coffering. Now, if that pattern in turn establishes an allusive connection with Islamic patterning, it's a kind of requisite payback. However, the semantic link it establishes with history is also a slippery one, as with all cases of signification, and so it is open to many other readings as well; the only difference, maybe, is that we encourage this kind of play within our work in general and raise it to a higher level of self-consciousness.

It's also important to recognize the immediacy of the structural problem we attended to: that when you're doing a long span with a coffered ceiling, you can tap into sectional strategies, establishing a correspondence between the maximum moment and the figural qualities of the ceiling, whereas when you're in the hotel zone where the layouts are rather conventional, the coffering is no different than a normative two-way slab. One has to look at the question of patterning in more devious ways. It is operating on two levels at one time, and we would use the technical alibi to imagine both structural and symbolic levels of play, in turn, also dealing with the possibilities this imparts in terms of investing in new means and methods of fabrication, using CNC possibilities, toward some new idea of digital craft. Imagine how the canopy, which was conceived as an environmental strategy, plays a part in the civic imagination of the public space by way of its structural, material, and geometric play.

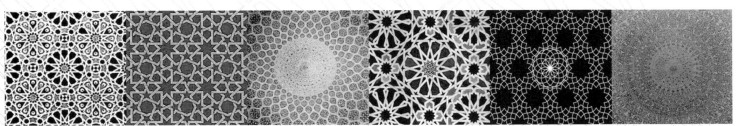

Typical souk and pattern of geometry.

Background: Study in coffering geometries.

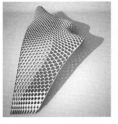 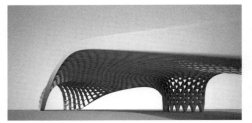 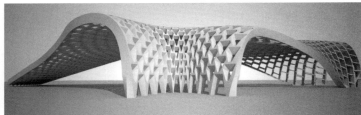

Studies in structural coffering.

P39: Would you expand on the relationship between pattern and type through various scales as is present in your Villa Moda competition entry? For instance, there has been some debate about the literal quotation of popular iconography and mimetic devices and their transformation in the hands of the architect practicing within the modern idiom. In some images you do not shy away from the mythical, populist, and direct references to the historical (old souks) and the mythical (flying carpets). Alejandro Zaero-Polo writes that "a double agenda grounds the practice within a more extended cultural background while claiming a body of technical expertise, rather than a position in the whimsical place of cultural production." Would you say this dynamic is present in your work?

NT: If you know our body or work, it's an operative technique throughout and probably one of the most dangerous areas for which we have received strong criticism. In the last fifteen years, many camps threw the baby out with the bath water, as they say, because they brushed the whole problem of iconography, of the problem of production of meaning and of the image under the carpet. In our practice, we probably dealt with this problematic as a consequence of construction techniques; in this sense, initially, we established a stronger link between pattern and construction in our earlier projects, while in the Villa Moda project we linked pattern to both construction and type. In each case we adopt an understanding of materials, their means and methods of construction, and their predisposition to innovation as a prerequisite or as a platform for the production of meaning, however multivalent that prospect may be. Then we try to slalom through the ethics involved in building—to what degree are we locating ourselves within the logic of a construction system and at what points are we precisely breaking with that logic in anomalous moments; moreover, we also try to identify those areas where a given system cannot fulfill the promise of programmatic or spatial conditions of exception. And so in most projects, we have tried to radicalize systems on the one hand, while also authoring the anomalies in extraordinary ways, on the other (I am thinking of the staircase in the New England House, for

instance). So, the double agenda is very much at work in the Villa Moda project, much as it was in Casa La Roca or the IFI project in Beirut.

P39: Do you consider it being tongue-in-cheek sometimes by using for, instance, the image of the flying carpet. It reminded me of how Foreign Office Architects used the Hokusai wave image to convince the larger audience about the iconicity of the Yokohama Terminal in Japan. In a sense, are you using a similar semiotic device to appeal to a larger group of people?

NT: I think the moment you reduce a project to a kind of icon—like a flying carpet—is the moment you kill the project. The project is never reducible to one reading, one interpretation. Yes, it is necessary for you to sell a project, and you will resort to many techniques to do that and to make it communicable. Selling it is a problem of communication and making people understand in one sound byte how something will operate. But, at the same time, there's a level of organizational and infrastructural complexity to projects like this that are generated internally and resonate within the discipline; that cannot be covered with a sound byte, one image, or a single reading.

Basically, the argument is that the form is not merely standing on its own terms; it is also finding its alibis in its structural, mechanical, and circulatory logics, and they, in turn, will lead to many other levels of interpretation. It's the delicate negotiation between all of these contingencies that will tend to suppress one's impulse to easily categorize it as the duck or an icon, as such. While we may dabble in the tongue-in-cheek, it is not interesting if the project is not considered in terms of the larger context of decisions of which it is a part. This, to me, is very important.

P39: From a historical perspective, your proposal for the Villa Moda immediately brings to mind the proposal of Alison and Peter Smithson for Kuwait City, a project that, with Candilis-Josic-Woods' Berlin Free University and Le Corbusier's Venice Hospital, marked the birth of the mat building. Was the formal and programmatic similarity a conscious decision and does it reflect a shared ideology about urbanism?

The identity of Villa Moda is based on the concept of an undulating canopy or large carpet that floats over the desert, shading and protecting the public spaces beneath.

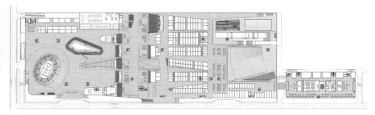

First floor plan showing arena, oasis, theater-plex convention hall, art souk/shopping area, aquatic spa center, and hotel.

The aquatic sport spa composed of a variety of pools, and both open and private areas.

NT: Obviously, mat buildings have made a re-emergence in the architectural scene over the last ten years or so, and we have obviously looked at the Smithsons, Candilis-Josic-Woods, and Le Corbusier. At the same time I would say some of the marked differences between this project and its modern predecessors are the way in which those tended to stratify urbanism as a way of organizing the mat. In this case we tried to re-adapt the type towards a more integrated and complex urbanism. At times it can result in a messier urbanism—as geometries and urban conditions collide—and yet the adopted technique attempts to bring continuity through both its circulatory elements and its structural premise. The ground in this project, for instance, departs from the sanitized way in which the Berlin Free University works; our ground weaves the parking, the theaters, the souk and the main concourse together as one seamless continuum. If the Berlin Free University is disengaged from the landscape, Villa Moda integrates the landscape into, through, and up the scheme, blurring the traditional separation between landscape and urbanism.

In this case, the landscape is central to the construction of this urbanism, and the congestion that it produces is central to our conception of the kind of crowd it is meant to sustain. In other words, we really do see a kind of density emerging here that can compete with the antiseptic qualities of the contemporary mall in as much as it competes with the gentrification of the old Souk that they have in downtown Kuwait City. So, maybe our critique of the mat precedents is their tendency to homogenize or organize through sterilization. Here, we are trying to integrate opposites, reconnecting levels that are traditionally divided between public and private spheres, bringing together programs that are conventionally divided, and developing a technique to produce urbanity.

P39: The so-called postcritical practice, more of a default rather than a conscious choice for the critical architect practicing within a speculative market, has been called into question due its "nimble" handshake with client and developer worlds. Do you think the postcritical position is a productive one, and does it carry a certain urgency or agency in today's context as a global practitioner?

NT: Can you first tell me a moment in history where there was a practice—critical or otherwise—that was not already embedded in a relationship with the "world" in the way that you're describing, in the realities of the real estate market, of institutional frameworks, of political engagements? Do you know of an architecture that has been able to critically disengage itself with that? Hasn't all of architecture been engaged with power, with economy, and with handshakes of all kinds?

When Stanford Anderson wrote about quasi-autonomy some fifteen to twenty years ago, he cited the inevitability of the architect's engagement in the world—he was referring to the "world" as defined by Edward Said, as I remember—but at the same time the way that you engage the world is through disciplinary techniques that are not reducible to the generalities of the so-called market, its politics, etc. In other words, you cannot escape the market, on the one hand, but at the same time the techniques that you adopt to engage it can almost only be through the techniques of your discipline, in this case being architecture and urbanism. Elaborating further, it would have to do with an understanding of typology, about methods of construction, techniques of perspective, among a range of other devices in which our own history has been invested.

It also has to do with innovations in material/construction performance that are rooted in certain scientific inventions and techniques that are evolving at this time—things that may be less relevant to the lay person or, say, the developer, who cares only about the bottom line (but not about how to get there). In this sense, I see the architect's best—or most critical—impact in the world being through technical inventions, spatial transformations, programmatic innovations, among a range of other disciplinary functions . . . all of which does not absolve her or him from their functions as citizens, but moreover clarifies how we are able to be effective in the world. Our own projects have been the result of various engagements with the world, and yet we have attempted to draw a relatively consistent thread of research through them, again, focusing on certain techniques and their peculiar makeup as a way of transforming the conditions of practice or the conditions of production—this, while striving to achieve a level of self-consciousness or inventiveness.

By way of example, our China project is wholly invested in bridging two cultures, the local and the global, and in that process effecting a certain change in practice. On the one hand, we were trying to adopt certain techniques from the Chinese construction system to ensure a certain quality, while also extending the evolution of their craft. At the same time, we were also invested in casting a new interpretation onto those very techniques, examining them against more current digital processes and ultimately producing a new form of knowledge through the building process as made possible from a global lens.

Second floor plan.

Third floor plan.

Background: Study in coffering geometries.

But if the implications of this question were to try to establish two strata of architectural practice, one, a critical practice, and the other a kind of simplistic practice that is engaged in the market, let's say Eisenman versus SOM, I reject that kind of dichotomy. I reject it on both ends: that SOM is not avant-garde and that Eisenman is not corporate.

P39: One other issue besides this debate about postcriticality and the question of architecture's autonomy is division between architecture and urbanism. *Perspecta* after all is the "Yale Architectural Journal," but our issue is focusing on urbanism, and it's very unusual in that way. So how do you define architecture versus urbanism?

NT: Yes, I spoke of this a bit earlier in our discussion, that is, how this project renders the relationship between architecture and urbanism ambiguous. As a building, this project is so large that it produces an urban effect, so much so it operates as a city. As the same time, it is clearly designed as a singular artifact—not, for instance, in terms of urban design guidelines—so it is also highly self-conscious about its objecthood, its autonomy, and the systems that make it possible to be implemented.

Two examples may help to clarify this argument. El Escorial, which is arguably a building, operates in much the same way: it serves as a strong architectural artifact within the landscape, it establishes a relationship between its construction system and the classical language, and its phasing points to the way it evolved as a city—all whilst it is seen as a singular icon. Rome, on the other hand, is used to illustrate the city as an organic phenomenon, something that grows over time, and establishes hierarchies between the public and private realm, is composed of a great range of functions and typologies, and is characterized by heterogeneity and urban differences --indeed made up of both great moments of self-consciousness and well as useful urban accidents, enriching the urban effect.

We could have used Cairo or Isfahan to make this point about cities, and in turn we could have used the mosque in Córdoba to make the mat argument, so I can imagine other models serving to make the case for the comparison between architecture and urbanism. In terms of production though, we have to imagine a slightly more contemporary set of examples, such as the Berlin Free University, where questions of mass production and repetition become more central to their conception and construction. For us, by way of comparison, the plausibility of mass customization became the vehicle by which to assemble urbanistic variety—orchestrating a great range of typologies, spatial variations, programs, etc.—all at the same time, using one fabricational system that is malleable enough to reconcile all of their differences: through a common structural, material, and spatial set of techniques.

So, I think your question is a central one and this project is attempting to bridge the gap between urbanism and building, on the one hand, and mass production and mass customization, on the other. Urban heterogeneity, here, is being linked to the techniques of mass customization, and in turn given a fabricational logic that rationalizes its speculated mode of production.

Project Description

VILLA MODA
Kuwait

Project Size
1,080,000 square feet

Principal in Charge
Nader Tehrani

Project Design
Nader Tehrani and Monica Ponce de Leon

Project Coordinator
Kurt Evans

Project Team
Ghazal Abbasy
Sean Baccei
Arthur Chang
Michael Filisky
Lisa Huang
Ji-Young Park
Ahmad Reza Schricker
Kyle Sturgeon

Site Characteristics
Desert landscape

Zoning Constraints
Max. height: 17 meters

Type of Client
Private/public joint venture

Program
Public (retail, commercial, conference and convention center, arena, cineplex, aquatic spa center, hotel) and residential

Construction System
Concrete framing with coffering

Funding
Private

Schedule
Design 2006–2007
Construction 2008–2011

Office dA Project Statement:

VILLA MODA Village: A domestic canopy for the public realm
Villa Moda presents the opportunity to speculate on an arena of urbanism in Kuwait, emerging typologies in its architecture, and a progressive attitude towards sustainability in the Middle East. With a footprint of 100,000 square meters, the Villa Moda development scheme will act as the new face for the New Kuwait Sports Shooting Club, situated on the 6th ring road.

At a scale situated between urban design and architecture, the project is comprised of spatial hybrids, and poses unprecedented ways of bringing programs together that are conventionally segregated, compartmentalized, or stratified. Contrary to dominant modern or current development paradigms, where districts are separated by zoning, functions, and uses, this scheme proposes a more cross-bred environment where alliances between programs may foster more interactive and urban living conditions, while offering a better economical strategy for the district as a development plan. Instead of proposing different buildings, separate blocks, and segregated zoning, we identify key programmatic overlaps to bring together certain public activities, while also using the resources of one program to strategically amplify the potentials of another. At the core of the philosophy of the design is the idea that the scheme can draw from the richness of programmatic layering, mixed-use functions, and multiple activities to sponsor a lively and economically diverse urban environment.

The basic organization of the proposal can be described by four decks of varied thickness and geometries: the basement with parking and technical support, a public ground as an extension of the city's terrain, a deep structural system above composed of coffering that in turn supports a housing district atop.

A Public Ground:
The ground plane is conceived as an extension of the city's public life, and access to it is organized along the north and south edges of the site. It is characterized by an undulating surface that dips and rises in accordance with the programs it sponsors. From west to east, the program of the public plane houses: an multi-use arena, a greenhouse/oasis, a convention hall, a cineplex, a souk/mall, a sport spa, and, lastly, a hotel for the new rifle club. The banding of these public functions on the ground plane takes advantage of their strategic adjacencies in order to activate the site.

A Domestic Canopy:
The activities of the multi-use environment on the ground plane are enhanced by residential units on the upper levels. The result is an integrated urban environment, where living, working, and entertainment benefit from a calibrated proximity to each other. The residential component of the program will take the form of a canopy that floats above the public ground, providing it shade and environmental protection, while also permitting the passage of light to the base through its courtyards. This single act organizes the site in the most telling way, informing its environmental, structural and social strategy.

The Structure:
The configurative logic of the coffering is made to coordinate with the varying programs, forms, and typologies that the structure spans. The structure is analogous to the sponge-like form and material-to-weight ratio of human bone: a trabecular structure in which material is concentrated efficiently in response to the applied or anticipated loading while minimizing weight. In areas of high moments, shears, or in response to concerns of serviceability, the form of the slab system morphs from a typical, orthogonal, uniform depth rib system into a system of deeper ribs, wider ribs, or more closely spaced ribs. The changing shape responds to the intensity of the loading and the need to provide strength and stiffness to the system.

Background: Reflect ceiling plan of Villa Moda geometries.

Metro Manila: Zones of Capital

Nina Rappaport

The unveiling of the model of Cavite Export Processing Economic Zone signed into law by former Philippine President Fidel V. Ramos, Cavite, 1995.

From left to right: Jose Concepcion (industrialist and former chair of the National Movement for Free Elections [Namfrel], a poll watchdog), Corazón Aquino (former president, 1986-1992), Juanito Remulla (former Cavite governor), Henry Sy (business magnate, the "retail king" of the Philippines), Juan Ponce Enrile (former secretary of state, now senator), Jesus Enrita (former AFP, now executive secretary, Vicente Paterno (former industry minister).

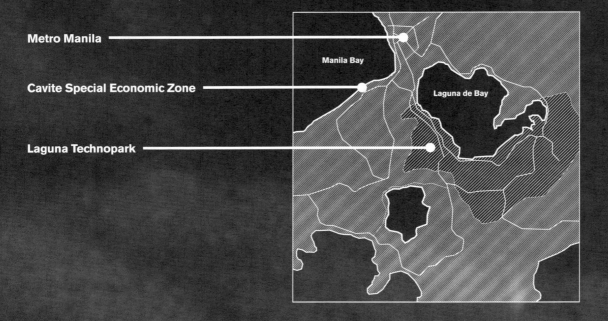

Metro Manila

Cavite Special Economic Zone

Laguna Technopark

Manila Bay

Laguna de Bay

In the postindustrial world, spaces of production have become either faceless sheds in offshore manufacturing zones in the East and South or taken the extreme opposite approach as the spectacular architecture of branded production in the West (take, for example, the new BMW Leipzig and VW Dresden factories). Placing manufacturing offshore, or on "others'" shores, has resulted in a return of pre-industrial working conditions similar to those that Max Weber observed and which led to worker reforms, the rise of unions, and worker empowerment in the mid-twentieth century. The so-called developing countries are aggressively pursuing global investment at the risk of abusing their labor forces and limited natural resources. Cities that were formerly trading ports are now rife with instances of global opportunism encouraged by political connections. Mega-scale infrastructural projects—catalysts for the growth of multiple sectors—are often steeped in hubris when disseminated as symbols of national growth, while their operative aspects facilitate activities that range from money laundering to exploitation.

One example of this strange push of fast-paced capital into local culture is in Manila, a depressed coastal city of 11 million on a sheltered inlet of the South China Sea. The Manila metro area struggles to keep pace in newly open Asian markets under the blanket of policies established by the U.S. to regulate commerce. The city developed as the capital of a colony of Spain, which destroyed the existing walled Muslim settlement and converted the inhabitants to Catholicism in 1571. A thriving port, Manila came under U.S. control in 1898 after the Spanish-American War; the Philippine-American War ended in a peace accord in 1902 but not without a fight from the Filipinos, who had not completely accepted American dominance as a colony. The elite families invented sophisticated trade mechanisms with the U.S. for sugar, and the ramifications are still felt today. A "sugar quota" enabled them to export sugar to the U.S. market at higher-than-market prices, thus beginning the Philippines' global trade.

After World War II, Manila became the capital of the newly independent Republic of the Philippines, assisted by the U.S. for the reconstruction of its economy, government, and educational systems and the creation of new export zones. What remains of the U.S. physical presence includes the former Clark Air Base and Subic Bay Naval Compound, which the U.S. were forced to leave in 1992. The land has subsequently been transformed into new industrial development zones under Filipino ownership and is now being developed as part of major infrastructural projects in which manufacturing spaces, transportation access, and labor forces are being combined.

Crime, terrorism, kidnapping, smuggling, poverty, and uprisings together with corrupt and controlling leaders make for a volatile situation in Manila that parallels the natural threats of earthquakes, typhoons, and volcanic eruptions. Yet its physical location makes it well positioned to foster a network of commercial exchange, airports, and ports, as well as trade policies to encourage foreign investors, mainly from the Japanese and Korean electronics and automobile industries. A governor, who is not elected by the people but appointed by the president, manages Metro Manila's 395-square-mile region (by comparison, New York City's metro area is 6,720 square miles). In the 1970s and 1980s, institutional abandonment of the city resulted as the landed elite developed a new suburban enclave, Makati, 127 miles southwest of the capital. In harsh contrast to the impoverished Manila shantytowns, new infrastructural systems, high-rise commercial towers, and wide streets were built for multinational corporations and their employees. Other landed families with ties to then-President Ferdinand Marcos created towns in the ring zones, which were later co-opted by the government to take advantage of the nearby industrial economic zone of CALABA (Cavite, Laguna, and Binan). The Philippines government recently carved the country into "super regions," which serve as catalysts for the development of new infrastructural transportation network systems. Rather than base these divisions on shared historical, social, or cultural interests, they are rely upon their potential for economic growth. One such "super region" is the Metro Luzon Urban Beltway, where an expressway is planned between the Subic Bay industrial development, which is focused around the deep-sea port, and the Clark Air Base, which will be an expanded aviation hub. Plans also call for new coastal roads, as well as a rail line that will connect eastern and western towns and ports to the inland roads linking the South China Sea to the Philippine Sea, paid for by the People's Republic of China.

At the January 2007 Association of Southeast Asian Nations (ASEAN) summit meeting, it was agreed that China would join ASEAN as part of a China-ASEAN Free Trade Area by July of that year. By 2015, the ten nations will form the ASEAN Economic Community, opening up trade to China and its market of 1.8 billion people and potential economic activity of $2 trillion. Already, the interim free-trade area has decreased import taxes and allowed goods to move more freely, but for the Philippines it will also mean increased competition with Chinese-made goods.[1] When Philippines president Gloria Arroyo opened the January ASEAN meeting, she praised "ASEAN's efforts to create one of the world's greatest trading blocs."[2] The country's economy is now on the rise, with a GDP growth the highest it has been since 1960 and increased foreign investment. Seventy percent of its exports are electronics. The Philippines is in fourth place for overseas remittances and outsourcing after India, China, and Mexico, and, like India, it is benefiting from its primary language of English through growth in the area of cyber-services.[3]

Part of the interest in what economists have called "the sick, old man of Asia" lies in a vision greater than the continuous struggle for a stable economy, the reduction of debt, and anticorruption and antiterrorism efforts. Since 1995, to promote the strategic development of factories around Metro Manila, the government has sponsored the institutionalization of industrial parks controlled and managed in Export Processing Zones (EPZ) by the Philippine Economic Zone Authority (PEZA). Offering seductive incentives to lure foreign and local companies, the managing entities have built infrastructural systems and amenities. There are no taxes for

1 The Economist (February 13, 2003).
2 Carlos H. Conde, New York Times (January 14, 2007): 17.
3 Business Times [Singapore] (November 10, 2006).

importing raw materials or exporting goods, and there is the promise of outsourcing in a region with low wages. EPZs began throughout the world in 1964 with support from the United Nations Economic and Social Council in order to help companies start up and get tax breaks in developing nations. Globally these industrial production zones have spawned a dis-connect between the local contract manufacturer and the multinational or international corporation. In the Philippines, they developed under Marcos in twenty-two zones, also called "ecozones," touted as integrated areas of commerce, tourism, and industry. Adjacent residential communities, which the PEZA advertises alongside the low wages required by the educated, English-speaking worker population, are also incentives to foreign manufacturers.

The industries coming to the Philippines both employ and exploit the lesser-skilled workers in repetitive jobs. The most desirable workers are females under 35 years of age, who are never hired for more than a few months to avoid requiring contracts and benefits. Slipping between the local employment laws and collective bargaining while ignoring the laws set up by the Organization for Economic Cooperation and Development (OECD), the minimum-wage workers receive little more than food and transportation to work, with no overtime pay. Local companies follow suit, hiring "casuals," or flexible hires, through worker employment agencies or cooperatives. Taylorized efficiency has taken hold, albeit without the paternalism of Henry Ford, who made a product his workers could afford.

The PEZA, a small regional planning office, has the governmental authority and freedom from regulation to develop industrial sites and "ecozones," including land management and sales, infrastructure such as roads, sewage, and water, and "city" services (i.e., police, security guards, lighting, and environmental needs). The economic zones could be traced to early-twentieth-century precedents such as Tony Garnier's *Cité Industrielle* or the Bata company town of Zlín in the Czech Republic, as well as Ford's development of Highland Park, a vertically integrated industrial complex located outside of Detroit. The PEZA is driven by economic control and desire for protection, its self-described goals being to "contribute to the acceleration of the creation of employment and other economic opportunities, particularly in the countryside, and to spur the growth of diversification of exports by encouraging investments."[4] Close to Manila, many of these industrial sites are leased to subcontractors who have no ties to the parent company and who hide their workers and environments from the new factory inspectors. These factories, rather than arising from advanced technology and industrial know-how, are actually "labor warehouses." The multinationals have no interest, material or ideological, in the country to which they have outsourced and make no investments in the people, place, or community.[5] As they don't pay local taxes or any import taxes, they are as virtual a manufacturing space as a simulated production line on a computer screen.

Two Special Economic Zones exemplify the issues of industrial development and global manufacturing: Laguna Technopark and Cavite. Laguna Technopark, located in the province of Santa Rosa thirty miles from Manila, is strategically sited to be near both the airport and the seaport as well as commutable from Makati. It was the first industrial estate in the country under the PEZA, as a joint venture between Ayala Land (owned by one of the elite Filipino families that developed Makati) and two Japanese companies, Mitsubishi Corp. and Kawasaki Steel. On its 956 acres, eighty-four other companies—including Hitachi, Honda, Isuzu, Matsushita, TDK, and Toshiba—are located. The electronic devices of the developed world

4 See http://www.peza.com.ph.
5 This is similar to what Richard Sennett discusses in *Corrosion of Capital* concerning commitment to regions.

are totally dependent on the regulated output of such factory complexes in controlled zones. One small item—1.8-inch disk drives for iPods—are assembled here by various manufacturers that ship over 20,000 drives a day from around-the-clock factories employing 6,000 people who come to work via 80 company-sponsored buses. One company, Nidec, makes the spindle motors for iPods, but suppliers are interchangeable as they all make the same product under different roofs managed by different contractors.

Laguna had been known as the "emerald province," a source of rice, vegetables, fruits and fish; it is now considered the Silicon Valley of the Philippines because of its numerous semiconductor plants. The Technopark traffic congestion and development have changed the area. Laguna has its own governing body, similar to a homeowners or business association, which addresses the leaseholder's issues. The gated park has a rectilinear plan within which the association manages roadways and digital communication. Buildings are required to have setbacks of five to ten meters in order to create "pockets of green." There are also banks, administrative buildings, medical facilities, and fire stations as well as their own customs office for ease of trade. Ayala Land has also built adjacent executive residential neighborhoods as planned suburban communities, with recreation facilities and golf courses. A private security detail ensures safety by regulating the flow of people in and out of the park, thus restricting the organization of laborers.

At Nikko Materials Philippines Inc., in a fall 2005 sit-down strike brought on because there was a deadlock in collective bargaining, the security force of the Technopark, the PEZA police, and one hundred security guards made actions against the workers and did not allow the local representative Renato Magtubo into the park. The water and power were cut off to the workers, who were locked inside. The manufacturers, attracted to profit, have made the workers into prisoners of the globalized development process. That strike also had ramifications within the park itself as the "company blacklisted the workers from going to other employers." The physical conditions of the spatial divisions, the factory buildings, and the zones thus impact the workers and their freedom. [6]

Striking is both a political and spatial act. It is spatial because workers strike over a specific task in a certain space, which they are often then restricted from entering or are forced against their will to occupy. Food and services can be withheld within that space, affecting the activities there. In the Philippines, Section 18, Article II of the constitution affirms labor as a primary social economic force and requires the state to protect the rights of workers and promote their welfare. When a strike occurs, the PEZA often has to play the conflicting role of the controller. As the activist Rosa Luxemburg wrote in 1906 in *The Mass Strike, the Political Party and the Trade Unions*:

The mass strike: its use, its effects, its reasons for coming about are in a constant state of flux…. Political and economic strikes, general strikes of individual sections of industry and general strikes of entire cities, peaceful wage strike and street battles, uprisings with barricades—all run together and run alongside each other, get in each other's way, overlap each other, a perpetually moving and changing sea of phenomena.[7]

The Cavite Special Economic Zone is in Rosario, twenty-nine miles from Manila, and was established first in 1980 as an "Export Processing Zone" and in 1995 as a "Special Economic Zone." It is best known for the protests of labor activist groups

6 Committee news of the committee affairs department vol. 14 no. 9 (September 6, 2006) and Asian Human Rights Commission (October 18, 2005).
7 Cited in J.P. Nettl, *Rosa Luxemburg*, vol 2. (London, Oxford University Press, 1966), 500.

against the sporting-goods manufacturer Nike, whose subcontractors treated workers inhumanely (Nike has since moved its production out of the Philippines). Discussed at length in Naomi Klein's book *No Logo*, Cavite is a 682-acre free-trade industrial area with over 280 factories and over 62,000 management and production workers. This means there are no taxes on materials coming in or on finished products going out. The incentives for foreign corporations "only reinforces the sense that the companies are economic tourists rather than long-term investors."[8]

Cavite's Office of the Governor has a "no union, no strike" policy, implying the free reign of multinationals. While seemingly normal on the outside, the workers' environments are places of social discord. In the fall of 2006, workers producing clothes for Korean apparel-maker Chong Won, which is contracted by Wal-Mart, went on strike and were then attacked by Cavite's zone police and private security guards as they were peacefully picketing outside the factory gates.[9] Some workers were injured, some have been fired, and others were denied food and water. The company had received an audit prior to this event, and the factory workers were made to lie about the length of their workday and conditions. The Philippine Workers' Assistance Center requested that Wal-Mart respect its code of conduct and Philippine labor laws. However, two months later, a worker was killed. The multinational corporations that have colonized the industrial parks of the Philippines continue to operate just beyond the political reach of Manila.

This question thus remains: How will the fast-paced growth of Southeast Asian capital cities and postindustrial globalization impact struggling cities such as Manila when globalization is actually creating competition between Export Processing Zones throughout developing countries? As the new business structure is not nationally based, it bypasses local centers, depriving cities like Manila of their political and economic capital.

Contemporary Mexico City: Recycled Sites, Regenerative Landscapes, and Revalued Post-Industrial Enclaves

Edward R. Burian

I remember some fifteen years ago, on a plane from San Jose del Cabo, Baja California, to Mexico City, I sat next to the pilot.

Almost from the moment we took off, he pointed at a brown mass in the air in the distance, and he told me...

Top: Panorama of the pre-conquest island city of Tenochtitlán, c. A.D. 1520. Bottom: Smog over the megalopolis of Mexico City trapped by the surrounding mountains of the Valley of Mexico on a typical day. Note the contrasting cleaner air above the layer of smog.

...'That is where we are headed.' —Arq. Agustín Landa, Mexico City, 2005

The sewer is the conscience of the city. —Victor Hugo

Top: Smog over the major boulevard of Ave. Reforma in Mexico City's center on a typical day. The megalopolis has some of the worst air pollution in the world. Bottom: Raw sewage several feet deep in the Chalco neighborhood in 2004 after a break in the unlined earthen canals that drain untreated raw sewage out of Mexico City.

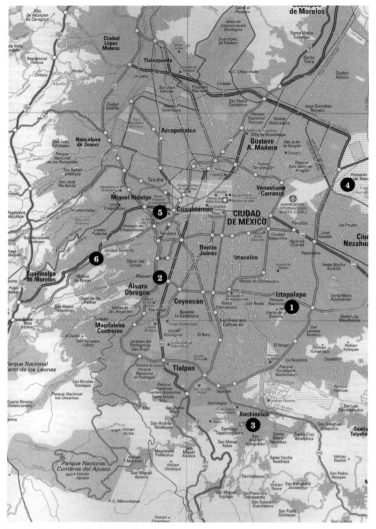

Map of the megalopolis of Mexico City showing projects.
1. Arq. Mauricio Rocha Iturbide, Center for the Blind, Mexico City, Col. Iztapalapa, 2000.
2. Landa, García, Landa Arquitectos, CEMEX Headquarters, Mexico City, Col. Mixcoac, 2004.
3. GDU, Arq. Mario Schjetnan Garduño and Arq. José Pérez Maldonado, Lake Xochimilco Restoration, Mexico City, Col. Xochimilco, 1998.
4. Arq. Alberto Kalach, Arq. Gustavo Lipkau, Arq. Juan Cordero, Arq. Teodoro Gonzalez de León, and team, "The Lakes Project," Mexico City, Col. Texcoco, 2000.
5. TEN Arquitectos, Arq. Enrique Norten, Hotel Habita, Mexico City, Col. Polonco, 2001
6. Diámetro Arquitectos, Arq. David Cherem Ades, Arq. Isaac Sasson Misri, Arq. Christain Herrera Kobashi, Arq. Carolina Barba Villanueva, Torre Punta del Parque, Mexico City, Col. Santa Fé, 2004

Four-year-old María Elena presses her face to the gritty glass window of her day-care center in the working-class Iztapalapa neighborhood in Mexico City, gazing longingly at the dirt outdoor play court with its shriveled, darkened tree and tire swing. The whir of electric air-purifying units as well as the squeals of children playing inside their classroom drowns out the roar of passing traffic. Today is a smog alert in the megalopolis, and the children are restricted from playing outside to protect them, as well as the elderly, from lung damage.[1] María Elena also misses playing with her favorite cousin, who is sick again with gastro-intestinal problems—a frequent source of absenteeism at the center—from inadvertently drinking untreated tap water or from eating contaminated food irrigated with untreated sewage. Around the walls of the day-care classroom are the children's paintings. But these

feature skies painted not blue but gray, the typical color of the sky over Mexico City, and most not with lush green trees they have seen on television but blackened ones that only sporadically appear on a few streets and in the few parks of the megalopolis.

The environmental conditions that María Elena and her 28 million fellow inhabitants of the metropolitan area of Mexico City (MAMC) endure are some of the worst on the planet. The capital city contains some 25 percent of the nation's population, and today it is the largest megalopolis in the world. However, recent discussions of contemporary architecture in the MAMC have focused primarily on innovative visual and formal compositions in an idealized environmental context that is largely portrayed in a fictional, unitary, forward march of technological progress. What is largely ignored and the focus of this essay are the challenges and opportunities of new kinds of sensory experience being driven by the MAMC's environmental devastation, the recycling, regeneration, and revaluing of former industrial and environmentally devastated sites, as well as the varying ethical and technological responses to the environmental devastation of the MAMC.

Mexico City as Paradoxical Reinvented Landscape, Inextricably Linked to Its Topography, Geology, and Hydrology

The Valley of Mexico, as it is usually termed, is actually a hydrographic basin with no natural drainage one and a half miles above sea level and surrounded by volcanic mountain ranges including the distinctive peaks of Popocatéptl and Iztaccíhuatl. These conditions formed a series of five large, shallow lakes fed by drainage, natural springs, and mountain snowmelt. The high elevation formerly produced a mild climate, with the highest portions of the valley to the west and south featuring the coolest microclimate and receiving more precipitation.

Competing pre-Columbian city-states developed around the perimeter of the lakes, with the Mexica (Aztecs) founding Tenochtitlán for mythological reasons in fulfillment of religious prophecy. The dense, gridded island city interlaced with canals developed an amphibious "metropolitan" culture of approximately 250,000 people with the advantages of natural defense, wet farming, water-based transportation, and extensive trade networks.[2] Tenochtitlán was destroyed in the Spanish Conquest (1521) and intentionally rebuilt, again for largely symbolic reasons, over the ruins of the Aztec capital to represent dominance and restored authority, and the newly rebuilt city was renamed, "Mejico."

However, the valley and its lakes were reinvented during the Spanish colonial era

and cause damage. Mexico City was ranked the most polluted when combining all three measurements and taking into account the overall number of children under five exposed to the polluted air. Levels of almost any pollutant such as nitrogen dioxide now regularly break international standards by two to three times. Levels of ozone, which protects us from solar radiation in the upper atmosphere but is dangerous to breathe, are twice as high here as the maximum allowed limit for one hour a year. And this occurs several hours per day, every day.

1 A study funded by the World Health Organization measured three important airborne pollutants: sulfur dioxide, nitrogen dioxide, and total suspended particulates (TSPs)—tiny particles of everything from dust to heavy metals that embed deep in lung tissue

2 The term *metropolitan culture* was used by George Kubler to describe the Aztec culture, which integrated outsiders' cultural concepts and aesthetics and was capable of a range of aesthetic expression, from the abstract to the figurative.

3 During the colonial era, the city flooded many times during the rainy season between 1555 and 1604. In fact, during one deluge in 1629, most the city was under six feet of water and remained submerged until 1634. Serious discussion of moving the capital were averted due to powerful real estate interests of urban property owners, and an earlier drainage scheme devised in 1608 to create and eight vided a 60-mile network of underground deep-drainage tunnels located up to 600 feet below-ground to avoid soil subsidence.

4 The existing springs of Chapultapec, Desierto de Leones, Lerma, and Santa Fé proved insufficient for the growing water needs of the metropolis.

5 See *Praxis* vol. 2, "Mexico City: the MegaCity," 74. The sinking had also caused the Gran Canal drainage project to reverse its slope and back up; a series of pumps were installed to lift the black water up-slope to each level.

6 This raw sewage is used for crop irrigation in Hidalgo state, which desperately needs the water for agriculture, but its residents have contracted cholera, parasites, and other illnesses by using it for farming.

7 In June 2004, the earthen edge of the canal collapsed in the former lakebed of the impoverished Valle de Chalco neighborhood, spewing tons of untreated raw sewage into the neighborhood up to six feet deep in some places; the catastrophe also cut off the main road linking the MAMC with Puebla.

(1521–1821) into a landscape of their own liking, reminiscent of the plains of Castille for raising livestock and arable land for farming, as well as for urban building sites. With the deforestation of hillsides and agricultural runoff, large deposits of silt filled the lake basin and resulted in the city flooding many times during the colonial era.[3] A number of projects to drain the lakes into the Tula River and ultimately out to the Gulf of Mexico were initiated. Only the *chinampas* gardens of Lake Xochimilco to the south survived as it provided food for the capital as well as native and imported flower horticulture. Yet as the city grew, at the end of the nineteenth century, it was still subject to flooding, and in 1900 a thirty-mile Gran Canal with a six-mile drainage tunnel was completed, and the project of lake drainage continues uncritically to the present.

During the dictatorship of Porfirio Díaz (1876–1911), the western edge of the valley was established as the preferred location for elite development with environmentally cooler and cleaner air, and the preferred direction for development for wealthy elites was established that continues today. A sixteen and a half-mile aqueduct was constructed from Xochimilco to supply the capital that served to further its environmental decline.[4] But by the 1970s, the constant pumping of the aquifer for drinking water and the construction of the city on the unstable lakebed had caused the city to sink in some places up to twenty-five feet.[5] This has been devastating for the water-supply infrastructure, causing many of the older supply pipes to break and lose up to 30 percent of the city's scarce, clean water. Today, the megalopolis pumps about 70 percent of its water from the aquifer up to one and a quarter miles below grade and piped as far away as 250 miles from the Lerma and Cutzamala basins, west of Mexico City. Furthermore, the serious risk of differential settlement and subsurface cracks could contaminate the aquifer and kill millions of people. The MAMC also mixes its storm drainage systems and wastewater, including human waste, street garbage, dead animals, and hazardous medical material. Ninety percent of this raw sewage is untreated and channeled north out of the city via unlined, open-air canals that have spilled in the past and that could also contaminate the aquifer.[6, 7]

During World War II, income flowed into Mexico to supply raw materials for the Allies, foreign investment followed, and Mexican intelligentsia and politicians advocated a policy of urban industrialization, rather than agricultural development. This marked the beginning of the explosive, runaway hyper growth of the MAMC, with the surrounding small towns becoming engulfed and leading to the MAMC's distinct quality of cities and enclaves amid the sprawling megalopolis. New factories and industrial sites were created in the 1940s in the least desirable areas of the dried former lakebeds in the east and the north, in Iztapalapa and Tlalnepantla, while in the 1950s the low-lying areas at the perimeter of the city to the northeast and southwest including Nezahualcóyotl and Chalco were also "informally developed."[8, 9]

The growing ad-hoc system of streets and highways with over four million vehicles has resulted in high levels of noise and air pollution. The roaring noise of vehicles, including many that cannot be properly maintained, results in noise levels up to 90 decibels, the sound level of jackhammers. The smog that envelops the valley of Mexico is only interrupted for a few days after the air is cleansed by seasonal rainfall. Since the 7,500-foot altitude reduces oxygen by almost a third, motor vehicles produce twice the carbon monoxide and hydrocarbon emissions they would at sea level. The surrounding volcanic mountain ranges trap smog and limit the flow of air currents to cleanse the air, and the average visibility of seven miles in the 1940s is less than a half-mile today. The continued deforestation of the Valley made the mild climate increasingly hotter and dryer. The air also contains dried fecal matter from millions of gallons of sewage dumped near the city in dried former lake-beds and from some three million stray dogs. Mexico City is one of the few places in the world where you can inhale a gastrointestinal disease like hepatitis or dysentery.

Planning in the MAMC after the 1968 Olympic Games until today is largely reactionary in terms of the reality of unplanned, uncontrolled growth, as opposed to regional, systematic planning protocols. Unoccupied private property was used illegally, either by the poor who constructed shacks with found objects with no utility infrastructure and no planned supporting amenities or as a dumping ground for trash and construction debris. Simultaneously, as the city continues to expand, at its perimeter, formerly abandoned and industrial sites closer to the amenities of the center of the city have become revalued and are being reused. Thus, typically both formal and informal development occurs then planning begins![10]

With an era of contemporary information technology from the 1990s, entire incremental stages of technology were able to be bypassed by the elite with a credit card and Internet access. As in many countries, the English-speaking, technologically savvy elite with either desirable skill sets or capital for investments, no longer will have much in common

8 An informal urbanism of poor workers' neighborhoods with few, if any, environmental concerns rose around the factories attracted by possible employment as well as usurping the electricity, water, and transportation infrastructure supplied to the factories. Tlalnepantala attracted numerous squatters in the 1950s with the new PEMEX Gas Storage facility. Tragically, this informal housing was built too close to the storage tanks and thousands were killed when the tanks accidentally exploded.

9 "Informally developed" is the euphemistic term for neighborhoods illegally built without drainage, roads, water supply, sewers, sewage treatment, electricity, telephone, schools, parks, landscape, street trees, or other infrastructure, typically on problematic sites. sixty percent of the population of the MAMC live in areas that were originally informally urbanized. Some 40 percent of the population are poor and live in one-room dwellings with an average of five people living in one room.

10 This is in spite of such notable achievements such as Luis Barragán's Gardens of Pedregal residential subdivision (1945–1949), the Ciudad Universitaria master-planned by Enrique del Moral and Mario Pani (1950-52), the large-scale multifamily housing projects of Mario Pani (1947-1962), and the public works projects of the Olympic Games (1968), which largely mark the end of proactive planning in the MAMC. The megalopolis has ceased to be economically self-sustaining as it costs more and more in urban infrastructure to produce less and less, even as it is supported with government subsidies paid by (with some resentment) taxes from across the country for food, water, and transportation, keeping real costs in the MAMC artificially low.

Arq. Mauricio Rocha Iturbide, Center for the Blind, Mexico City, Col. Iztapalapa, 2000. Trash and illegal dumping on the existing site prior to construction.

Arq. Mauricio Rocha Iturbide, Center for the Blind, Mexico City, Col. Iztapalapa, 2000. The exterior rubble wall of the project relates to traditional local tectonic practices and also provides a tactile experience for the blind.

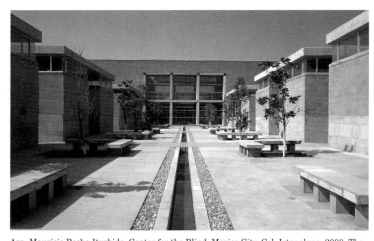

Arq. Mauricio Rocha Iturbide, Center for the Blind, Mexico City, Col. Iztapalapa, 2000. The central court with its water channel and planted trees orients the project's users in terms of sound, smell, coolness on the skin, as well as helping to cleanse the air.

11 For insight into the phenomena of globalization and the diminishing concept of nationhood, see an essay by Kaplan, Robert, "Fort Leavenworth and the Eclipse of Nationhood," *The Atlantic Monthly* (September 1996): 75–90.

12 See Keller Easterling *Enduring Innocence: Global Architecture and Its Masquerades.* (Cambridge, Mass.: MIT Press, 2005)

13 Not surprisingly, this discussion of the sensory-based experience of architecture parallels architectural discourses in relationship to phenomenology developed by the work of philosophers such as Husserl, Heidegger, Bachelard, Merleau-Ponty, and Levinas. These philosophical discourses from the 1960s onward were interpreted by architectural theorists such as Christian Norberg-Schulz, Juhani Pallasmaa, Kenneth Frampton, Robert Mugerauer, Michael Benedikt, and perhaps not surprisingly by Alberto Pérez-Gómez, a native of Mexico City, among others.

14 This position is related to the work of cultural geographers and ecologists who have also utilized some concepts from phenomenology including Edward Relph, Michael Zimmerman, and David Abram. In my mind, what is important here is the analytical dimension of processes in conjunction with sensory experience. The term *architecture of reconciliation* is derived from "reconciliation ecology" from Michael L. Rosenzweig's *Win-Win Ecology: How the Earth's Species Can Survive in the Midst of Human Enterprise* (Oxford University Press, 2003).

15 The notion of the "fragmented body" is related to an essay by Arthur and Marilouise Kroker, *Theses on the Disappearing Body in the Hyper-Modern Condition*, in their book, *Body Invaders: Panic Sex in America* (New York: St. Martins Press, 1987). For general discussions of postindustrial cities, see the recent publications of Keller Easterling, Edward Soja, and Stephen Graham, among others. These provide insights regarding the social construction of the megalopolis in relation to the systems, networks, processes, and underlying agendas of late-capitalist

with most of their less-educated, low-income fellow citizens. Instead, they will have more in common with elite networks of international project teams that will be assembled for specific projects around the world. This will further weaken the notion of being economically, intellectually, or emotionally invested in the megalopolis or the nation.[11] This has led to the establishment of new reinvented landscapes in the protected, post-industrial enclaves for globalized trade, conspicuous consumption, and escape from pollution in the hills and ravines at the western-most edge of the city, such as Lomas de Santa Fé, that "aspire to be worlds within themselves."[12]

Contemporary Conditions and the Changing Status of Sensory, Body-Oriented Experience

In response to the MAMC's contemporary conditions, new kinds of architectural experiences are being created, which can be understood in terms of the "grounded body," a primarily sensory relationship to the contemporary conditions of place; the "restorative body," a sensory *and* analytical relationship to place in an "architecture of reconciliation" that promotes environmental healing, bodily well-being, and an awareness of environmental restorative processes; and the "fragmented body," a distanced relationship to local conditions in the post-industrial city, an abandoning and hyper-exteriorization of the non-grounded "floating" body within a controlled "techno-landscape."[13, 14, 15] Thus, the projects examined here are non-monolithic in relating to their degraded environments in the MAMC. They exist as a number of distinct modes of sensory body experience related to varying kinds of environmental degradation, economic class, differing technologies, and ethical and architectural intentions, as opposed to a transitional economy in which the lower levels of technology are being replaced in upward mobility.

The Recycled Urban Industrial Site and the Grounded Body: Reconciling the Protected Interior Court

The **Center for the Blind** by Arq. Mauricio Rocha Iturbide Buildings provides educational, therapeutic, and recreation services for the blind and education about the blind for the sighted in an effort to integrate the blind more fully into urban life. The project is located in the low-income, informally developed Iztapalapa district now enveloped in the midst of the megalopolis, where 25 percent of the MAMC population resides and where infrastructure has only been built in recent years.[16] For years the site was utilized for the illegal disposal of construction debris and is surrounded by busy,

noisy streets on two sides and adjacent to a public metro station for ease of access for the blind population it serves. The recycled debris-filled site and noise from traffic were the main points of departure in the design strategy of presenting a rubble wall to the street. This wall features a construction system that recalls the pre-Columbian, colonial, and mod-

development in developed countries and, in particular, the automobile and the impact of electronic information technology. However, I believe it is important not to merely apply the methodology of Easterling, Soja, and Graham to an underdeveloped country such

Arq. Mauricio Rocha Iturbide, Center for the Blind, Mexico City, Col. Iztapalapa, 2000. Sketch of section at the edge of site where earth is bermed at the perimeter wall to act as sound absorption and also as a landscaped sensory experience for the blind.

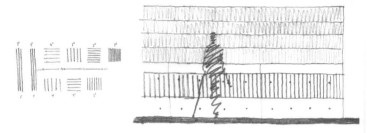

Arq. Mauricio Rocha Iturbide, Center for the Blind, Mexico City, Col. Iztapalapa, 2000. Types of wall surfaces to aid the blind in orientation.

as Mexico and the diverse neighborhoods of Mexico City with multiple, parallel, and distinct technologies, economies, and access to capital and information technology.

16 Iztapalapa has the greatest concentration of blind citizens, reflecting the environmental degradation of the district leading to diseases and birth defects of the eye. Ironically, reflecting the pressures of globalization of the economy in Mexico City, there is also a manufacturing plant in Iztapalapa for Yale de Mexico, a clothing line which produces casual sportswear and employs about one thousand people, presumably mostly women, as seamstresses, see www.yale.com.mx.

ern vernacular traditions of the city. Constructed with hand labor using local stone, it acts as an acoustical barrier at the scale of the city and as a retaining wall, while a garden adds mass to absorb sound. This is particularly important for the attuned sense of hearing of the blind in terms of architectural experience. The garden peeks out above the wall, giving a visual clue to the sighted and partially sighted, as well as olfactory clues to the blind. Like a mask, the wall both conceals the facility to the street and neighborhood yet also represents the condition of being visually impaired to the sighted. Its roughness provides a tactile cue of the center itself to the blind. In contrast to the relative abstraction of the perimeter wall, the complex inside the wall is carefully scaled and reinterprets the plaza, court, and garden to make a small pedestrian city.

Utilizing roughly formed concrete and masonry with inexpensive wooden formwork allows this public project to meet the public client's requirement of using low-skilled labor to create local employment. It is also cost effective in its use of the ample supply of sand, gravel, and aggregate available from the lake-bed geology of the MAMC. The pavilions

that define the courts feature articulated concrete frames that are in-filled with local concrete block, a variation on the typical self-built home in the MAMC. These are expressively built by hand, with poured-in-place concrete to create a series of layered experiences, while the vertical layering of the walls act as a filter from general to increasingly specialized activities, which enhances the senses of touch, sound, and smell for the blind and partially sighted. Tactile orientation for each building at arm's length is provided by vertical and horizontal lines poured into the concrete walls. Each room is differentiated to the user by varying the size, proportion, intensity of light, and the weight and texture of materials. Outdoor circulation is cost effective and shaded to create coolness. Orientation for the user is achieved by overhangs of varying width alongside and between buildings, and a small stream runs through the central courtyard that also cools and cleans the air.

By overcoming the "tyranny of vision," the project creates a place of attentive body experience.[17] The nuanced, multisensory design of the project creates an empathetic relation between body and world, heightening other senses and not dominated by the eyes. Paradoxically, blindness offers an alternative, more intimate way of sensing and knowing the world that can be whole and complete. Vision touches only with the eyes, reaching only to the surface of things, enlarging the world, and extending the length of the body that limbs cannot touch; it is analytical and reflective and distracts from the integrated sensory experience of "things as they are."

Many of the blind report that they can experience place with an attentive, multi-nodal sensing that includes the "pressure" of proximate animate and inanimate objects, touching sizes of openings and walls in close proximity, sensing solar position, smelling odors, and "feeling" a dimensions by hearing.[18] In this sense, the project creates a sound-scape that is active, present, and generative; while conceptually and experientially rich, yet is formally and materially modest.[19]

17 This recalls the phemenological writings of Norberg-Schulz of "dwelling as being at peace in a protected place," and "the world that brings into presence is the world that it gathers."

18 This is what Merleau-Ponty called "body-subject," the innate ability of the body to perform movement with neither conscious awareness or effort.

19 This ability to feel pressure without seeing is best explained to a sighted person by the experience of "feeling" someone coming up behind you. In football, the quarterback who is able to "feel" pressure of unseen onrushing defensive players is a remarkable gift. Many blind people report that they have the most problems "hearing" the dimensions of a room on windy days. See Miriam Helen Hill's essay, "Bound to the Environment: Toward a Phenomenology of Sightlessness."

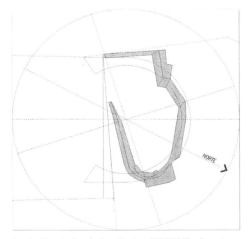

Landa, García, Landa Arquitectos, CEMEX Headquarters, Mexico City, Col. Mixcoac, 2004. Plan diagram of existing gravel pit on the existing site with the project shown dotted.

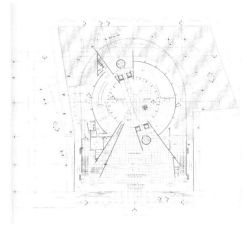

Landa, García, Landa Arquitectos, CEMEX Headquarters, Mexico City, Col. Mixcoac, 2004. Ground floor plan with interior court.

Landa, García, Landa Arquitectos, CEMEX Headquarters, Mexico City, Col. Mixcoac, 2004. The existing gravel pit inspired the radial organization of the project, shown here during construction.

The **Corporativo CEMEX Headquarters** designed by Agustín Landa of Landa, García, Landa reuses an industrial site that contains a concrete batch plant located in southwestern Mexico City in San Antonio Mixcoac, now embedded in the middle of the city. An abandoned circular gravel pit was selected as the site and provided the inspiration and the organization of the project. Given the industrial character of the site and the existing circular depression, the project is half buried and imbedded into the earth. The scheme turns inward into a circular, reflective water court shaded by a freestanding concrete frame within a nested series of discrete enclosure systems.[20] The offices are composed as a radial concrete office block that opens to the south and forms half of a focused cylindrical atrium, the other half being formed with the open-air circulation system which extends around the building. The floor of the atrium is a shallow reflecting pool that provides an inward, focused view for the office workers, while access to the circular office block is across a radial bridge from the entry. The abstraction of the interior court's massive radial walls and the sheet of reflective water can be understood in multiple ways, including as a geographic condensation of the ancient landscape of the Valley of Mexico surrounded by mountain ranges with lakes on the valley floor.[21]

In this regard, the project makes a place inherently (and literally) "within itself," where the court and shaped roof are experienced as boundary, horizon, and frame for understanding the MAMC. However, in private discussions with the architect, Landa has called the organization "a womb."[22] A womb not only suggests a feminine perspective but also a common shared human experience of being born from mothers, implying a deeply sheltered, intimate, nurtured, protected place and an escape from the stress of the increasingly degraded environment. Even the indirect lighting of the court from above recalls the Spanish phrase *dar a luz*, or "to give to the light," which refers to giving birth.

But this womb is complex and dualistic, and Landa has explained his approach to the circular court as a critical act in mediating the city.

Landa, García, Landa Arquitectos, CEMEX Headquarters, Mexico City, Col. Mixcoac, 2004. The circular court with glass membrane that divides it into a portion open to the pollution and noise of the megalopolis, and an enclosed portion with noise control and conditioned air.

[20] Here, Landa extends and reinterprets the nested series of a discrete enclosure system deployed by Kahn for his unbuilt project for the Hurva Synagogue Project for Jerusalem (1968).

[21] This point was first pointed out by my colleague in Monterrey, Arq. Miguel Virgen Gonzalez. This also embraces many concepts advanced by Norberg-Schulz in regard to "being at peace in a protected place" and his concept of "genius loci," the spirit of a particular place having a constancy over time.

[22] This private discussion took place after I participated in a review of his design studio at the ITESM Monterrey in the fall of 2004.

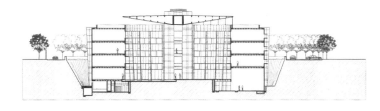

Corte transversal Transversal section

Landa, García, Landa Arquitectos, CEMEX Headquarters, Mexico City, Col. Mixcoac, 2004. Section.

GDU, Arq. Mario Schjetnan Garduño and Arq. José Pérez Maldonado, Lake Xochimilco Restoration, Mexico City, Col. Xochimilco, 1998. Project restoration plan.

The idea of having one half open and one closed responds to the desire of having a duality within the building—one half gets some rain, and the other does not; in one half you can feel the wind and hear the noise of the city and in the other you do not. So while the heart of the building is enclosed, it is not completely oblivious to its surroundings. The tension between interior and exterior invites those who walk through it to remember where they are while at the same time feel protected from the outside. This is perhaps a response to my experience of Mexico City today . . . I realize that those who live there do not notice the terrible environmental and urban chaos they live in. The sky is eternally gray, and people are always sick. The contrast in the building's court is to call attention to this and not be merely an experience of a blissful refuge.[23]

The project explores the material, processes, and tectonic qualities of concrete itself. Secondary views of the batch plant are framed in narrow slits, while the gravel and aggregate for the building come from the site. Unlike the typical rough-formed concrete of Mexico City, the highly refined, shiny concrete work creates a material equivalence with the mirror-like refection of the interior water court.[24] Landa explains that the entire complex was executed with the same formwork that "was made out of wood with a special oil to prevent the formwork sticking to the concrete."[25] This was achieved with a close working relationship between the craftspeople, the builder, and the architect's team.[26]

23 From my personal e-mail correspondence with Agustín Landa, October 6, 2005.

24 In contrast, in the F2 Residence (2001) by Adria, Broid, Rojkind, Mexico City, rough-formed concrete is employed as an expression of local handcraft and tectonic culture (60 percent of concrete sold in Mexico is for self-built homes). See Raul A. Barrenche, *Modern House Three* (London: Phaidon, 2005).

25 From my personal e-mail correspondence with Agustín Landa, October 6, 2005.

26 The concrete work was crafted by the master-builder Miguel Cornejo and his dedicated teams of craftsman with meticulously detailed form-work, form-ties, and resolved intersections, while many of the building's construction details were developed between the architects and Guillermo Hernández, who worked with Sr. Cornejo.

Landa, García, Landa Arquitectos, CEMEX Headquarters, Mexico City, Col. Mixcoac, 2004. Rear facade with strip windows, radial system of solar control, and articulated service towers.

A Mexican family enjoying a holiday on Lake Xochimilco, c. 1940.

27 Mario Schjetan and GDO also utilize the notion of a working landscape in the restoration and intervention of a degraded site in northern Mexico City in the district of Azcapotzalco, a former pre-Columbian city-state on the shore of the lakes, which are now dried lakebed and urbanized amid the megalopolis. Here, a contaminated former industrial site has been transformed into a large-scale high-tech office campus of sixteen hectares. At the level of environmental mitigation, the project pays particular attention to hydrology, water recycling, capturing rainwater, and replenishing the deep aquifer. Other projects by Schjetnan and GDO include the restoration of Chapultapec Park, the largest public park in the city and home to many of the city's major museums, with almost sixteen million visitors per year. Half of the budget for the project was raised from contributions from the private sector.

28 A tree nursery was introduced on the site, and it produces some 30 million trees for planting around the MAMC.

29 This recalls Heidegger's "constructing" and "cultivating" in terms of making the processes that restore and sustain this place as visible, designed experiences. A reexamination of the worldview of indigenous people reveals their closer attention to the nuance of the physical world, a more profound relationship to the history of place, and their bonds to the land that were as much ethical and religious as biological. In this respect, the project continues the agenda of the "racial affirmation"

The Regenerative Landscape and the Renewal of the Body: The Restoration Environmentally Degraded Sites

The **Xochimilco Restoration** is a fragment of the remaining pre-Columbian lake system that was declared a UNESCO world heritage site in 1987, prompting a large-scale environmental restoration project. Designed by Mario Schjetnan of Grupo Diseno Urbano (GDO), the project encompasses 7,400 acres.[27] This working landscape provides a process of healing and is a microcosm of the larger destroyed landscape of the Valley of Mexico. Dealing with more than merely visual issues, the project engages environmental, social, educational, and economic issues.

A number of remedial environmental issues needed to be addressed, including the *chinampas* islands sinking due to the aquifer's depletion, contaminated surface waters, illegal residential development encroaching on the perimeter of the lake, increasing storm runoff, canals choked with aquatic plants, and islands located at the interior of the canal system that were difficult to reach and were underutilized for agriculture.

The design solution was primarily hydraulic: Water was pumped back into the aquifer to stabilize the site, reservoirs were created to retain storm water, while polluted water was cleansed at treatment plants and returned to the lake to regulate water levels. The eroded *chinampas* islands were stabilized with a mesh of logs filled with dredge and stabilized with traditional *salix* trees. Flowers and agriculture for growing vegetables were reintroduced to the site, with some islands reserved for grazing. Furthermore, more than one million trees were planted.[28] Aside from the relatively sophisticated water treatment plant, Schjetnan uses hands-on, low technology for this restoration project.[29]

At the edge of the restored lake, a 740-acre park creates floral, recreational, and interpretive uses. A new terraced entry features stone-lined aqueducts that discharge treated water into the lake; a plaza contains a water

tower in the form of an Archimedes screw. A new interpretive center includes an auditorium and exhibition galleries featuring the region's ecology, archaeology, and agriculture, with a roof terrace that offers panoramic views over the lakes and canals, as well as views of the Popocatéptl and Iztaccíhuatl through the smog that typically envelops the city. A 1,300-foot pergola leads to a waterside promenade, and an arboretum and flowerbeds represent the productive agricultural activities of the restored *chinampas*. Other portions of the new park have playing fields, ball courts, and wetlands to collect storm runoff. The traditional shallow-bottomed pole canoes carrying visitors continue to navigate the canals amid the restored *chinampas* and working gardens, while other canoes sell food and feature musicians.

Schjetnan's Xochimilco restoration project recalls Edward Relph's phenomenology of "a field of care" and "sparing," which focus on empathy for a place with deep concerns for the processes of life integral to, defining, and shaping a given place,[30] as well as the experiential bonds that people establish with a place.

GDU, Arq. Mario Schjetnan Garduño and Arq. José Pérez Maldonado, Lake Xochimilco Restoration, Mexico City, Col. Xochimilco, 1998. Public garden space and water recycling at restored edge of lake.

The Lakes Project is an even more ambitious, broad-based proposal to reconstitute the series of lakes at the outskirts of Mexico City to recharge the depleted aquifer, halt the sinking of the city, and restore humidity to the now arid microclimate, potentially increasing precipitation that would cleanse the air. It engages issues of public health and environmental degradation, reintroduces a proactive planning framework, and optimistically proposes a comprehensive social and political agenda for the MAMC. The strategy also envisions the interrelationships of urbanization, infrastructure, and lost open space for parks and recreation, as well as recognizing the cur-

of post-revolutionary Mexico. There is also an implied acknowledgement for Heidegger's claim that "memory is the source of poetry," in the sense that the indigenous people of the Valley of Mexico who originally created Xochimilco had not developed "philosophies of separation" from nature but developed empathetic wet-farming practices in relationship to the original landscape of the place. For a discussion of architecture and the policy of racial affirmation in post-revolutionary Mexico, see my interview with Alberto Pérez-Gómez and essays by others in my book, *Modernity and the Architecture of Mexico,* (Austin: University of Texas Press, 1997), 40-44, 51-60, 83-87, 91-105, 109-114, 119, 141-147, 182-185, and 192-193. Whether indigenous, urbanized people of the MAMC still are able to maintain these relationships to nature is another question.

30 See Peter Hays, *Main Currents in Western Environmental Thought* (Bloomington: Indiana University Press, 2002), 154–155.

GDU, Arq. Mario Schjetnan Garduño and Arq. José Pérez Maldonado, Lake Xochimilco Restoration, Mexico City, Col. Xochimilco, 1998. View of public facilities from restored lake.

Arq. Alberto Kalach, Arq. Gustavo Lipkau, Arq. Juan Cordero, Arq. Teodoro Gonzalez de León, and team, "The Lakes Project," Mexico City, Col. Texcoco, 2000. Photo collage of the reconstituted lakes that form a new edge and amenity to low-income neighborhoods, and new setting for cross-city freeway systems.

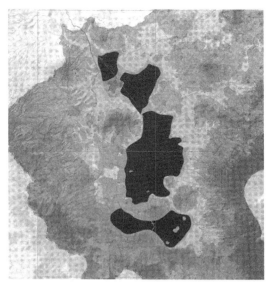

1865

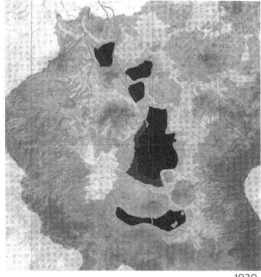

1930

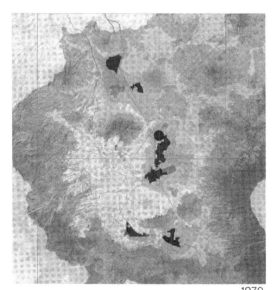

1970

Arq. Alberto Kalach, Arq. Gustavo Lipkau, Arq. Juan Cordero, Arq. Teodoro Gonzalez de León, and team, "The Lakes Project," Mexico City, Col. Texcoco, 2000. The shrinking system of lakes over time in the Valley of Mexico.

rent ecological crisis as an opportunity for rethinking development in the city. The genesis for the project was a proposal by soils expert Nabor Carillo in the 1960s that realized the benefits of reversing the 400-year project of draining the lakes to reconstitute the lakes to address the problems of flooding, water supply, and sinking of the ground, which was rediscovered by Arq. Teodoro González de León and Arq. Alberto Kalach twenty-five years later.[31]

In the proposal, Lake Texcoco, the largest of the former lakes, is partially reconstituted to control flooding and receive treated wastewater. Although large, only 10 percent of the original system of lakes is reconstituted by treating only 7 percent of the black water the city produces. The project uses the lowest-lying land that still floods, is too salty to cultivate, and whose soil is too soft to economically support buildings. The lake proposal creates a void in the dense urban fabric and acts as a catalyst to organize the adjacent urban fabric. The eastern edge of the lakes provides reforestation, low-rise development including university and public buildings, and the creation of "green fingers" in restored ravines that would both feed the lake and where the aquifer could be recharged through its porous volcanic rock (currently hundreds of ravines are overrun and used as trash dumps). The western edge would be reforested and the existing low-income settlement revitalized. A new entrance to the city is created with

31 In 1985, following part of Carillo's proposal, the government constructed a 2,500-acre basin on part of the largest of the lakes, Lake Texcoco. Arq. Gonzalez de Leon used Carillo's proposal for a design studio at the UNAM, which among other tasks produced a "X-ray of the city" that for the first time mapped topography in relationship to existing hydraulic engineering. They later formed Taller Ciudad de Mexico with José Castillo, which published *La Ciudad y sus Lagos* (1998). See essay by Megan Miller in *Praxis: Journal of Writing and Building* vol. 2 (2001): 72–87.

32 The Mexico City international airport has outgrown its current site. Plans to relocate the airport to a rural area outside the city were met with strong vocal protest, and that relocation plan was abandoned.

33 See *Praxis* 2 (2001): 72–91.

34 The project has also started an ongoing discourse about planning across all of Mexico, related to waste, sound business practices, politics, and culture. The project is also fascinating in terms of the employment that might result from its construction. The labor involved might require a variety of skills from highly skilled to low-skilled labor, and potentially hundreds of thousands of low-skilled workers could be employed.

35 Critics of the project have generally criticized the macro scale, the feasibility to procure land at the edges of the lakes, and a fixed physical intervention that some claim avoids urban complexity. Specific criticisms include the scale of water treatment required and relocation of the low-income population of Chalco to form Lake Chalco.

a much-needed new international airport on an artificial island in the lake, with transportation infrastructure of freeways and mass transit lines above the lake's surface.[32] Furthermore, the reconstituted lakes would act as a large mirror, suggesting new ways of experiencing the megalopolis. The airport would also partially finance the proposal and spur development along the edge of the lake. Thus, the project engages both local ecological realities, as well as the reality of global networks.

Rather than a nostalgic relationship with history, Kalach conceives of the proposal as a large infrastructure project that could direct growth and organize the informal development that he believes is inevitable. He envisions tall buildings that could float on the soft soil like boats, new hybrid building programs related to water treatment, and buildings capable of becoming more self-sufficient in terms of storing water, treating waste water, and producing electricity.[33]

Unlike many utopian planning proposals, this project is not meant to be universally replicated but instead deals with local conditions as well as the pressures of globalization in specific place.[34] The project is presented as a kind of pragmatic, ambitious public-works project that has a confidence in the positivist scientific method, technology, and a self-conscious modernist attitude about the composition of the lakes. This place could be experienced in contemporary ways, as a new entrance to the city by jet airliner, along high-speed freeways that cross the lake, for pedestrians around the lake, and in new types of floating buildings at the edges of the lakes with new hybrid functions. There is also the sense that this project would provide, in Relph's collective, social terms, a new symbol, common focus, and social space for the MAMC, where the community would give it meaning and identity. Instead of being viewed in the light of "restoration ecology" to produce an imagined, utopian (and undoubtedly impossible) ecological restoration of the Valley of Mexico, this project can be understood as an intervention of "reconciliation" between the built megalopolis and its underlying geology, geography, landscape, and hydrology. This is one of the few proposal for the MAMC to address its ecological crisis, bringing this to the forefront of architectural discourse in Mexico, and also acknowledging local realities and globalization. Whether the proposal will be adapted in whole or in part remains to be seen, however, inaction regarding the aquifer and waste treatment is not a viable option for the MCMA.[35]

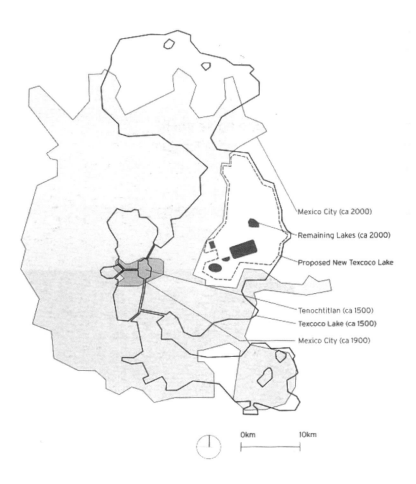

Arq. Alberto Kalach, Arq. Gustavo Lipkau, Arq. Juan Cordero, Arq. Teodoro Gonzalez de León, and team, "The Lakes Project," Mexico City, Col. Texcoco, 2000. Plan diagram showing the growth of Mexico City and the shrinking of the lakes over time, in relationship to the Lakes Project proposal.

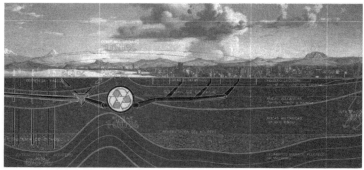

Arq. Alberto Kalach, Arq. Gustavo Lipkau, Arq. Juan Cordero, Arq. Teodoro Gonzalez de León, and team, "The Lakes Project," Mexico City, Col. Texcoco, 2000. The shrinking system of lakes over time in the Valley of Mexico.

TEN Arquitectos, Arq. Enrique Norten, Hotel Habita, Mexico City, Col. Polonco, 2001. Existing abandoned apartment building on the site that was recycled.

TEN Arquitectos, Arq. Enrique Norten, Hotel Habita, Mexico City, Col. Polonco, 2001, Exterior façade during daytime.

TEN Arquitectos, Arq. Enrique Norten, Hotel Habita, Mexico City, Col. Polonco, 2001, Exterior façade at night.

Revalued Post-Industrial Enclaves and the Fragmented Body: The Rebranded Boutique Hotel and the Recycled Elite Enclave Connected to the Global Economy

Enrique Norten's **Hotel Habita** renovates an existing, decaying concrete-frame apartment building from the 1950s in the "yuppie" Polonco neighborhood, which has been transformed into an upscale niche-market boutique hotel catering to guests tied to a global economy.[36] The program includes a rooftop spa, a gourmet restaurant, and renovated guest rooms with high-tech amenities that required few interior modifications.[37] Thus, in spite of recycling, much of the focus was more limited conceptually in terms of compositional issues, including visually editing the city and "re-imaging" the hotel from the street in terms of experience and marketing. A new glass façade cladding was conceived as conceptually "thick" and extended the existing terraces of each guest room, adding five additional feet of depth to each room, while the façade itself is transformed from the street with varying degrees of reflectivity, opacity, translucency, and transparency, which transforms from day to night.

The glass cladding system employs an 11-foot-3-inch-by-4-foot-11-inch module with a transparent interior glass skin and a translucent exterior designed by the architects to meet the budget and local labor's skill sets. The rigorous use of industrialized glazing materials of varying transparency both protects guest from the gaze of the city and frames selected and edited specific views of the city, like a veil.[38]

Protecting the guests from the gaze of others provides privacy, exclusivity, and a sense of excitement about what is only shadowy revealed. The selective views edit the unsavory aspects of the city, allowing for a rereading of the city as a series of fragments analogous to the distinct neighborhoods of the MAMC and recalls the split screen of cinema and television. Each guest room becomes a framed viewing device like a kind of painting. These are simultaneously a translucent flat-glass pane with shadows and blurs of the city, as well as edited, focused horizontal strips that capture three-dimensional deep space.[39]

36 Polonco had been among the most chic, desired places for tourists and wealthy, status-seeking *chilangos* (natives of Mexico City) during the 1950s to 1990s, with its nightlife, restaurants, discos, and shopping for international *haute couture*. While the area is still prominent, it has lost some its cutting-edge appeal in recent years.

37 See article by Ashley Schaffer in *Praxis: Journal of Writing and Building* vol. 2 (2001): 65.

38 While veils have long appeared in traditional women's clothing in Mexico, this veil is closer to a *chimera*, or wedding veil. The glass curtain wall also reinterprets modernist compositional devices and the light-scrim art installations of Bruce Nauman, James Turrell and others.

39 Abstraction in this case allows each user to project their own memories, while sensing the materiality and light effects of this experience. Norten uses materials to achieve the image of an industrialized system of production, which are ironically put together by handcraft that reflects the reality of the local economy of Mexico.

TEN Arquitectos, Hotel Habita, Mexico City, Col. Polonco, 2001. Interior of room with diffused light and edited and screened view of surrounding urban context.

TEN Arquitectos, Hotel Habita, Mexico City, Col. Polonco, 2001. Rood terrace with edited view of surrounding city.

Lomas de Santa Fé was once a large trash dump where entire families of *pepenadores* (trash scavengers) daily scrounged for food and items for resale under horrific environmental conditions. Today, this landfill has been radically transformed, but unlike the many previous visions of Mexico City as a *public* symbolic representation, in this case as a *private* enclave for global commerce, exclusion, and conspicuous consumption. Santa Fé features the head offices of GE, EDS, IBM, Daimler-Chrysler, Televisa, Coca-Cola, Hewlett Packard, 3M, Standard & Poor's, several foreign embassies, business hotels, Starbucks coffee shops, trendy *nouveau* Japanese and Indian restaurants; while the Centro Comercial Santa Fé is one of the most exclusive shopping malls in the MAMC and is hailed as the largest in Latin America.[40] Lomas de Santa Fé has quickly transformed for a variety of reasons: its adjacency to wealthy development on the western edge of the MAMC that has long been the direction of affluent development; its strategic location on the road to the affluent weekend retreat of Toluca; limited access by means of toll roads that limit both public access and crime; the recent construction of the private, elite Universidad Iberoamericana campus; its isolation from the MAMC in a steep ravine that still manages to maintain some lush landscape on its steep landscape during the rainy season; relatively clean air to breath, due to its higher elevation; and its proximity of only nineteen miles to the Mexico City international airport. Lomas de Santa Fé is loosely organized as a linear strip development on the access roads that parallel the freeway that links the MAMC with Toluca in one of the few conservative pro-business *delegaciones*. This development is composed of high-rise towers with heliports and occasionally interspersed with gated, expensive low-rise housing that rises up the hillsides guarded by private security forces. This development is so disconnected from the MAMC's infrastructure grid that water has to be trucked in; it also has its own power plants, and the restricted public bus system limits access to maids, gardeners, guards, and support personnel.[41] Paradoxically, despite the technological imagery and highly individualized forms of the towers and blocks, they are programmatically nearly identical and almost all built with inexpensive hand labor with rough, poured-in-place concrete frames.

The most formally ambitious and innovative is the **Torre Punta del Parque** by Diámetro Arquitectos. The project consists of two narrow, thirty-one-story tower blocks. The complex is entered via an automobile ramp between the two tower blocks and skewed from

Diámetro Arquitectos, Arq. David Cherem Ades, Arq. Isaac Sasson Misri, Arq. Christain Herrera Kobashi, Arq. Carolina Barba Villanueva, Torre Punta del Parque, Mexico City, Col. Santa Fé, 2004. Exterior façade.

the street with a reflecting pool and a garden that are linked to the reception areas and public functions with parking below. The typical residential floor plan has two apartments and is organized with a zone of service at the back, with kitchen and maid quarters expressed as a wall with irregular punched openings; while each apartment's diagonally protruding major rooms are expressed as a horizontally glazed dominant element of the façade that opens to spectacular views of the city and the volcanic mountain ranges beyond when the smog clears after a rain. Access to each of the apartments further reinforces social separations based on class, with two elevators giving residents access to the living area of each unit, while a separate service elevator and service stairway is provided for the women who work as maids and enter through the kitchen. Thus, no unnecessary social interaction between employees and residents occurs.[42] A series of dramatic figural elements interrupt the eighteenth floor of each tower. One tower contains a four-story-high clubhouse with a bar, fireplace, and indoor swimming pool, while the

40 Patrick Oster in *The Mexicans* writes about young women from elite families who work on the Mexico City Stock Exchange negotiating multi-million-dollar deals. Being unmarried, they still live at home but on weekends fly to New York City to buy designer shoes.

41 See article by Liane LeFaivre, "Urban Age Convenes in Mexico City," in *Architecture* (May 2006): 35–36.

42 This arrangement is typical in Mexico City. The older high-rise towers constructed in the 1970s had no service elevators *at all* and forced the women who worked as maids to carry heavy bags of groceries and other household items up many flights of stairs, thereby limiting their interaction with others. If any interaction occurred it was likely to be only with their gender and social class.

other features a spa and gymnasium. These are linked with a twisted connecting bridge and *mirador* (a place to look out).

This kind of development creates a sensory experience of the fragmented body. The public domain of the pedestrian experience has ceased to exist as almost all movement is by automobile, the service access roads have no sidewalks, and the bridge between the towers inhibits public interaction at the street level. The twisted bridge is not a place of repose and contemplation, but rather a foreboding precipice, with the fear of falling out or collapse during an earthquake. Like the reality-TV game shows that have infiltrated Mexican television, this place gives the elite dwellers a thrill in their lives which are detached from the dangers of life in the streets.

In Santa Fé, the body's organs have become exteriorized with iPods for ears, computer simulation for the eyes, computer memory for the mind, and treadmills for the legs. No longer are muscles in the body toned by physical labor; instead, they are toned by exercise machines for an aestheticized body that seemingly floats in the air. Many elite women in Santa Fé also undergo the knife to rid themselves of their *mestitzo* (mixed race) noses to acquire the more European one celebrated in the media, Botox to eliminate wrinkles, while pills and lipo-suction blur the relationship of nutrition and food. The question arises if this or some other architecture will evolve that enhances the body reborn in its technified form?

Conclusion:
Environmental Apocalypse and
Remedial Interventions

Given the environmental disaster that looms for the MAMC, the architecture of the megalopolis needs to be more than merely interesting shapes and the cool, detached, cynicism of formal exercises. The current dilemma brings to the forefront the ethical role of MAMC architecture, which at the most basic level needs to sustain human life by preserving the water, air, and land that supports its plant and animal life.[43]

Simply put, remedial environmental infrastructure/working landscape interventions are desperately needed.[44] These include street trees, restored creeks and river edges, recycled gray water, planted roofs on existing housing that use recycled materials to provide cooling and food, as well as hydraulic infrastructure including water purification, aquifer restoration, waste-water treatment, and strategies to curb air pollution.

These projects exist at a scale that will require leadership by public officials and the business community, as well as by the architecture and design professions to avert the coming environmental apocalypse that awaits the MAMC. In this sense, it may be possible to muster the political will to find the common ground in both the private and pubic sector with an appeal to the survival of the family across classes and neighborhoods, in which women will undoubtedly play a vital role.[45] The bonds and relationships that exist in the close-knit extended family are the basic "glue" of the MAMC; from the pre-industrial technology of the shack dweller to the postindustrial yuppie condominium in Santa Fé; that are one of the core strengths and shared values of the society.

The contemporary environmental disaster faced by the MAMC today was echoed in the remarkably prescient *nahuatl* lyrical poetry of the "*Cantares mexicanos*," written just two years after the collapse of Tenochtitlán in 1523.

Our water has turned bitter,
Our food is bitter.
The walls are black,
The air is black with smoke,
The guns flash in the darkness.

43 The most realistic hope for the air pollution in the MAMC is the development of non-polluting vehicles in developed countries that ultimately would be adopted in Mexico City. If the MAMC can manage somehow to survive for the next fifty years, this seems a distinct possibility. Today, the polluted air of the MAMC would even be worse if the poor of Mexico had motor vehicles.

44 For remedial design proposals for Mexico of working landscapes and infrastructure, see the concluding chapter in my forthcoming book, *The Architecture and Cities of Northern Mexico, 1821–2006*. It examines the undervalued architectural culture of the northern Mexican states of Nuevo León, Coahuila, Chihuahua, Durango, Sonora, Sinaloa, Tamaulipas, and Baja California.

45 It may well be the women of the MAMC who provide the backbone and ethical leadership needed to confront these issues. Rosario Robles Berlanga served as the first female mayor of Mexico City (1997–2000), women are the leaders of an emerging Green environmental party in Mexico City, and women have served as the ethical compass of the Mexican family for generations.

This essay is dedicated to the millions of hard-working people of Mexico City who daily endure the environmental degradations of the megalopolis. Thanks are extended to my colleague, Prof. Alberto Pérez-Gómez of McGill University, who generously commented on an earlier, more detailed version this essay. I would also like to thank Mark Lochrin as well as Dr. Mike Cusanovich, the staff, and students at the University of Arizona Science and Engineering Library in Tucson, AZ who kindly assisted me in scanning the images for this essay.

Multi-National City: From Silicon Valley to New Delhi

Reinhold Martin

Hafeez Contractor
City of Logos, DLF Square Tower
DLF City, Gurgaon, 1999.

Multi-National City (MNC) is the name we give to the city of corporate globalization. In the research from which this text is excerpted and adapted, we follow three architectural itineraries through three such cities and their histories: Silicon Valley in northern California, New York's internal suburbias, and Gurgaon, a new corporate city outside of Delhi.[1] These itineraries in turn follow the feedback loops of globalization in both space and time. "Multi-National City" therefore refers to each city individually, as well as to the single, pulsating megacity to which they all belong. This city, made up of diffuse and constantly transforming networks, comes into focus with each feedback loop, only to fade into another loop. Here, we offer an informal tour of some of its monuments.

1 This essay is based on research done in collaboration with Kadambari Baxi and is excerpted and adapted from Reinhold Martin and Kadambari Baxi, *Multi-National City: Architectural Itineraries* (Barcelona: Actar, 2007).

Herbert Baker
Council House
New Delhi, 1927.

Herbert Baker and Edwin Lutyens
Imperial Complex
New Delhi, 1927. Detail.

RSP Architects and Planners
International Tech Park Ltd. (ITPL)
Bangalore, 2002.

We use the term *multi-national* rather than the more current "transnational" or the more conventional "global" to emphasize the internal multiplicities to be found within what is often understood as a homogeneous monoculture that spreads through the circuitry of corporate globalization. Such multiplicities often take the form of displacements, where an apparently homogeneous "space of flows" turns out to be full of holes, gaps, and discontinuities.[2] For example, a figure that seems anachronistic or untimely in one context—as the term *multi-national corporation* might seem in the United States, with its overtones of the 1970s—is all too timely in another. Thus in postmodern India, land of the acronym, the term *multi-national corporation* is commonly shortened to MNC, which inscribes the dream spaces of an emergent globality materialized in shopping malls, call centers, office buildings, and gated residential enclaves.

So we borrow the letters *MNC* while insisting on their ambiguity. The Multi-National City, with its promise of new freedoms for some, remains shadowed by the multi-national corporation, much like delirious, metropolitan New York was in an earlier era shadowed by big business. That's what globalization is: a simultaneous coupling and distancing in both space and time, in which, as Arjun Appadurai has put it, "your present is their future."[3] In other words, under globalization the world is anything but "flat," and what appears homogeneous and smooth is actually heterogeneous and fractured. These fractures mark differentials of all kinds, including structural exclusions that come into focus with respect to the very real, imagined communities conjured by and in the MNC. For the MNC is also a continuous interior, a network of airports, parking garages, lobbies, elevators, offices, and living rooms in which, from one perspective, "you" are on the inside and "they" are on the outside, while from another, "they" are inside and "you" are outside, perhaps trying to get in.

Capital, Part 1

In this context, where the representational significance of capital cities might often seem overshadowed by representations of multi-national capital (and nations might seem to give way to networks), we never really know *what* a particular building signifies. We only know *that* it signifies, after the fact. For example, three months after the events of September 11, there was a smaller, unrelated attack on the former headquarters of modernity's most extensive empire. On December 13, 2001, unidentified militants attacked a meeting of the Indian Parliament at the circular Parliament House in New Delhi. The building, known under the British Raj as the Council House, was designed by Sir Herbert Baker and completed in 1927. At the time of the attack, it was controlled by the Bharatiya Janata Party (BJP), the Hindu nationalist party that held a parliamentary majority from 1998 until 2004. Then-Prime Minister Atal Bihari Vajpayee compared the attack to the 9/11 events in New York, and his government implicated Pakistan. India and Pakistan lurched toward nuclear war, which was eventually averted through negotiations. In retrospect this attack, like 9/11, appeared all the more real for its symbolism, especially since the BJP had risen to power in the aftermath of an even more vivid piece of architectural iconoclasm when, on December 6, 1992, militant Hindus flattened the Babri Masjid, a sixteenth-century mosque in Ayodyha, setting off riots in which thousands died.

When it was built, the New Delhi imperial complex, designed by Sir Edwin Lutyens in collaboration with Baker, had been hailed as a happy, conciliatory synthesis of Western neo-classicism and the "Indo-Saracenic" style. An amalgam of motifs, including *chattris* (pavilions) and *jhallis* (carved stone screens) cribbed from the palaces and fortresses of northern India's earlier Mughal rulers, it still stands as a monument to empire as such. Yet the construction

of New Delhi, with its geometric, axial plan drawn as if from scratch, was also the result of the British Raj withdrawing its official seat from Calcutta, a site of intensifying civil unrest, to a site near Shajahanabad ("Old Delhi"), the former seat of Mughal rule. It seems the British imagined that this move, together with a regionally inflected architecture, would bring them closer to the hearts and minds of their colonial subjects.[4] But the many peoples that made up British India lost their patience, and at midnight on August 14, 1947, the twin states of India and Pakistan were born.

Capital, Part 2: Bangalorism

A mirage: Out on an open plain, eighteen kilometers from the postcolonial grandeur and congestion of central Bangalore in southern India, stands the International Tech Park Ltd. (ITPL). Its sleek stone surfaces give form to what Silicon Valley calls "outsourcing," which is served by a system of flexible, skilled labor that in India is called "body shopping." ITPL was designed by Singapore-based RSP Architects Planners & Engineers (Pte.) Ltd. and built in stages from 2000 to 2004. It consists of five buildings with five different names: Discoverer, Innovator, Creator, Explorer, and Inventor. Stakeholders in the original development included Tata Industries Ltd., the government of Karnataka, and a consortium of Singapore-based investors. In that sense and many others, Bangalore is a different kind of capital city, marking the dynamic displacements of multi-national capital itself.

World-Class

The 28-hectare, full-service ITPL campus is advertised by its managers as a state-of-the-art "World in a Park," complete with mall, health club, and a residential complex nearby. A testimonial by one Fran Feldman, a general manager at America Online India (an ITPL tenant), summarizes its attractions:

---

2 The expression *space of flows* refers to the work of Manuel Castells. See in particular Castells, *The Rise of the Networked Society* (Cambridge: Blackwell, 1996), Chapter 6, "The Space of Flows," 326-428. The MNC also differs conceptually from the "global city" as elaborated by Saskia Sassen. See Sassen, *The Global City: New York, London, Tokyo* (Princeton: Princeton University Press, 1991), in that the power differentials driving its circuitry draw on the discontinuities and displacements inherent in networks of all sorts, rather than simply managing them through mechanisms of command and control.

3 Arjun Appadurai, *Modernity at Large: Cultural Dimensions of Globalization* (Minneapolis: University of Minnesota Press, 1996), 31.

4 Suhash Chakravarty, "Architecture and Politics in the Construction of New Delhi," *Architecture + Design* vol. 2, no. 2 (January-February-1986): 76. See also Thomas R. Metcalf, *An Imperial Vision: Indian Architecture and Britain's Raj* (Berkeley: University of California Press, 1989), and Norma Everson, *The Indian Metropolis: A View Toward the West* (New Haven: Yale University Press, 1989).

Karan Grover
Digital Park
Bangalore, 2002.

In our quest to expand our ability to provide world-class customer service to our 36 million members worldwide, AOL chose ITP in Bangalore as the site to set up our largest call center outside of the United States. We enjoy the state-of-the-art facilities and the quiet atmosphere of the beautifully landscaped Tech Park, as well as the additional facilities located in the basement which provide our teams additional outlets for food, fitness, shopping, and fun.[5]

This little piece of India's "Silicon Plateau" reportedly sprang from a 1992 meeting between then-Indian Prime Minister P.V. Narasimha Rao and Singaporean Prime Minister Goh Chok Tong. Though a public/private venture, it was inspired in part by the Indian government's systematic investment in the information technology industry under 1991's Software Technology Parks (STP) scheme, which was the result of a policy white paper written in 1986 titled "Computer Software Export, Software Development and Training." Under STP, software firms that did a one-hundred-percent export business were entitled to five years of tax-free existence. And in New Delhi, bureaucrats seem to dream in block letters. So by 2004, there were forty-one official information technology centers scattered through-out the country administered by Software Technology Parks of India (STPI), under the Indian government's Department of Electronics (DOE). In parallel with the Electronics Hardware Technology Park Scheme (EHTP), STPI offered services, support, and financial incentives to companies devoted to increasing India's high-tech exports, a project that is officially described as "encouraging, promoting, and boosting the software exports from India."[6]

Digital (Park)
Not far from ITPL, in Bangalore's recently developed Electronics City (phase 2), is a campus

In postmodern India, land of the acronym, the term multi-national corporation is commonly shortened to MNC, which inscribes the "dream spaces" of an emergent globality materialized in shopping malls, call centers, office buildings, and gated residential enclaves.

called Digital Park. Its name is in keeping with Bangalore's reputation as the ultimate garden city—so designated by its former British rulers, who should know, since they invented the garden-city concept. Designed by architect Karan Grover in accordance with an "ecology-friendly theme" and built to accommodate 4,200 employees, Digital Park, like ITPL, consists of five buildings with five different names, this time themed according to five elements: Prithvi (Earth), Jal (Water), Akash (Space), Vayu (Air), and Agni (Fire).[7] The ecological theme further extends to the campus infrastructure, which is said to recycle every drop of relatively scarce water that passes through it. Bird-watching (on-site) is encouraged. Opened in 2002, it became the home of Hewlett-Packard GlobalSoft Ltd., formerly Digital GlobalSoft Ltd., which was once a subsidiary of Digital Equipment India Ltd., the Indian subsidiary of Digital Equipment Corporation (DEC) until 1998, when that company was acquired by Compaq Computer Corp., which in turn was acquired by Hewlett-Packard in 2004. In memory of this history perhaps, the signs atop the complex of ecologically themed buildings in Digital Park continued to carry the original Silicon Valley company's straightforwardly mythic name: Digital.

Euphoria in the Cafeteria
Like its Silicon Valley counterparts, as well as the even more pastoral campuses of its indigenous neighbors in Electronics City (phase 1)—the Indian software giant Infosys and its competitor Wipro—Digital Park's environmental friendliness extended to in-house coffee, tea, and dining. An anonymous composition, "Euphoria in the Cafeteria," celebrates the social life on campus:

All work and no coffee break,
Dull software engineers you'll make!
So move out from the office interior,
And head for the cafeteria!
So, what will it be? Coffee or tea?
Anything's fine, to break the monotony![8]

Such corporate lyricism is a reminder that there is more than technology being produced here and in other digital parks around the world. And where Digital's environmentally sensitive ethos and its happy cafeteria represent efforts to reinforce employee identification (and loyalty) through what is called "internal branding," in Bangalore and beyond, such hospitality also extends to the customer, which is more often than not another corporation.

Thus did Bangalore-based Sundaram Architects (Pvt.) Ltd. provide Infosys Technologies Ltd. with a prominently placed Corporate Care Center containing eight conference rooms for customer consultation and an "experience theater," in which the history of software could be experienced in front of what was once the largest video wall in Asia. Unwilling to settle for a mere cafeteria, Infosys also provided its employees, known internally as "Infoscions," with a building by Sundaram Architects called The Food Court, which actually housed three food courts, a gymnasium, an Infosys company store (which also sells selected Microsoft products), and a bank, with a curvilinear swimming pool outside. The company likes to claim that four-thousand quadratic equations were crunched to produce its parabolic concrete-shell roofs, which shade stylistically in the direction of the Brazilian communist and architect of concrete shells, Oscar Niemeyer.

5 See http://www.intltechpark.com/about_itpl/testimonials.htm.

6 See http://www.stpi.soft.net/aboutstpi.html#goal.

7 See http://www.myiris.com/shares/company/reportShow.php?url=AMServer%2F2001%2F09%2FDIGEQUIA_20010903.htm.

8 See "Digital: A Trusted Partner", http://www.koramangala.com/korabuz/y2k2/sept1r.htm.

NRI

An NRI is a non-resident Indian. Often, the NRI and what the United States government calls a resident alien are the same person. After Silicon Valley's economic bubble burst in 2001, many NRIs returned to India, with many relocating to Bangalore. More than a few wound up eating lunch (and sometimes dinner and sometimes breakfast) in The Food Court at Infosys. There, on November 13, 2002, the lucky ones met Microsoft's chief software architect, Bill Gates, on his first visit to India. "It was long overdue," said his Indian counterpart, Infosys co-founder N. R. Narayana Murthy.[9]

Meanwhile, on any given day, aspiring NRIs who are—by definition—not (yet?) resident aliens can be seen in the waiting room of the United States Embassy in New Delhi, waiting. Obtaining a U.S. visa is a grueling and often humiliating process. Still, it is done. But it is not done inside the actual embassy building; rather, the waiting takes place in an ancillary building on the embassy grounds. The embassy building itself, hidden behind layers of security both physical and virtual, is reserved for those in the foreign service whose duties include doing whatever it is that embassy workers do, besides denying visas.

Despite the barricaded streets surrounding it, the U.S. Embassy remains a landmark in New Delhi's lush diplomatic neighborhood. Once the United States's largest listening post in Asia, from an architectural point of view, the building, which was designed by Edward Durell Stone and completed in 1954, stands as the monumental achievement of a postwar turn toward modernism by the U.S. State Department Foreign Buildings Operations (FBO) office. The first of many embassies designed under this regime, Stone's project was subject to a directive issued by a special board advising the FBO on architectural matters:

> To the sensitive and imaginative designer [an embassy commission] will be an invitation to give serious study to local conditions of climate and site, to understand and sympathize with local customs and people, and to grasp the historical meaning of the particular environment in which the new building must be set. He will do so with a free mind without being dictated by obsolete or sterile formulae or clichés, be they old or new; he will avoid being either bizarre or fashionable, yet he will not fear using new techniques or new materials should these constitute real advance in architectural thinking.[10]

9 Amy Waldman, "Bill Gates Finds a Seattle in India," *New York Times*, International, November 14, 2002, 1.

10 Pietro Belluschi, FBO Architectural Advisory Committee memorandum, January 27, 1954, quoted in Jane C. Loeffler, *The Architecture of Diplomacy: Building America's Embassies* (New York: Princeton Architectural Press, 1998), 124–125. Also quoted in Edward Durell Stone, *The Evolution of an Architect* (New York: Horizon Press, 1962), 138.

Edward Durell Stone

United States Embassy
New Delhi, 1954. Fence, 2002.

Stone was hardly one for the "bizarre or fashionable." To prove this, he provided the State Department with a glass box set on a plinth. Inside, the box was penetrated by a courtyard-as-tropical water garden (though the local climate is technically semi-arid). Outside, it was wrapped entirely in a patterned screen of perforated terrazzo block. In keeping with the FBO directive, Stone designed the screen as a gesture to that same local climate but perhaps also to an image of the East lodged in his (and his clients') imaginary, reinforced by what he called the "oriental opulence" of the gold-leafed colonnade surrounding it. Like the imperial headquarters built by Lutyens and Baker in New Delhi three decades earlier but with significantly less subtlety, this corporate glass box with a sensitive skin was a piece of architectural diplomacy—an effort to convince whomever would listen that the U.S. was a good neighbor.

In the old days, entry to the U.S. Embassy was gained on axis, across a grand lawn with a circular reflecting pool and fountains, up a grand stair, and under the colonnaded porch. Today, visitors are forced to skulk off-center toward to a guard booth in front of a threatening wall, only to be dispatched around the back to the outbuilding where future NRIs wait indefinitely for visas. Those fortunate enough to be invited up the steps are greeted by a grim, well-armed Marine standing inside a bulletproof glass booth, inside Stone's glass box inside the perforated terrazzo shell. In late 2002, conspicuously taped to the Marine's booth, was a "Wanted" poster: Osama Bin Laden, directly across from whom hung an awkwardly grinning triumvirate: the American president, vice president, and secretary of state. A face-off.

IIC

As perhaps a measure of Stone's success, an alter ego to the U.S. Embassy and its aggressive regionalism was soon to be found in the more genteel regionalism of the India Interna-

Le Corbusier

Assembly Building
Chandigarh, 1963.

tional Centre (IIC), which opened in 1962. For starters, its patrimony traces back to New York and San Francisco, rather than to Washington, D.C. Funded by the Rockefeller Foundation in the wake of that family's contribution to the United Nations Headquarters, the IIC was designed by Joseph Allen Stein, an American architect from Berkeley who had become head of the new architecture school in Calcutta a few years earlier. Stein would go on to design the Ford Foundation Headquarters next door in 1968, even as Kevin Roche was completing his own, more famous Ford Foundation in New York in 1967.

A conference center and forum dedicated to international cultural exchange, the IIC's architecture exudes a cosmopolitan optimism that lands softly on its site adjacent to Lodhi Gardens in central New Delhi. Again there are screens and verandahs, but now they are rendered in a local material: blue-glazed tile crafted in Delhi. Still, the paradox of identity is inescapable. Unlike the UN, which laid claim to modern architecture's supposed universality, the "international" nature of the IIC was to be secured by its site specificity, which extended to its users to the degree that, as the inaugural brochure put it, "the Centre will be a forum for the exposition of the cultural patterns prevailing in the different parts of the world by the men and women most competent on the subjects—nay, embodying in themselves each such pattern."[11]

chandigarh.com

Meanwhile, back in Bangalore, The Food Court at Infosys was hardly the first ghost of an earlier, heroic modernism to haunt that city's subtropical landscape. In 1977, work began on the Bangalore campus of the Indian Institute of Management (IIM), designed by Stein's future partner, Balkrishna V. Doshi, and completed in 1985. The IIM acronym was already known to those following modernism's international meanderings in the 1960s, when Louis I. Kahn

11 India International Centre Inaugural Souvenir, 1962, Quoted in Stephen White, *Building in the Garden: The Architecture of Joseph Allen Stein in India and California* (Oxford: Oxford University Press, 1993), 146.

Joseph Allen Stein
India International Centre
New Delhi, 1962.

designed an IIM campus in Ahmedabad, begun in 1962 but completed only after Kahn's death in transit in 1974. Doshi had worked in Paris on Le Corbusier's plans for Chandigarh, and, after setting up his own practice in Ahmedabad, he assisted in bringing Kahn to India to design the IIM. Doshi's own Bangalore IIM was an ode to Kahn, with its iterative, cubic spaces fabricated from the modest means of raw concrete, with local granite block in place of Kahn's mythic brick. But it was even more overtly modeled after Fatehpur Sikri, the sixteenth-century Mughal imperial compound inhabited by Akbar and his court. Simultaneously princely and prosaic, Bangalore's IIM thus telescoped the precolonial with the postcolonial—royal gardens and local granite—in an environment that scrambled Kahn's hierarchies into episodic spatial sequences interwoven with plantings, all designed for a new class of managers who would eventually manage the country's entry into the "new economy" growing up nearby in the new digital gardens of Bangalore's technology parks.

Notwithstanding the persistence of Kahn, the most visible of modern architecture's ghosts haunting India's new modernity remains that of Le Corbusier, whose spirit still roams the verdant avenues, monumental halls, and modest housing of Chandigarh, capital of Punjab, which now does double duty as the capital of neighboring Haryana as well. Chandigarh still embodies the possibility of building entire cities and even entire worlds from scratch. And it was of this city that its prime sponsor, Prime Minister Jawaharlal Nehru, could declare with a politician's tact:

I do not like every building in Chandigarh. I like some very much. I like the general conception of the township very much. But what I like above all is this creative approach: not being tied down to what has been done by our forefathers and the like but thinking out in new terms, trying to think in terms of light and air and ground and water and human beings, not in terms of rules and regulations laid down by our ancestors.[12]

In practice, these new terms were first laid out by Albert Mayer and Matthew Nowicki and after them Le Corbusier, assisted by Pierre Jeanneret, Jane Drew, Maxwell Fry, M. N. Sharma, A. R. Prabhawalkar, B. P. Mathur, Piloo Moody, U. E. Chowdhury, N. S. Lambda, Jeet Lal Malhotra, J. S. Detghe, and Aditya Prakash, all of whom together extended to Nehru an open hand in symbolic, concrete solidarity.[13]

In contrast, among the offshoots of Bangalore's corporate gardens—illegitimate heirs to Chandigarh's sparkling, technologically enhanced future—is the 111-acre Chandigarh Technology Park (CTP), located just outside the city and anchored by an Infosys campus.

12 Jawaharlal Nehru, "Mr. Nehru on Architecture," *Urban and Rural Planning Thought* 2.2 (April 1959): 49, as quoted in Vikramaditya Prakash, *Chandigarh's Le Corbusier: The Struggle for Modernity in Postcolonial India* (Seattle: University of Washington Press, 2002), 19.

13 The names of those who assisted Le Corbusier on Chandigarh are given in Prakash, *Chandigarh's Le Corbusier*, 14.

For the MNC is also a continuous interior, a network of airports, parking garages, lobbies, elevators, offices, and living rooms in which, from one perspective, "you" are on the inside and "they" are on the outside, while from another, "they" are inside and "you" are outside, perhaps trying to get in.

Another golden opportunity for bureaucratic abbreviation, CTP, like its Bangalore counterpart ITPL, was developed under the STPI scheme and administered by the Department of Information Technology (DIT), Chandigarh. But other, equally fantastical names were not far behind, and on May 20, 2004, Denver-based Quark Inc. broke ground on a nearby 46-acre campus, a home for seven-thousand new Quarkians (yes, that's right, Quarkians), complete with multiplexes and shopping. Chandigarh was chosen over Bangalore in part for a "quality of life" deemed attractive to engineering talent in short supply even in India. The move was led by future Quark CEO Kamar Aulakh, himself a graduate in engineering from Chandigarh's Punjab University, who made sure the new campus would be state of the art. Thus could Quark boast to prospective employees of its India Development Center (IDC):

A modern, twenty-first-century office, Quark takes every care to ensure that the workplace is energetic and lively. It is a "flat" organization without archaic, bureaucratic designations. The Quark culture is designed to help individuals realize their true potential in a comfortable environment. Employees are known as "members" of their departments, and there are no superficial barriers between one employee and another. Quark is committed to making every employee feel at home. This is reflected in almost every aspect of the work culture—from the fresh, clean architecture of its glass building to the elegant interiors, and from the relaxed dress code to the well-stocked pantries and cafeterias.[14]

In explaining to these prospective employees "Why Chandigarh?" Quark further emphasized

the benefits of a planned city with modern amenities and comparably low levels of air pollution but also felt obliged to apologize for the city's relative lack of historical attractions. So instead of its shabby modern architecture and the not-so-shabby utopia it imagined, the environmentally friendly Quark chose to emphasize Chandigarh's greenery. According to the company, the city possesses an abundance of "theme-based gardens and parks," including Leisure Valley (running through the center of Le Corbusier's plan), the Rose Garden, the Terraced Flower Garden, and the Botanical Garden. There is also Sukhna Lake, which is surrounded by a "golf course of national repute" and winter home to "exotic migratory birds" from Siberia, among other wildlife.[15] All of which suggested a science-fiction vision of ecotopian bliss, in another kind of city in another kind of universe parallel to Le Corbusier's. The Quarkians called this Quark City.

A 5,000-acre office-cum-residential township, Quark City, with Quark's IDC as its anchor, was expected to bring twenty thousand new jobs to the Chandigarh area, thereby overcoming that city's previous shortcomings in attracting IT companies, despite Le Corbusier's best efforts in laying the technological groundwork. Thus could Quark Inc. proudly boast of the projected economic impact of its proposed new city:

A messiah in the form of an MNC may yet usher affluence and advancement to the region while providing an international platform that the enterprising people of the region had been waiting for.[16]

The MNC had arrived.

An Error

Le Corbusier, who no doubt would have preferred to be recognized as Chandigarh's first messiah, also waxed lyrical about the city's natural setting. There are many stories told about his adventures there, but perhaps the best is told by Le Corbusier himself, under the title "Birth of the Legend":

On 28th March, 1951, at Chandigarh, at sunset, we had set off in a jeep across the still-empty site of the capital—[P. L.] Varma, [Maxwell] Fry, Pierre Jeanneret, and myself. Never had the spring been so lovely, the air so pure after a storm on the day before, the horizons so clear, the mango trees so gigantic and magnificent. We were at the end of our task (the first): we had created the city (the town plan).

I noticed then that I had lost the box of the Modulor, of the only Modulor strip in existence, made by [Jerzy] Soltan in 1945, which had not left my pocket for six years . . . A grubby box, splitting at the edges. During that last visit of the site before my return to Paris, the Modulor had fallen from the jeep onto the soil of the fields that were to disappear to make way for the capital. It is there now, in the very heart of the place, integrated in the soil. Soon it will flower in all the measurements of the first city of the world to be organized all of a piece in accordance with that harmonious scale.[17]

Despite Le Corbusier's faith in his own virility and in the fertility of his Modulor seed inadvertently sown in Chandigarh's virgin soil during a moment of uncontrolled ecstasy, there was a problem: The proportions shown on that first Modulor tape were wrong. There was a microscopic error in the architectural genome that, if left unattended, would lead to unimaginable mutations.

The error was first brought to Le Corbusier's attention sometime in 1950 by one R. F. Duffau. It concerned, as Duffau put it, "the graphic demonstration out of which the first terms of the Modulor series are derived."[18] The geometrical relationships drawn on Le Corbusier's tape—the one with which he fertilized Chandigarh's soil—did not correspond to the mathematics. The error amounted to 1/6,000, or .017 percent, but it was enough to send Le Corbusier's diagrammatic Modulor figure (at Chandigarh, a universal "Indian"?) into inhuman contortions. It had to be corrected. And so it was, in 1955, after the designs for Chandigarh had been all but completed.

14 See http://www.quarkindia.com/careers/lifeatquark/workculture.html.

15 See http://www.quarkindia.com/careers/chandigarh/.

16 Quark press release, "Big Bang Theory," http://www.quarkindia.com/presscenter/india_news/ie20031911.html.

17 Le Corbusier, *Le Modulor 2 1955 (Let the User Speak Next): Continuation of "The Modulor" 1948* (Cambridge: MIT Press, 1968), 33-34.

18 Ibid., 45.

If we are to take Le Corbusier at his word—that the original tape, containing such an error, still somehow spawned Chandigarh's monumental "harmonies"—are we to believe that Chandigarh actually harbors a genetic mutation, a deviation from the Modulor ideal? Far from originating in some indigenous trait to be regarded with neocolonial disdain—faulty craftsmanship, inadequately comprehending local assistants, etc.—was this error in the code lodged in the very mind's eye of the master himself?

In other words, is it possible that far from representing the realization of Le Corbusier's urban visions, Chandigarh represents something of a productive aberration? In fact, Le Corbusier's reflections on the use of the Modulor are full of such aberrations. At Chandigarh, for example, there is the discrepancy between the conceptual, "arithmetic" dimensioning of the High Court (12 by 12 by 18 meters) and the *"texturique"* (or visible) proportions of the Modulor, as applied to the *brise-soleil*. Of this discrepancy Le Corbusier admitted, "It will be seen that, between arithmetic and *texturique,* there appeared some 'residues', to be reabsorbed in the normal way."[19]

Once such discrepancies were overcome in "the normal way," design by Modulor had its practical advantages, as demonstrated by the small, medium, and large versions of the unbuilt governor's house. The product of a "free imagination," the original design came in over budget. "We had built to the scale of giants," Le Corbusier said, so he and his team simply took out the Modulor scale, halved the generating cube, and adjusted everything accordingly, making a second round of adjustments to "put the Governor back into a House of Man."[20]

"Third World Paradigm" (Dots)
Who was this figure drawn on Le Corbusier's Modulor tape? There had been some variations proposed by others, as dutifully recorded by the master. These included a monkey (by students at London's Architectural Association) and a woman (by Le Corbusier's associate Justin Serralta). But despite these overdetermined graphic challenges, the Modular survived as Man himself. And it was not until the 1970s that this universal Man would mutate into another figure—more Gandhi than Nehru—lodged in Chandigarh's unconscious: the "Indian."

In 1962, prior to designing the IIM campus and just after returning from his stint in Le Corbusier's office applying the Modulor to Chandigarh's monuments, Balkrishna V. Doshi helped found the Centre for Environmental Planning

and Technology (CEPT). He also served as the first director of its school of architecture, then as director of the school of planning, and finally as dean of all of CEPT. He even designed the architecture school, with its open brick-and-concrete studios, from which have issued generations of architects hung over from drunken bouts with the auras of Kahn and Le Corbusier and, later, with the aura of Doshi, along with that of his friendly rival, Charles Correa.

Correa, a graduate of the University of Michigan and MIT, started big. Since the mid-1960s he has been a leading figure in the preparation of a master plan for Navi Mumbai (New Bombay), an enormous city-from-scratch across the river from Mumbai/Bombay. He incorporated many of the issues confronted in the master plan for New Bombay into *The New Landscape* (1985), a manifesto for urbanism in a modernizing Third World, its title borrowed (without acknowledgement) from a work by one of his MIT teachers, Gyorgy Kepes. In the book, Correa reiterated an ambiguous lesson on density as taught by another of his MIT teachers, Constantinos Doxiadis, that replaced Le Corbusier's Modulor figure with a colored dot: Diagram the population of a village with 250 red dots and one blue (someone "different from the rest"); next, a town of one thousand, with four or five floating blue dots; then a town of twenty-five thousand. Two blue dots finally meet, by chance. And now in a city of a hundred thousand, "we have several colonies where blue people reside . . . and furthermore, some of the red dots on the fringes of these colonies are turning . . . purple!"[21] Celebrating India's dense cities as cauldrons of social transformation (Gandhi's "Quit India" movement and the Calcutta resistance of the 1920s), Correa also notes an outsourcing in reverse, saying, "Today in the Gulf, a surprisingly large proportion of development is in the hands of Third World [urban] technocrats."[22] Still, "There is a syndrome common to almost all Third World urban centres. They each seem to consist of two different cities: one is for the poor; the other (interlocked with it) is for the rich." Correa calls this juxtaposition (also of red and blue dots) the "Third World paradigm."[23] In conclusion, he doubles it up with another ambiguous story of his own:

In the 60s, when European hippies first started coming to Bombay, a lot of rich Indians complained bitterly about them. At dinner parties they would refer to those "terrible, dirty people with lice in their hair, begging." In response one would say, "It doesn't bother

Charles Correa
Life Insurance Corporaton of India (Jeevan Bharati)
New Delhi, 1986.

you when you see Indians under those conditions. Why do you get so upset when you see a European?" Finally, a friend gave me the answer, "Naturally, a rich Indian goes berserk when he drives his Mercedes and sees a hippie. The hippie is signaling him a message: I'm coming from where you're going—and it's not worth going there. That upsets him terribly." But come to think of it, surely it is a message that should work the other way around as well! The hippie should realize that the Indian in his Mercedes, gross as he may be, is also sending a message, in fact, the very same one: "I'M COMING FROM WHERE YOU'RE GOING."[24]

To this elliptical allegory of modernization, Correa appends an image of Bombay's new luxury high-rise housing looming over a squatter settlement in the foreground, captioned "The Metropolis as Mirage."

Sandstone (Red)
Simultaneously, Correa nurtured a professional practice oriented toward a maturing nation-state as well as to multi-national capital. A snapshot of this is visible in his own contribution to the Bangalore skyline: the 21-story Visvesvaraya Centre, developed by the state-owned Life Insurance Corporation of India (LIC) and completed in 1980. Like Doshi's early work, Correa's office complex extended Le Corbusier's "voyage to the East" beyond the master's lifetime into a set of raw concrete towers topped with periscopic heads that poeticized a hulking proto-industrial mass inhabited by bureaucrats. But concrete was an inadequate carrier for the meaning that Correa sought, and along with such innovations as the folded concrete pavilion designed for Hindustan Lever in 1961—Correa's own Lever House—the Visvesvaraya Centre was relegated to the margins of subsequent monographs.

19 Ibid., 217.
20 Ibid., 222.

21 Charles Correa, *The New Landscape* (Bombay: The Book Society of India, 1985), 84-85.
22 Ibid., 87.
23 Ibid., 103.

24 Ibid., 132-133.

Raj Rewal
State Trading Corporation Headquarters
New Delhi, 1976.

Ralph Lerner
Indira Gandhi National Centre for the Arts
New Delhi, 1999.

Instead, Correa reasserted the promise of meaning in far more literal terms in his contribution to the Delhi skyline in 1986: the main offices of his Bangalore client, the LIC. Here Le Corbusier and Kahn were replaced by Kevin Roche and I. M. Pei as apparent sources, except that Pei's signature triangular massing was now clad in the red sandstone typically quarried in the Delhi area or in neighboring Rajasthan, offset against expanses of Roche's signature mirrored glass and topped off by a functionless space frame spanning the empty plinth below.[25]

Yet this was no mere repetition of Western models. On the contrary, like the man in the Mercedes, both Correa's writings and his architecture are rife with the tensions of "Indianness" written into that red stone. These tensions were already there in the sandstone monuments of the earlier Mughal imperium; they were also prominently on display in the politically motivated sandstone detailing of Baker and Lutyens in New Delhi, only to be sublimated into the concrete and brick abstractions of Le Corbusier and Kahn. Thus did the red sandstone specter of "Indianness" resurface—literally—in the Delhi LIC (or Jeevan Bharati) and other Correa projects. Shortly thereafter, reddish-beige sandstone was again applied to British skin in Delhi, in the form of the screen wall fronting Correa's British Council, a center devoted to "cultural exchange" and opened in 1992. That same year also saw the opening of India's Permanent Mission to the United Nations in a recently postmodernized New York, again designed by Correa. There, on Forty-Third Street in midtown Manhattan, a red granite base, inlaid with an entrance door "made in India of wood and brass by traditional Rajasthani craftsmen," transmogrified into metal panels coated in reddish enamel as it wrapped the narrow tower above.[26] But even as Correa continued to use it superficially as he went on to explore the iconography

of nine-square mandalas in other projects, red sandstone was, together with modular patterns modeled on indigenous settlements, being refined as a blunt instrument for smashing concrete modernism by the doyen of the Delhi scene, Raj Rewal.

Mini-Mega
Two other Delhi monuments testify to the durability of red sandstone (with beige trim) in evoking the local in the interest of the global. The first of these is Rewal's 1976 State Trading Corporation (STC) headquarters in central Delhi, near the neo-Roman circus of Connaught Place, on which Correa's LIC buildings stands. A mini-megastructure frozen in stone, the STC complex consists of three towers, the tallest of which is fourteen stories, with stacks of Virendeel trusses spanning between them. The towers were designed to accommodate the offices of a semi-governmental agency overseeing the export of Indian products. At the base was the government-run Cottage Industries shopping emporium, in which tourists, NRIs, and middle-to upper-class residents could purchase a wide variety of craft products. As representations of a traditional India from which a new modernity rises, these crafts provided a cultural foundation for the futuristic exertions of Rewal's architecture, grounded in red stone.

The second, equally demonstrative project by Rewal to exhibit megastructural tendencies—this time at a more genuinely mega-scale—was the Standing Conference of Public Enterprise (SCOPE) office complex, completed in 1989. Here, interlocking mid-rise polygons housed a bewildering, seemingly infinite variety of government offices in 75,000 square meters of sandstone-clad space punctured at regular, geometrically controlled intervals by vertical cores. Again, the building intimates a specifically "Indian" architecture, the link of which to

its geographical region is supposedly secured by the very earth of which it is made—the global phenomenon known as "local stone."

But the concluding chapter in the saga of red stone was written by another megaproject of the 1980s that went unrealized amid New Delhi's lush greenery until the 1990s: Ralph Lerner's Indira Gandhi National Centre for the Arts (IGNCA). A postmodern return to the symbolisms of Lutyens and Baker, the IGNCA was also evidence of a new stage in India's modernity, in which the raw materials of imperial imagery—Mughal motifs, taken up by the British—were recycled once again. This time, the recycling was passed through the lens of a rigorous, academic historicism by an American architect who had successfully tapped into the Indian geopolitical imaginary at a moment when this leader of the historically "nonaligned" nations was beginning to represent itself as having confidently emerged from the shadow of colonialism with solid historical foundations of its own. And, as in the equally postmodern efforts of Correa and Rewal, at the IGNCA these metaphorical foundations were built—again—of red sandstone.

Owing largely to shifts in the political fortunes of its namesake's Congress Party sponsors, the IGNCA was only partially realized. Still, throughout its lengthy construction period, visitors to the site could hear the continuous background sound of masons chipping slowly at the recalcitrant stone that was expected to sing eventually of India's new global status. Alas, as the Indian economy was systematically "opened up" during the same period, government receded as the architectural custodian of Indian "culture," even as the far-right Hindu nationalist Bharatiya Janata Party (BJP) began its ascent to power fueled by a deadly culture war that began with the demolition of the Ayodyha mosque. Emerging in its wake and singing the song of "Indianness" all the while (what the BJP called "India Shining") was a new cult of lifestyle that began at home rather than in public. The earlier "housing colonies" built and presided over by the Delhi Development Authority (DDA) were gradually replaced by private, corporate enclaves, now called "housing estates." Alongside these sat subdivisions filled with new houses executed in populist, post-Chandigarh styles, including the aspirational style that one observer has called "Punjabi Baroque."[27]

Import-Export
But as with the STPI initiative, government-led efforts to redefine "India" with the help of archi-

25 Vikram Bhatt and Peter Scriver, *After the Masters* (Ahmedabad: Mapin Publishers, 1990), 144.

26 Charles Correa, *Charles Correa* (London: Thames & Hudson, 1996), 110.

27 Gautham Bhatia, *Punjabi Baroque* (New York: Penguin Books, 1994).

tecture did bear some fruit. For example, during his pre-sandstone. concrete phase, Rewal designed a pair of permanent exhibition pavilions for the grounds of the International Trade Fair in New Delhi (Asia '72). The project was the result of a competition whose brief was as much symbolic as it was pragmatic: to represent India's progressive industrialization to the world, for export. The resulting pavilions, the Hall of Nations and the Hall of Industries, each spanned large, open exhibition spaces with truncated, pyramidal concrete space frames, designed in collaboration with the engineer Mahendra Raj. Seen against the imported steel image of Correa's (later) LIC space frame, these were monuments to the lopsided ratio of (high) material cost versus (low) labor cost in India, which meant that Rewal and Raj had to perform the alchemical feat of transforming high-priced steel—the traditional material of the space frame—into labor-intensive concrete.

Global Village
By 1990, Rewal's pavilions had been joined on their site by the National Crafts Museum, designed by Correa. The museum incorporated into its precincts an earlier collection of rural huts constructed by the All India Handicrafts Board for Asia '72. Correa thus laid it out as a kind of abstracted village with the occasional figural motif, such as the red-tile awnings that surround the interlocking courtyards. The museum's collection brought together for the first time representative crafts from the farthest reaches of the cultural amalgam called "India," with its 28 states and 325 languages, so that tourists, residents, and visiting craftspersons alike could compare various traditions and techniques and draw their own conclusions as to national identity. As its first director, Smita J. Baxi, described it, the museum was conceived as a prototypical component for a "university of crafts" that as yet had no campus—a center of knowledge about the diverse crafts practices and their histories that formed yet another fragile foundation on which India's modernity could be built.[28]

But more than merely making available a pan-Indian heteroglossia of craft traditions for the first time to a general public, the museum literally enacted it, with actual, rural craftspeople performing (and selling) their crafts in the courtyards. This live performance reproduced the interpenetration of the rural and the urban—indeed, their necessary coexistence, often on the same piece of land—which is all too apparent in the vast squatter settlements and "unauthor-

Achyut Kanvinde
National Science Museum
New Delhi, 1990.

ized" housing sectors that cover Delhi and other major cities. Such settlements had been inhabited earlier by Salman Rushdie's "midnight's children," displaced by partition, and were later inventoried by Correa in *The New Landscape*. They are now home to a new generation of rural migrants who are busy redefining cities around the world. It is often said (with middle-class annoyance) that Delhi's sometimes daily power outages are due in part to the electricity pirated by these settlements from the city's overtaxed, ancient infrastructure. Yet from those settlements emerges daily a vast corps of domestic workers to service the fast-growing middle-class households of a fast-growing service economy, closing the circle each day.

National Science
The other side of the coin that joined the production of culture with the new economy was also revealed in 1990, when Rewal's pavilions and the National Crafts Museum were joined on their site by the National Science Museum, designed by Achyut Kanvinde. In a move that complemented the project of the Crafts Museum, the National Science Museum and its companion, the Nehru Science Center, in Mumbai (also designed by Kanvinde), were intended to introduce a broad Indian public to national and international advances in the sciences, encouraging the developing nation's youth to pursue careers in science and technology. Such careers were further nurtured in the state-run Indian Institutes of Technology (IIT) located in each province, one of which was the fruit of Kanvinde's first major professional commission. Together, these institutions and others materialized Nehru's commitment to modernization as an engine of nation-building, a project that explicitly included modern architecture, again with Kanvinde's assistance.

Having been sent by his (still British) government in 1945 to Harvard University's Graduate School of Design to study under Walter

Gropius, Kanvinde returned to a liberated India in September 1947. At the time, an orientalist hangover still held sway on the architectural front in the form of calls for an anti-modern "national style" made by the still-British head of Bombay's Sir J. J. College of Architecture, Claude Batley, among others. Equipped with a modernism that matched Nehru's as well as Gropius's, Kanvinde met with the prime minister to make known his distress at this state of affairs. Subsequently, in a March 1959 address to architects made at Kanvinde's invitation, Nehru officially endorsed modern architecture as an appropriate vehicle for India's national aspirations.[29] Three decades later, in the National Science Museum, Kanvinde synthesized these still-vivid aspirations in a cascade of program captured in a modular, concrete frame. Orchestrated around the imagery of infrastructure, Kanvinde's cascade spoke—with Gropius but also with megastructuralists such as Kenzo Tange as well as with Nehru—of the foundational power of science, technology, and industry.

All That Is Solid . . .
Thus was the landscape of late-twentieth-century Delhi built on two types of foundations, concrete and sandstone, on which the nation's emerging role in the global economy could be seen to rest. One offered the presumably solid footing of techno-scientific calculation, while the other offered the more ephemeral but no less real footing of imagined cultural identity, more often than not rendered in dusky reds, trimmed with beige.

Other, hardly incidental contributions to this landscape were made by other, hardly incidental architects. At one end of the spectrum, for example, there was Kuldip Singh's solid monument to the public sector, the Delhi Town Hall, sculpted out of concrete in a manner that recalls Correa in Bangalore, as well as any number of other late-Corbusian modernisms worldwide, but with deeper recesses that register the blazing heat of the Delhi climate or perhaps the deep thoughts of the bureaucrats inside. While at the other end of the spectrum, also in central New Delhi, is a monument to the private sector: the golden, shiny headquarters of Delhi Land and Finance, now renamed the Delhi Land Finance (DLF) Group. An essay in branding that exchanges "Indianness" for international glitz, the DLF headquarters presents a cartoon façade that, unlike the ponderous recesses of Singh's Town Hall, drowns its central, pseudo-classical "portico" in the brash liquidity of multi-national capital momentarily frozen in mirrored glass.

28 Smita J. Baxi, "The Crafts Museum at New Delhi," *Museum* vol. 31, vo. 2 (1979): 99.

29 Kazi Khaleed Ashraf and James Belluardo, eds., *An Architecture of Independence: The Making of Modern South Asia* (New York: Architectural League of New York, 1998), 14.

Hafeez Contractor
DLF Group Headquarters
New Delhi, 1997.

Hafeez Contractor
in advertisements from *Architecture + Design*, 2002.

Hafeez Contractor
in advertisements from *Architecture + Design*, 2002.

DLF City
Gurgaon, c. 2004.

Hafeez

The DLF construction company was founded in 1946 and immediately rose to prominence as a builder of speculative housing to accommodate the massive influx of midnight's children moving to Delhi as a result of the 1947 partition. This private company—which is actually older than its more visible government counterpart, the Delhi Development Authority (DDA), founded in 1957—would eventually build twenty-one urban "townships," housing nearly a million people in and around the city.

The architect for the DLF headquarters (DLF Centre) in New Delhi is arguably India's most prolific and most famous practitioner: the inimitable Hafeez Contractor. By mid-2004, Contractor (or Hafeez, as he is affectionately known) had designed four million square feet of residential space, 2.5 million square feet of commercial space, and half a million square feet of shopping for the DLF Group. Most of this was in Gurgaon, a burgeoning "cyber-city" that had sprung up

over the past decade near the airport, on the semi-rural outskirts of New Delhi, which was itself once on the semi-rural outskirts of Delhi proper, having now been encircled in dense sprawl by subsequent waves of urbanization.

By some accounts, Gurgaon harbors the largest privately owned conurbation in Asia, mostly in the form of the very large, irregular enclaves that together make up DLF City. As a set of non-contiguous spatial islands held together only by their brand name, DLF City is the Multi-National City in microcosm. It is an entirely private city financed by speculative capital. There is virtually no public transportation.

Not afraid of theorizing, its developers celebrated what they call the city's "walk-to-work concept, making global corporates feel at home," a concept, they continued, often heard but "rarely possible in today's congested metropolis." Not only does this city supposedly reduce transportation costs (even as many workers endure two-hour commutes in company vans), according

Hafeez Contractor
DLF Princeton Estate
DLF City, Gurgaon, 2004.

(MSAUD) from the United States. In fact, the degree is from the Graduate School of Architecture, Planning and Preservation (GSAPP) at Columbia University, which probably makes Contractor that school's most prolific alumnus. But in terms of the cultural capital out of which the Multi-National City is built, it remains more important in the Indian context to identify oneself as having studied "abroad" (in the U.S., in Contractor's case) than to name the specific institution. And like many of the founders of India's burgeoning IT industry to which DLF City caters, Contractor returned to India after his studies, foregoing the temptations (or hardships) of life as an NRI in New York, and founding his own practice in Mumbai in 1982. Among his other works are any number of office buildings, including large projects for large multi-nationals like Citibank, Colgate-Palmolive, and Proctor & Gamble; residential complexes with names like Broadway Avenue (Mumbai), City of Joy (Mumbai, projected), Dreams-AT (Mumbai, projected), Seawoods Estate (Navi Mumbai), Place Orchard (Pune), Vastu (Mumbai), and Lake Castle (Mumbai), and institutions, including IIT Mumbai and a projected twenty-acre campus for Infosys in the Chandigarh Technology Park (CTP).

"Very, Very American!"
DLF City faces stiff competition just to the east of New Delhi from an official high-technology sector developed under the STPI scheme, the township of Noida. Among the new buildings on the Noida skyline is the headquarters of Adobe India, rendered in bright colors that, according to the company, reflect "the vibrant and fun-filled work environment" inside.[31] The building, which opened in 2003, was designed by the New Delhi–based firm Spazzio. It contains an indoor gym, recreation room, library, and medical room, with a cafeteria that serves from 8 a.m. to 10 p.m., as well as outdoor volleyball and tennis courts. Work hours are flexible and are set by each employee, "according to their lifestyle." What is more, work is supplemented by an institutionalized regime of "fun" presided over by a self-organized, employee-run Sports and Cultural Council that, like its counterparts in Silicon Valley, dedicates itself to reproducing the carefree abandon of college life.

All of this postmodernity led the *Times of India* to declare the building "Very, Very American!" Here, in direct contrast to the deployment of red sandstone elsewhere for its "Indianness," cultural identity is imported. Among those architectural characteristics that (in addition to its overseas corporate parent)

earned the building the designation "American" was the fact that the window glazing was from Glaverbel Belgium, the exterior aluminum panels were from Alucobond Germany, and the modular furniture was from the Canadian manufacturer Teknion—everything imported. "Definitely American."[32]

Princeton, Gurgaon
Both Noida and DLF City/Gurgaon emerged from the latest phase of modernization serviced so adeptly by Hafeez Contractor. They did so by accommodating a middle-class flight from the city and from the newly urbanized rural masses. In that sense, the MNC is paradoxical: a city that abandons the city, as the city, in turn, absorbs the village in the form of miles of urban poverty. This is a turning inward that is accomplished by moving outward, beyond the airport, which in the case of DLF City yielded five phased residential enclaves and a series of corporate offices, with requisite posturban amenities. These gated enclaves go by such names as DLF Windsor Court, DLF Hamilton Court, DLF Regency Park, DLF Richmond Park, DLF Belvedere Towers, DLF Belvedere Place, DLF Silver Oaks, DLF Wellington Estate, DLF Oakwood Estate, DLF Ridgewood Estate, DLF Beverly Park, DLF Carlton Estate, and DLF Princeton Estate.

Their televisual names connect these objects to other objects in places like suburban New Jersey, where new condominium developments in the greater Princeton area offer an independent, home-owning lifestyle to the expanding NRI class of international, English-speaking technical workers trained in India's IITs and IIMs. Conversely, the "opening up" of the Indian economy during the 1990s brought tax breaks for NRI investors. And so, together with the upwardly mobile middle class who imagine themselves as walk-to-work executives, among the main clientele of DLF City is the NRI, for whom apartment units in DLF Princeton Estate

to the DLF Group, it "reduces executive stress," thereby increasing productivity; while on the home front, "it makes for much fuller family life," since "time available with the family is a lot more than would otherwise be possible."[30] Hidden in these proclamations is a tension in which the bonds of the traditional, extended Indian family are threatened by the demands of commuting to the new utopia of the office park and by the multiple allegiances of corporate life. This occurs both at the level of the so-called executive (the implied patriarch) and of the offspring, whose new job at the call center down the road (or two hours away) may require her to work evenings. In the Multi-National City, not only is your past their present, but your day is their night—the waking hours, that is, of potential credit-card customers on the other side of the globe.

And in more than one way, Contractor can be called a multi-national architect. His firm's PR materials identify him as holding a Master of Science in Architecture and Urban Design

30 Text formerly on http://www.dlf-group.com/. Accessed June 2002.

31 See http://www.adobeindia.com/templates/ui/contentpage. asp?pageid=18.

32 Nita Trikha, "Very, Very American!" *Times of India*, June 4 2003, Cities: Delhi, 1.

Hafeez Contractor
GE Capital Call Center
with DLF Princeton Estate beyond DLF City.

may represent both a potential investment in a rising real estate market and a kind of displaced homecoming—a base from which to visit the family while still maintaining a safe distance.

Inside Outsourcing

Other such avatars of the outsourcing of identity in Gurgaon include DLF Square Tower, DLF Gateway Tower, and DLF Plaza Tower. There are also assorted shopping malls, as well as that all-important lifestyle amenity for walk-to-work executives unable to tolerate for very long their own families: a golf course. Adjacent to DLF City Phase V, the golf course and country club comes complete with five lakes, "greens that play true," floodlighting for night golf, and a downloadable application form that—like the city itself—helped construct the very golfers it serves, offering varying rates to "overseas corporate members," NRIs, individual residents, individual expatriates, and corporations, although it remains unclear whether these categories are in fact mutually exclusive.

Also adjacent to DLF City Phase V on Vishwakarma Road is the General Electric call center. Dedicated mainly to the back-office marketing and service operations of GE Capital, the call center is representative of the strange topologies of outsourcing. Anguished debates during the 2004 U.S. presidential campaign about sending so-called American jobs overseas missed the point entirely, since a key job description for many call-center operators has been the ability to produce a simulacrum of the "American" overseas. Here is an account from India's version of *Time* magazine, *India Today*. Meghna is a 23-year-old call-center operator somewhere in Gurgaon.

When her phone rings, she becomes "Michelle." The caller is in Philadelphia, asking for a credit extension. "Meghna is unruffled. Months of training, which included watching

Hollywood blockbusters to pick up a wide variety of American accents and reading John Grisham thrillers to clear any linguistic obstacles, have paid off. Her computer screen even flashes the weather at Philadelphia as she tells a caller what a perfect day it is. Meghna signs off saying, "Have a good day." Outside her window it is pitch dark.[33]

Inside outsourcing, then, "Hari will become Harry, he will work this Diwali, and he will have a holiday on July 4."[34] So observed Ajit Isaac, CEO of Bangalore-based PeopleOne Consulting, a "full-spectrum human-capital services company" financed by JP Morgan Ventures. This is outsourcing: the paradoxical reproduction of national and cultural identity on the *inside* of an *exterior* space—inside the call center, out in Gurgaon, at night. In that sense, in mirrored symmetry with the NRI and the "resident alien," the call-center operator is a prototypical subject of the Multi-National City, a cyborg who switches identities by plugging into technological networks that scramble time and space into a topological knot.

And whether in Gurgaon or in Bangalore, outsourcing's strange topologies would not be possible without the technical infrastructure that provides the uplink—in the case of Bangalore's ITPL, the prominently placed satellite dish that, like the building's smooth surfaces, fulfills both a functional and symbolic role simultaneously.[35] This is a role prefigured, perhaps, by the cryptic symbolism of Le Corbusier's sculptural dome atop the Assembly building at Chandigarh, city of Nehru's technological dreams.

There is also a large satellite dish poised prominently atop the GE Capital call center in Gurgaon, signaling the building's status as a machine for producing multi-nationals of all kinds. On the inside, the cubicle space is divided into territories corresponding to regions serviced: North America, Europe, Africa, and so on—the globe, internalized.

The interiors of GE Capital were designed by the Delhi-based firm of Framework Interiors, whose production was singled out in 2002 by the Indian periodical *Architecture + Design* as exemplifying "Multinational Design for the Multinational Mind." The mind-set of Framework Interiors is no different than that of their American counterparts. They apply such Silicon Valley-style office-planning methods as the relaxed, "open" office with designated social areas; or "hotelling," in which workers "plug and play" into different workstations on a daily basis, as well as "internal branding," or packaging the corporation from the inside out to encourage brand loyalty

Hafeez Contractor
DLF Square Tower
DLF City, Gurgaon, 1999.

in the employees more than the customers. And naturally, the architect of the GE Capital call center in which Framework Interiors exercised their craft was Hafeez Contractor.

Again, despite the inclination of many Euro-American architects and critics to regard such developments as Gurgaon as emerging spontaneously out of the exotic, ahistorical jungles of globalization—Shanghai as "primitive hut," to name another—these cities are nothing if not historical. Contractor's unapologetic postmodernism is not only a remixed echo of earlier postmodernisms that Euro-American architects used to call historicist. In addition, looming large over private, postmodern cities such as Gurgaon is the hulking mass of Chandigarh: the modernist promise of a new future emanating from the recently decolonized public sector. In that sense, Contractor materializes a kind of Corbusian alter ego who will build in any style whatever, thereby also refusing the reactions to international modernism that advocate a more "authentically" Indian architecture. As a result, Contractor's postmodernism and the televisual image of the West that it projects (a kind of architectural equivalent to the pan-Asian Star TV) are certainly agents of power. But they also represent an inadvertent challenge to the jargon of authenticity associated with the rigid postmodernisms of national identity carved in stone.

In addition to the GE Capital call center, among Contractor's output in DLF City proper is DLF Square Tower, with an upside-down pyramid (the DLF logo) at its base—the figurative skyscraper top that once marked the skyline of "delirious New York" now inverted to become the ubiquitous emblem of the MNC: the glass atrium. But DLF City is not without a skyline. the bulk of DLF Square Tower hovers over the vast fields formerly tended by villagers who are rendered increasingly invisible by its looming postmodernity. The entrance to DLF City and to the new districts of Gurgaon into which it is embedded is marked

33 Raj Chengappa and Malini Goyal, "Housekeepers to the World," *India Today*, vol. 1, no. 46 (12-18 November 2002), 10.

34 Samar Halakarnar, "Bangalore: The Buzz Is Back!" *Indian Express*, 8 November 2002, 15.

35 On the "broadcast urbanism" of satellite and telecommunications networks woven into the IT imaginary in India, see Keller Easterling, *Enduring Innocence: Global Architecture and Its Political Masquerades* (Cambridge: MIT Press, 2005), 135-159.

by Hafeez's DLF Gateway Tower, completed in 1999. The DLF Group duly celebrates this building's state-of-the-art technology, including "The 100-percent power backup facility [that] makes sure that office efficiency is maximized at all times," a claim that reminds us that the politics of the MNC is often a politics of infrastructure.

Generators (Backup)

In Delhi's residential neighborhoods, the use of individual backup generators in the event of a power outage is widespread, to the degree that the economic structure of a given neighborhood is starkly visible during a blackout by virtue of whose lights are on. Industry has followed suit, offering not just backup generators in buildings like DLF Gateway Tower but also the class prestige that goes along with them, which is analogous to the Westernized names of the DLF housing estates.

During blackouts in Gurgaon the efficacy of backup generators can in principle be measured by the glow of the glass atriums that feature prominently in other Contractor buildings, such as DLF Atria and the Ericsson headquarters. An equally potent architectural status symbol is the mirrored-glass-curtain wall that covers half of what the DLF Group calls Gateway Tower's "futuristic exterior." Again, your past is their future or perhaps it's the other way around. One commentator writing in India's *Architecture + Design* describes—with tongue in cheek—a mirrored-glass, spherical office building in Bangalore as "a globe building for a 'global' corporation," and therefore a Venturian "duck," albeit absent the usual irony.[36] Gurgaon has its own version, minus the spherical form: the Global Business Park. Are we to conclude, then, that this and other such buildings, including Bangalore's Digital Park, are decorated sheds, where the equation "glass = global" is applied as a billboard to the otherwise unremarkable shell of an otherwise unremarkable office building?

Clients in India's IT parks have indeed been known to request a specific percentage of curtain wall for their buildings, but the global curtain wall is more than merely a sign with structure behind it: it is a surface with specific topological properties—a two-sided sign. These enigmatic mirrors both reflect and fold the Multi-National City back onto itself, doubling up both its strange exteriority and its strange intimacy, thereby defeating the logic of inside and outside, us and them, even as they reproduce it. This is not merely a matter of a false transparency, a false universality, where you can see out but you can't see in, and vice versa. It is a matter of that math-

DLF City, Phase V
Gurgaon, 2004.

ematical property familiar to all digital architects, known as: the "normal." Normal to one side of the mirror is its reflective opacity; normal to the other, its transparency. This double valence is doubled many times across the world, mirroring the doubled-up infrastructure of the backup generator and, like a revolving door, offering both entrances and exits in and out of the MNC.

Capital, Again

Has the capital city simply been replaced, then, by the city of multi-national capital? No, but neither can these two collections of monuments be held apart any longer. Let us return momentarily to New York, a city that in the American context has seen much of its internal, psychic dynamism siphoned off to entropic quasi-cities like Silicon Valley. In the early 1970s, when New York was entering a period of crisis and the United States was revising its policies in Asia, the architectural historian Manfredo Tafuri found it convenient to juxtapose Manhattan's flexible gridiron with Pierre-Charles L'Enfant's neo-Baroque planning in Washington, D.C., which was among the models on which New Delhi was based.[37] For Tafuri, New York's capacity to accept any image whatsoever stood in contrast to the symbolic "values" still implicit if unattainable in the American city, even in Washington. Instead, it seemed to Tafuri, in the United States and increasingly in Europe, the architectural representation of stable, civic values had given way to the networked canalization of capital. Compare Euro-America to other parts of the

world, however, and you might arrive at slightly different conclusions.

For in the Multi-National City the issue is not so much, as Tafuri would have it, that architecture and urban planning have been definitively separated (though indeed they have), with architecture reduced to a mere signifier floating aimlessly on the multi-national sea. Instead, the issue is architecture's persistent capacity to channel multivalent flows into apparently stable basins—in this case, capital(ist) cities and their monuments, on which both nations and corporations float. Specifically, the issue is the feedback loops that work to secure the closure of these basins. The latter turn out to be nothing less than gated communities at a global scale, and their closure turns out to exist as much in the cultural imaginary as it does on the ground. Every building imagines a city, and architecture is all the more real for the dreamscapes that it conjures. Like other capital cities from other times, the Multi-National City that we have just visited represents one of those dreamscapes. Its reality is secured by the frequency with which it recurs, until dream and reality become indistinguishable. But as with the promises still built into Chandigarh's empty plazas, the harsh actualities of the MNC have not simply replaced the dream that architects and urban planners used to call utopia; instead, among the MNC's most significant consequences could be, lest you become too convinced of its inevitability, that you awaken one day and wonder who, in the end, is the dreamer.

36 Vijay Narnapatti, "Glass-Box Slick: Dressing Up the Corporate Image, Bangalore Context," *Architecture + Design* vol. 19, no. 6 (November-December 2002), 94.

37 Manfredo Tafuri, *Architecture and Utopia: Design and Capitalist Development* (Cambridge: MIT Press, 1976), 30-40.

From Washington, D.C., to the Emergent American Neighborhood: Strategies of Surveillance, Tactics of Encroachment

Teddy Cruz

Along the newly reconstituted global border that a post-9/11 world has produced between the First and Third Worlds, we are witnessing how societies of overproduction and excess are barricading themselves once more in an unprecedented way against the sectors of scarcity they produce out of political and economic indifference.

Graphics of the Department of Homeland Security: Secure Border Initiative (SBI).

Border Calculus

T (IA travel) >> T (apprehend)

To be successful, 3 criteria must be met:
- Sufficient detection and tracking coverage
- Sufficient tracking in depth to allow agent time to react before alien reaches a vanishing point
- Sufficient capacity to handle numbers of apprehended

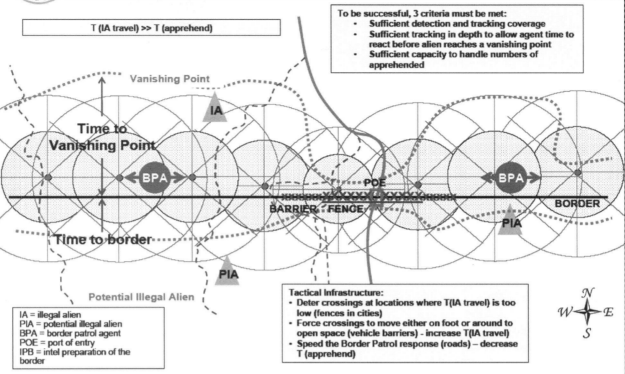

IA = illegal alien
PIA = potential illegal alien
BPA = border patrol agent
POE = port of entry
IPB = intel preparation of the border

Tactical Infrastructure:
- Deter crossings at locations where T(IA travel) is too low (fences in cities)
- Force crossings to move either on foot or around to open space (vehicle barriers) - increase T(IA travel)
- Speed the Border Patrol response (roads) – decrease T (apprehend)

Mobile Systems Communications

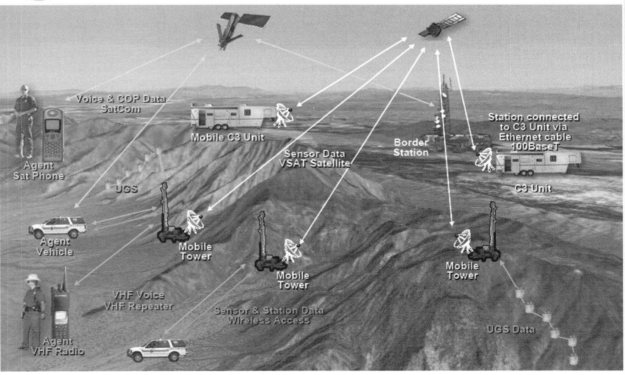

But these current, sweeping neo-liberalist economic policies of privatization and homogenization worldwide are also producing sectors of resistance to "American-style" globalization from the Middle East to South America. Latin America is one of those sectors, reconfiguring itself ideologically and economically across national, continental, and global scales. The political transformations emerging in many South American capitals, including La Paz, Brasília, Caracas, Lima, and La Asunción, are eroding the established institutions of control and influence that had traditionally aligned many of these countries with Washington, D.C. Presidents such as Bolivian Evo Morales announcing the insertion of illegal coca production into the official national economy, Brazilian Inácio Lula da Silva awarding property titles to thousand of slum dwellers in Rio de Janeiro and São Paulo, and Venezuelan Hugo Chavez waging a demagogic war against the Bush administration and promising to give huge oil revenues to the poor of his country, all point to a very different socio-political and economic landscape in Latin America that was hard to imagine barely ten years ago.

Opposite the geo-economic scenarios that predicted the "take over" by the large-scale economic power of multi-nationals, transforming many of these capital cities into enclaves of neo-liberalism, these recent changes have proven those reductive speculations wrong. The interest of these governments in observing the role of the informal sector and the search for alternative socio-economic policies grounded on local systems of production to mitigate social inequalities has put forward, once more, the tensions between urbanisms of the formal and the informal, division and mixture, wealth and poverty, at local and global levels.

In a certain way, this blockade against Washington's unilateral politics influencing many of these countries' capitals begins to shape an expanding cartographic figure of resistance whose "spill" ends at the border between Latin America and the United States. In this context, the deflection of the Washington–Latin America axis is further bent through the prism of the current politics of fear manifested at the border between the United States and Mexico. As the U.S. Congress passes regula-

tions to build 700 more miles of border wall and pours billions of dollars to increase surveillance infrastructure at the different border checkpoints across the continent, it is clear that the policies of control emerging from Washington are consolidating anti-terrorist and anti-immigration agendas into a xenophobic urbanism of exclusion and division.

In the context of these transformations, the centralization of police power in the District of Colombia has made Homeland Security the new national planning department and the Patriot Act its social and environmental blueprint, making many disenfranchised inner-city neighborhoods across the U.S. become the focus of police repression and disinvestment, transforming the 11 million illegal laborers who live there into criminals. While we observe this renewed centralization of unchecked and unchallenged political power, imposed from above as a new totalizing land-use ordinance, we can also see a resurgence of pockets of resistance distributed at the ground level in the shape of informal densities, economies, and politics to reclaim the public domain.

What are the implications of these forces of control on the one hand and of non-conformity on the other in the reshaping of the American city? As an extension of the current tensions between the U.S. and Latin America, the San Diego-Tijuana border can serve as a magnifying lens to observe the clash between Washington's NIMBY [Not in My Backyard] politics of fear and the nationally emerging immigrant neighborhoods, whose spatial tactics thrive on non-conformity and an alternative public realm.

Washington, D.C., as Macondo: Magical Realism the American Way (An Autobiographical Note From the Border)

One of the most dramatic phenomena of our time is the unprecedented blurring of fiction and reality in the public sphere. The popularity of reality TV and documentary filmmaking has confirmed the return of the real to a central place in the collective imagination, but as the media spins it out of control what we see emerging is actually a form of magical realism, fueled by a morbid obsession with the

contradictions of everyday life. As a Guatemalan immigrant living in California, I cannot avoid being amused by this radical shift in American media culture, primarily because the practice of interweaving the fictive and the factual to reveal socio-political realities has been prescribed as the locus of Latin American culture. It seems to me that there has been a significant reversal: as the literary and visual arts of Latin America, from Mexico to Argentina, move "beyond the fantastic" into a new kind of social realism grounded less in the poetics of metaphor and more in operative activism, Americans have traded in their fantasies of grandeur for the magical dimension of the quotidian.

Could we then say that magical realism is no longer culturally specific to Latin America, as it has mutated from Macondo to Washington, D.C., and California in the last six years? Considering some of the socio-political shifts that have occurred during this period, I would say yes: George W. Bush turned into the leader of the Western world, an action-movie hero became governor of California, a New York real estate mogul was promoted to reality-television star, and Pat Buchanan wound up being the visionary of the decade. Even more ominous is the fact that the anti-immigration fantasies of the latter's 2000 presidential platform have become a reality, Homeland Security is now the construction manager of the new post-9/11 transcontinental border wall, and vigilante armadas from Arizona to California are the new gatekeepers of America.

In November 2000, as I watched the three Bushes, George, George W., and Jeb, celebrating the results of one of the most controversial elections in United States history, there was some foreshadowing of these developments. The Bush patriarch and his children sitting leisurely in the same room represented a strange cross-section of American political power: an ex-vice president and then president, a governor of one of the richest states in the U.S. and now newly elected president, and a governor of the controversial state where the polls, under his leadership, have (twice now) rivaled Third World elections for their lack of credibility. As I watched this scene on local TV news, a caption scrolled by warning Californians of possible power blackouts during the

Capitol-migration: the politics of cheap labor.

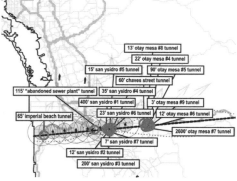

Illegal cross-border tunnel found in 2006.

next months. The juxtaposition was surreal. I hallucinated that I was back in Guatemala, between oligarchy and infrastructural uncertainty. But I never imagined at the time that such blackouts were the Machiavellian manipulations of Enron, which would perpetrate the largest U.S. corporate fraud.

Living in the San Diego-Tijuana border zone, I have found it difficult to separate Arnold Schwarzenegger's governorship of California from his Hollywood image. This problem was exacerbated a few months ago when I heard him emphatically disclose to a conservative talk-show host that the U.S. should close its borders and that a vigilante armada in Arizona known as the Minuteman operation was the answer to the problem of securing the border against illegal crossings. Televised images followed: infrared night-vision scenes provided by cameramen patroling with the vigilante groups (a graphic demonstration of how their sophisticated weapons and tracking gadgets were helping to forcefully capture immigrants crossing the Arizona desert) were intercut with the governor being interviewed as the Minutemen's ideological ally, turning the talk show into a sequel to Schwarzenegger's *Predator*. The uncanny echo of the governor's action classics in events that have continued to unfold following the 2000 election of George W. Bush is just one by-product of an ongoing right-wing political process promoting the politics of fear that has in every respect transformed our concept and experience of the public domain since 9/11.

In his recent essay, "Vigilante Man," for the *Socialist Review,* Mike Davis exposed the Minuteman in Arizona as a theater of the absurd and a canny attempt to move vigilantism into the mainstream of conservative politics. And even if the Minuteman's founder, a former kindergarten teacher from Southern California, failed to make good on his promise to the media that a thousand heavily-armed superpatriots would confront illegal aliens along Arizona's border (only 150 actually attended), Davis warns us that "vigilantes have always been to the American West what the Ku Klux Klan has been to the South: vicious and cowardly bigotry organized as a self-righteous mob. Almost every decade, some dismal group of self-proclaimed patriots mobilizes to repel a new invasion or subversive threat . . . . Their wrath has almost always been directed against the poorest, most powerless, and hard-working segment of the population: recent migrants from Donegal, Guangdong, Oklahoma, or, now, Oaxaca... But with a Vigilante Man in the governor's mansion in Sacramento, the next Minutemen provocation ('tens of thousands of volunteers blockading the Mexican border in California this coming fall') may be tragedy, not farce."

What Davis refers to here is the fact that, from the summer of 2005 until now, the Minutemen have moved westward toward the San Diego-Tijuana border to reenact the history of vigilantism in this region. The last time such an organized civilian army acted on this border was in the early 1990s, when California then-Governor Pete Wilson's anti-immigration Proposition 187 inspired hundreds of civilians to form the "Light-up the Border Coalition." People parked at the border wall with headlights and flashlights aimed at Tijuana in protest of the deficient militarized surveillance at the border and the increasing number of illegal workers infiltrating San Diego's North County suburbs.

In a certain way, the status of the Mexican border today is just one more casualty of 9/11 in the sense that the events of that day permanently altered Washington's position on its international borders, throwing longstanding and politically charged immigration issues relating to illegal labor into high relief against the backdrop of terrorism. Contradictions inherent in revamped protectionist agendas were further dramatized in 2004 when George W. Bush rolled out his new immigration policy. He proposed temporary work visas to allow illegal aliens to work legally in the U.S. for a period of three years; after a renewable three-year term, the workers would have to return to their home country. This "open door" policy professes to "legalize" the status of hard-working people who currently fill a seemingly insatiable demand for cheap labor (in California alone, if every nanny, housekeeper, waiter, busboy, cook, gardener, janitor, and construction and agricultural worker stopped working for twenty-four hours, the whole state would come to a standstill). However, labor organizers contend that by denying the possibility of citizenship, the proposed policy merely (re)produces a labor underclass. Is this just a rerun of the Bracero program that invited over 12,000 documented Mexican workers into the country in 1942? While it is true that in little more than two decades these workers transformed the growing fields of America into the most productive in the world, one shouldn't forget that the Bracero program was abolished in 1964, when the Department of Labor official Lee G. Williams indicted it as a system of "legalized slavery."

Public reaction to the dysfunctional nature of the border is reflected in the actual death of one pedestrian attempting to cross the border from Tijuana into San Diego early one morning in May 2005. A man hanged himself from one of the Tijuana's pedestrian bridges, currently under construction as part of an effort to address the chaotic flow of foot traffic on the Mexican side of the checkpoint. The body dangled directly over hundreds of cars waiting in twenty-four lanes of bumper-to-bumper rush-hour traffic to cross into San Diego, while countless vendors swarmed through the traffic jam selling curios. Some speculated that he had grown increasingly desperate after many failed attempts to reach family, whom he had been separated for months. Whatever the reason, this surreal scene became emblematic of the lack of interest on the part of the U.S. government concerning the border, upon which many citizens and businesses depend, and highlighted the absence of binational agencies to protect the human rights of the millions of people who cross this border annually, legally or not.

The new millennium's utopian dream of a borderless world made of cities whose urbanism is founded on cultural contact and exchange, whose social landscape is enriched by advanced informational technologies, whose infrastructure is shared, and whose inter-institutional and jurisdictional alliances and collaborations are ensured has been compromised. So, re-entrenched anti-immigration sentiment in the U.S. converges with the ongoing post-9/11 anti-terrorist agenda at the Mexican border into its most recent sequel, which posits Homeland Security and the Minutemen against the invasion. The general perception of this "eminent invasion from

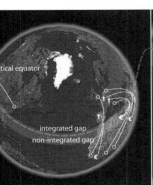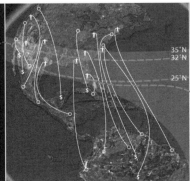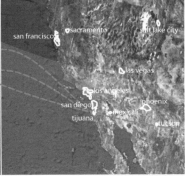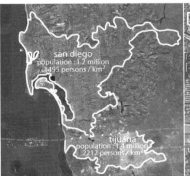

Political equator.

Washington's spectral power reaching toward its borders seeks to thicken the United States' "property line" against its Mexican neighbor, transforming San Diego into the world's largest gated community.

south of the border," as county Commissioner Robert Vasquez of Idaho called it in a *New York Times* article in May 2005, is what has galvanized anti-immigration and anti-terrorism as the new locus of patriotic nationalism in the U.S. and the manifesto for a new urban code that promises to spread the already rampant NIMBY-ism in many American cities, producing unprecedented urbanities of labor and surveillance.

The tensions at play at the busiest border in the world, then, have only recently been exacerbated as this socio-cultural and economic funnel is suppressed, with Washington, D.C., arriving to close the gaps and fortify, or "harden," the San Diego–Tijuana border.

Funded by billions of federal tax dollars that are pouring into San Ysidro through the Department of Homeland Security (DHS), the federal government has embarked on the construction of a larger, more militarized, and more technologically sophisticated checkpoint than we have seen anywhere. Through the design program of the General Services Administration (GSA), an architectural firm has been recently selected for the commission. The project consists of a large-scale transformation of the existing security infrastructure at the border and the installation of a highway of surveillance along the wall. This operation includes the replacement of the existing inefficient steel-wall border, whose corrugation runs horizontally, allowing people to easily climb it (its solidity made it a perfect place to hide), with a sophisticated version built out of concrete columns strategically spaced in order to maximize visual control and minimize human spillage; all this is crowned by an electrified fence. Accelerated by a mandate from the federal government, the highway of surveillance is already under construction, overriding every environmental policy that has protected the land reserves along the Tijuana

River Estuary for decades.

Needless to say, the impact of this hardening of the border falls first and foremost on the adjacent border communities of San Ysidro and Tijuana, not to mention the natural ecology and landscape of their shared territory. These new protectionist strategies fueled by a collective obsession with security, paranoia, and greed are defining a radically conservative cultural agenda that is incrementally reinforcing a rigid grid of containment instead of a fluid bed of opportunity. In other words, the hardening of the wall in recent years has occurred in tandem with the hardening of a social legislation toward the public, producing a discriminatory urban policy of exclusion and division. The perennial alliance between militarization and urbanization is re-enacted here and epitomized by the solidifying of the border wall between the cities of San Ysidro and Tijuana.

While in the context of the history of urbanism this alliance between systems of control and urban development is nothing new, what dramatizes its effect in the post-9/11 city is its complicity with the increasing neoliberalist global economic policies of privatization and their effect in producing a crisis of public infrastructure and affordable housing. This is how Washington, D.C., exists at the Tijuana–San Diego border, doubly inscribed in this binational territory: on one hand, in the shape of advanced surveillance apparatus made of high-tech walls and robotic aircraft; on the other hand by top-down, discriminatory forms of urban economic redevelopment and planning legislation as expressed in unchecked eminent-domain policies supporting large-scale privatization. Washington's spectral power reaching toward its borders seeks to thicken the United States' "property line" against its

Mexican neighbor, transforming San Diego into the world's largest gated community. In this context, Washington's conservative economics promoting an "ownership society" and the deregulated free-market forces that support it also promise to engender divisive tensions in terms of social and economic inequalities and the erosion of public institutions across communities, nation-states, and hemispheres. At no other urban juncture in the world, for example, can we find some of the wealthiest real estate, as the one found at San Diego's northern edges, barely twenty minutes away from some of the poorest settlements in Latin America, as found at Tijuana's southern fringe. At this critical juncture between hemispheres, Washington is both private developer and border patrol.

Countertactics of Encroachment: The Fictional Cartographies of an Urbanism Seventy Feet Deep

When Kevin Lynch was commissioned by a San Diego environmental group to come up with a "regional vision plan" for the U.S.-México border zone in 1974, he dreamed of a "Temporary Paradise." Addressed to the City Planning Commission of San Diego, his bi-national planning strategy focused on the network of canyons and watersheds that traverse the landscape on both sides of the San Diego-Tijuana border. Lynch could never have predicted that neither the natural landscape nor city planners would define the real action plan for transborder urbanism, and that instead it would be an emergent network of underground tunnels masterminded by drug lords and "coyotes," who would quietly and invisibly efface the formidable barrier that separates the two cities. Now, thirty-four years later, at least thirty tunnels have been discovered, a vast ant-farm–like maze of subterranean routes crisscrossing the border from

Levittown retrofitted: density=amount of social exchanges per acre.

Los Angeles, for example, is home to the second-largest concentration of Latin Americans outside the capitals of Mexico, Guatemala, and El Salvador. Current demographic studies predict that Latin Americans will comprise the majority of California's population in the next decade.

California to Arizona, all dug within the last eight years.

An archaeological section map of the territory would reveal an underground urbanism worming its way into houses, churches, parking lots, warehouses, and streets. The most outlandish and sophisticated of these tunnels, discovered by U.S. border officials in January 2007, is clearly the work of professionals: up to seventy feet below ground and 2,400 feet in length, its passageways are five to six feet high and four feet wide to permit two-way circulation. Striking not only for its scale, the tunnel is equipped with ventilation and drainage systems, water pumps, electricity, retaining reinforcements, and stairs that connect various levels. Beyond its use by drug traffickers, it was also "leased" during off-hours to coyotes transporting illegal aliens into the U.S., making it perhaps the first mixed-use tunnel at the border. Some might see this as a marvel of informal transnational infrastructure, but most locals understand it as an example of the vigorous Mexican-American economy at work.

Beyond the sensationalism that might accompany these images, what is exposed is the presence of an informal economy and the politics of density that surrounds it. As we represent the locations of these illegal tunnels on official border maps, a different image of the border appears: the linear rigidity of the artificial geopolitical boundary is transformed back into a complex set of porous lines perpendicular to the border, as if they were small leakages that began to percolate through a powerful dam. As these lines puncture the border in our fictional cartography, they almost restore the primacy of the network of existing canyons, juxtaposing the natural with the socio-economic flows that continue to be under the radar in many official documents of urban planning and border representation.

Indeed, an accurate bi-national land-use map does not exist. If we were to cut-and-paste the existing land-use documents from Tijuana and San Diego, a borderline—without marking the border wall itself—would again appear between the two cities; the larger land-use chunks of San Diego next to the smaller pixilation of Tijuana's infrastructure would suggest two different ways of administering density and mixed use. This fictional cartography invites speculation about how to represent the transformation of some of the San Diego neighborhoods impacted by informal patterns of development. This new map would show the higher pixilation of Tijuana's three-dimensional, multicolor zoning forming an archipelago of exception as it crosses into the sea of the current homogeneous sprawl that defines this city's periphery.

From the Global Border to the Neighborhood: Levittown Retrofitted with Difference

After years of being absent from our main institutions of representation and display, we are all drawn to the city, yearning to recuperate it as a site of experimentation and cultural production. The current desire in our cultural institutions to move from the city as a static repository of objects—whether seen as autonomous architectural artifacts or as sculpture in the middle of the plaza—to a notion that is inclusive of the temporal dynamics across social and ecological networks, as well as the politics and economics of density and urban development. This has been unavoidably provoked by a new world that begins to redefine the role of architecture in its relationship to the territory. The changing geo-political boundaries across continents, the unprecedented shifting of socio-cultural demographics, the migration of labor and the redeployment of centers of manufacturing across hemispheres are condi-

tions that are provoking many architects and artists to construct alternative practices, particularly within geographies of conflict such as the Tijuana–San Diego region. This return to the city and to critical thresholds such as Tijuana might be ultimately a reflection of our need to critically challenge the erosion of public culture in the hands of Washington's current fear of social density.

But as we return to the city, it is clear that across the fields of government, academia, and private development, the focus of attention continues to be twofold: the return to the downtown core, on one end, and engaging the challenge of sprawl, on the other; while the territory that continues to be ignored is the space in between, the mid-city. Even though the return to the center is a welcomed agenda after the past decades' urban flight to the periphery, the economic strategies that are generally driving these redevelopment energies are engendering a project of gentrification on a massive scale. The downtown revitalization projects in many American cities, a widespread phenomenon occurring from New York to San Diego, are ironically importing into city centers the very suburban project of privatization, homogenization, and "theming," accompanied by "loft-like" luxury housing, stadiums, and the official corporate franchises that always tag along with this kind of development. At the other end of the spectrum, the interest in suburbia is also a welcomed, mainly when the institution of architecture and urbanism have been overtly discriminatory against such environments, calling them uncivilized and benefitting the center as the privileged site of urban culture. But many efforts to engage sprawl end up merely supporting a repetition of gentrification. The proliferation of McMansions continues to be made possible by the construction of freeway infrastructure subsidized by tax dollars and

indulged by architecture's own indifference to the economic forces that shape these developments. Even populist agendas such as New Urbanism become instruments of government-supported privatization, dressing suburbia with a fake façade of difference.

The emphasis on these two extreme areas of development in many cities around the world mirrors the urgency for many metropolitan centers to work with new economic models of revitalization through privatization. But when the new economies of globalization hit the actual territory, it divides into two projects: grand redevelopment (every city wants its Times Square, its stadium) and the project of marginalization (the service sector needed to support such projects). At a time when large-scale redevelopment projects are becoming the basis for the skyrocketing of the real state market in many city centers across the United States, creating a formidable economic bubble of land speculation, practically no one is asking *where* the cook, janitor, maid, busboy, nanny, gardener, and many of the thousands of immigrants crossing the border to fulfill the demand for such jobs will live and what kinds of rents and housing markets will be available to them. There are not too many options when we are reminded that, according to the last housing census, San Diego is the second-least affordable housing area in the country, with only 11 percent of households capable of affording a median-price home at $500,000.

Even if the socio-economic inequalities produced by the division between the redevelopment centers and the service sector are increasing exponentially, immigrants continue flowing toward the north, searching for one of the strongest economies in the world, the state of California, with the assurance that such economic power still depends on the cheap labor only provided by them; it's a demand-and-supply logic. Los Angeles, for example, is home to the second-largest concentration of Latin Americans outside the capitals of Mexico, Guatemala, and El Salvador. Current demographic studies predict that Latin Americans will comprise the majority of California's population in the next decade. As the Latin American diaspora

travels north, it inevitably alters and transforms the fabric of certain neighborhoods in cities like Los Angeles and San Diego. Immigrants bring with them diverse socio-cultural attitudes and sensibilities regarding the use of domestic and public space as well as the natural landscape. In these neighborhoods, multi-generational households of extended families shape their own programs of use, taking charge of their own micro-economies in order to maintain a standard for the household, generating non-conforming uses and high densities that reshape the fabric of the residential neighborhoods where they settle. Alleys, setbacks, driveways, and other underutilized infrastructures and leftover spaces are appropriated and activated as the community sees fit. This results in the emergence of a temporal public domain encroaching into private property: Social spaces begin to spring up in large parking lots, informal economies such as flea markets and street vendors appear in vacant properties, and housing additions in the shape of illegal companion units are plugged into existing dwellings to provide affordable living. Together, these plug-in programs and architectures pixilate with a finer socio-economic grain, the discriminatory land use that has maintained the social and the formal at a distance.

Therefore, it is not a coincidence that the territory that continues to be ignored is the mid-city. This is the area where most of the immigrants coming from Latin America, Asia, and Africa have settled in the last decades, making these neighborhoods the service communities for the newly gentrified center and the expensive periphery. Not able to afford the high-priced new luxury condos of downtown or the McMansions of the new sprawl, waves of immigrant communities have concentrated themselves in the older mid-city neighborhoods in recent years. The temporal, informal economies and patterns of density promoted by immigrants and their socio-cultural and economic dynamics have fundamentally altered what was the first ring of Levittown-type suburbanization of the 1950s, transforming its homogeneity into a more complex network of illegal socio-economic relationships. By criti-

cally observing how these temporal and contingent urbanisms have contaminated the rigidity of zoning within these older fabrics, can we anticipate how the one-dimensionality of the McMansions now sprawling in the third, fourth, and fifth rings of suburbanization will be retrofitted to accommodate difference in the next five decades?

In other words, our institutions of representation across government, academia, and development have not been able to critically observe and translate the logic of these temporal and informal dynamics at play not only at the border itself, but also within the city at large. The official documentation of land use at any municipal agency, whether in San Diego or Tijuana, for example, has systematically ignored the non-conforming and self-organizing processes behind these environments, continuing instead to advocate a false, bi-dimensional land-use convention based on abstract information rendered at the planners' table, whereby retail is represented with red and housing yellow, safely located adjacent to one another in the best of scenarios, since they are typically very far apart.

If, on the other hand, one were to map the *actual* land use in some of the San Diego neighborhoods that have been impacted by immigration, examining them parcel by parcel, block by block, what would emerge is a land-use map with at least ten or more zone colors, reflecting the gradation of use and scale of the diverse social composition and non-conforming small businesses and social exchanges that characterize these culturally intensive areas of the city. We would also find a three-dimensional zoning based not on adjacencies but on juxtapositions, as dormant infrastructures are transformed into usable semi-public spaces and larger-than-needed parcels are illegally subdivided to accommodate extra dwelling units. In other words, the appropriation and negotiation of public and private boundaries remains anathema for conventional code regulation, ignoring the potentialities that this stealth urbanism can open up. How conventions of representation should be changed to absorb the ambiguity of these forces remains the essential question in the negotiation between the formal and the informal city.

Tactics of encroachment: the impact of immigration on the American neighborhood.

As our institutions of planning are unable to mediate the multiple forces that shape the politics of the territory and resolve the tensions between the top-down urban strategies of official development and the bottom-up tactics of community activism, it is the micro-heterotopias emerging within small neighborhoods in the form of informal, counterspatial and entrepreneurial practices that are defining a different idea of density and land use. Making visible the invisibility of these non-conforming forces and their operational potential to be a bridge between the formal and the informal, the wealthy subdivisions and the enclaves of poverty, seems to be the only point of departure to construct a different idea of sustainable land use. We need to engage new conceptual and representational tools that can allow us to transcend the reductive understanding of density as an abstract amount of units/inhabitants per acre and instead reaffirm it as an amount of social interactions and exchanges per acre.

This is how Tijuana's informal urbanism could become an instrument to research and further understand the patterns of density and programmatic intensity that are redefining the American metropolis. The cataloging, for example, of the small, prototypical nonconforming appendages, spatially and programmatically, that have erupted illegally from the official planning of the mid-city would reveal that the future of the sprawling city's edge will be determined by an urbanism of retrofitting, pixilating the large with the small. Small programs, spaces, and infrastructures will be injected into the homogeneity of these large-scale environments as a result of the micro-political and socio-economic transformations in urban policy from the ground up, at the scale of the neighborhood.

It is out of territories of political conflict that critical architectural practices can emerge. These are territorial projects whose main focus is not the object of architecture but the subversion of the information imprinted artificially on the land, the alteration of the boundaries and limits established by the institutions of official development. In the context of this paradigm shift and in order to respond to the mutation of the socio-cultural demographics across the world, it is clear that one of the most important issues is the politics of density through the articulation of new housing prototypes that can promote alternative categories of land use, affordability, and new modes of sociability.

But the future of affordable housing and its critical relationship to social and ecological networks in the United States is currently not in the hands of the federal or state governments, which have overtly indicated their indifference to social institution, environmental practices, and public culture in the city; nor is it in the hands of private developers, who in general continue to perpetuate the equation of minimum investment/maximum profit and perceive investing in the public realm to be anti-democratic because it reduces their economic "freedoms."

Instead, the most experimental work in housing is in the hands of progressive, community-based, non-profit organizations, as well as small communities across the continent. These agencies daily engage the social dynamics of many mid-city neighborhoods, mediating between their bottom-up histories and identities and the top-down planning policies that shape their destiny. It seems appropriate that these organizations become the future developers of affordable housing and a new public realm within these environments, because they are in a unique position to comprehend the value of social capital as an engine for economic development.

As Washington's discriminatory urban and environmental policies continue negating social density while supporting rampant privatization, the counter economic and social organizational practices produced by many non-profit social service organizations are the only alternative to create potential sites of negotiation and collaboration across agencies, institutions, and jurisdictions. They effectively search to transform top-down legislation and lending structures in order to generate a new brand of bottom-up social and economic justice.

Community Based Non-profit Organization: A Neighborhood's Temporal City Hall

The current need to engage the politics of land use, then, has been provoked by the re-alization that no advances in housing design can be accomplished without advances in the transformation of housing policy. In other words, the ultimate site of intervention is planning regulation itself and the "contamination" of zoning in the form of alternative densities and transitional uses that can directly respond to the political and economic informalities at play in the contemporary city. It is in fact the political and cultural dimension of housing and density as a tools for social integration that can inform an urbanism of transgression that infiltrates itself beyond the property line, a migrant micro-urbanism that can alter the rigidity of the discriminatory public policies of the American city. The effort has been to create a participatory practice that can enter the politics of information and public debate in the border cities: What do we mean by density? What is the meaning of housing? The site where these questions converge is within the micro-scale of the neighborhood.

Conventional ideas of housing generally define it as an equation, a number; in the same way, density has been understood solely in terms of building size and mass. Both of these notions need to be redefined, not as singularities but as a set of relationships in the broader socio-political and economic framework. Housing and density are not just a number of units but dwell in relationship to the larger forces at play in the city. Housing needs to be thought of in relationship to transportation, politics, economics, and, in particular, the temporal programmatic contingencies that transform the neighborhood's dwelling unit into a machine of socio-economic exchanges.

These are the notions that are fueling the alternative housing projects currently developing on both sides of the San Diego-Tijuana border, focusing on the neighborhood as a site of exception to shape new processes of intervention in collaborations with progressive non-profit organizations. The goal is to achieve maximum effect with minimal gestures, taking existing patterns of use as a point of departure to develop urban solutions to change obsolete planning policy, zoning regulation, and lending and housing subsidy structures.

Case study 1:
A Micro-Policy: Affordable Housing Overlay Zone (AHOZ)

During the last four years, I have been collaborating with Casa Familiar, a non-profit community-based organization located in the border city of San Ysidro, adjacent to the San Diego-Tijuana border checkpoint, to construct what we have called "practices of encroachment." Casa Familiar's executive director is Andrea Skorepa, an urban activist who has become the matriarch of this small and forgotten border community made up primarily of Hispanic immigrants. Skorepa is searching to redevelop this community's historic core with alternative housing projects that can be a catalyst for the transformation of existing policy. This relationship between urban practice and social-service agency has allowed us to recognize that the foundation for any meaningful architectural intervention within the shifting dynamics of mid-city neighborhoods such as this one depends on shaping a tactical process of collaboration.

The neighborhood is transformed into an experimental think tank, a site to investigate actual economic and spatial tactics that can encroach on the established procedures of stagnant federal, state, and local government institutions in order to mobilize dormant sources of funding and blur certain obsolete boundaries separating public and private resources. A tactical new zoning policy can be proposed to the city, one that is initiated from within the community and not from the planners' table, and mediated by the non-profit organization, an urban legislature emerging from the internal energies of the neighborhood that can accommodate and support a more inclusive and complex micro-urbanism.

The tactical design and organization of a series of community dialogues and workshops generated the idea of a micro-zoning policy that could provide the fertile political ground from which alternative hybrid projects and their sources of funding could emerge. This new policy framework would ignite new opportunities for economic development from within the community in order to avoid gentrification. The negotiation of certain junctures between public and private property and funding could generate small, alternative public infrastructures, as organizational frameworks for new social and cultural programs for the neighborhood. Some of these micro-infrastructures will frame and support the non-conforming, informal economies typical of these communities, as well as their organic patterns of development. This framework could also include new networks of connectivity, so that this small community can redefine its role within the busiest border in the world.

Out of this initial process emerged the Affordable Housing Overlay Zone (AHOZ), becoming such a socio-political and economic framework. The AHOZ is an instrument of development by which the community, through the non-profit organization, will partner with the municipality and selected financial institutions.

Through the AHOZ, we proposed to the municipality of San Diego to consider partnering with Casa Familiar, giving it a new role in developing alternative, affordable housing prototypes that can advance notions of density and mixed use for communities such as San Ysidro. This process would include alternative models for funding and entitlement processes (construction permit management) oriented toward the disenfranchised members of the community and allowing the neighborhood to become a developer of its own housing prototypes.

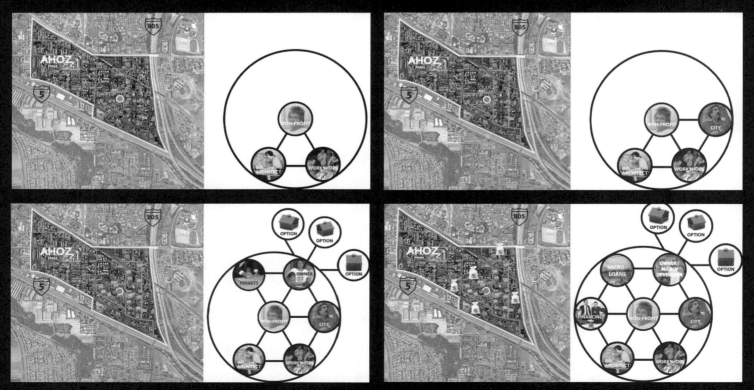

Designing collaboration across agencies and institutions=neighborhood urbanism.

AHOZ Micro-Policy:
Ten points (Designing the Conditions)

Premise: In San Ysidro housing will not be just units spread indifferently across the territory.
Here, housing is dwelling in relationship to a social and cultural program managed by Casa Familiar.

1. The non-profit organization becomes an urban think tank. It manages an initial research project to identify and document properties on which illegal construction has taken place in the last decades, as small extended families share resources in building non-conforming additions. These stealth companion units usually are located in the back of a parcel flanking an alley.

2. The municipality allows a small overlay zone within which these illegal and fragile units could be legalized, allowing their replacement by new ones without penalizing the property owners (the municipality makes visible the invisible, inserting these illegal units into a new category of zoning).

3. The non-profit, with the support of special grants, funds the design of a series of small, ready-made housing additions that can be combined in a variety of scenarios and assembled within the community (it is in these neighborhoods where the service-construction sector lives).

4. The non-profit acts as mediator between the city and financial agencies, managing and facilitating construction permitting and loan processes.

5. A property owner selects a particular combination of dwelling, and the non-profit assists in expediting its permitting process (the non-profit becomes a micro-City Hall). The municipality pre-authorizes the construction documents for these new dwellings, allowing the non-profit to facilitate the end process and manage the actual construction permit.

6. The property owner promises to participate in the construction of the unit, therefore allowing sweat equity hours of labor to become equity in the development, pro forma. (The property owner becomes a micro developer, participating in the process).

7. How are these units made affordable? The non-profit manages a series of micro credits. This is achieved by breaking the loan structure allocated to large, affordable housing projects— out of tax credits and other subsidies—into small pieces that can be distributed throughout the community. Let's imagine shattering the large loan for a conventional condominium project over parking into smaller pieces and then distributing these micro credits across the neighborhood.

Note: The reason private developers have not built affordable housing projects in neighborhoods such as these ones —even during a period of unprecedented construction boom in California —is a discrepancy between zoning policy and economic development. In other words, for a developer to make an affordable housing project profitable, he or she would have to be competitive in terms of tax credits and subsidies. In order to make it feasible, this project would have to have an average of fifty units, but fifty units are not allowed by code in many of these communities, and mixed used is prohibited by zoning. Housing affordability in the U.S. is trapped by this contradiction.

8. The construction of housing units at the back of parcels supports the activation of a network of alleys into a circuit of pedestrian and landscape corridors.

9. Some of the amenities included in these community housing projects are small, open-ended social-service infrastructures as support systems for non-conforming community uses, such as informal public markets and gardens.

10. The guidelines proposed by the AHOZ are distilled into a series of new relationships, so that private developers who want to benefit from the higher densities proposed by this overlay zone would have to comply with the social and public programs that accompany these developments.

In a special resolution, in January 2005, Casa Familiar's micro-policy was authorized by San Diego's mayor and city council, paving the way for the design of a pilot housing project that could anticipate new densities and mixed uses in the mid-city.

Case study 2
Living Rooms at the Border (Designing the Project)

Living Rooms at the Border is a small housing project that emerges from the micro policy and serves as a catalyst to anticipate San Diego's needed densities and mixed uses, while becoming a political instrument to enable Casa Familiar to further transform zoning regulation for the border city of San Ysidro. Both the micro-policy and this small architectural project convey to the municipality the need to foster the relationship between socio-political and economic strategies and spatial tactics in order to shape a new notion of affordability. In terms of spatial organization, the objective of this project, then, has been to distill the essence of patterns of use within conventional parcels in this neighborhood, where property owners encroach and activate the left over. Also, the project learns from the improvisational tactics of transgression by which people inside this community appropriate the undifferentiated public right of way, transforming alleys into complex, informal networks of pedestrian and economic activity.

This informal negotiation of boundaries and spaces becomes the basis for incremental design solutions that have a catalytic effect on the urban fabric. In a small parcel where existing zoning allows only three units of housing, this project proposes, through negotiated density bonuses and by sharing kitchens, twelve affordable housing units, the adaptive re-use of an existing 1927 church on the site as a community center, offices for the non-profit in the church's new attic, and a community garden that serves as an armature to support this community's non-conforming micro-economies. The parcel becomes a system of interrelated spaces that can anticipate and organize social encounter. Housing units take a different meaning within this service infrastructure as they are "stitched" with socio-cultural programming choreographed by the non-profit organization.

In a place where current regulation allows only one use, we propose five different uses that support one another, suggesting a model of social sustainability for San Diego, one that conveys density not as bulk but as social choreography and neighborhood collaboration.

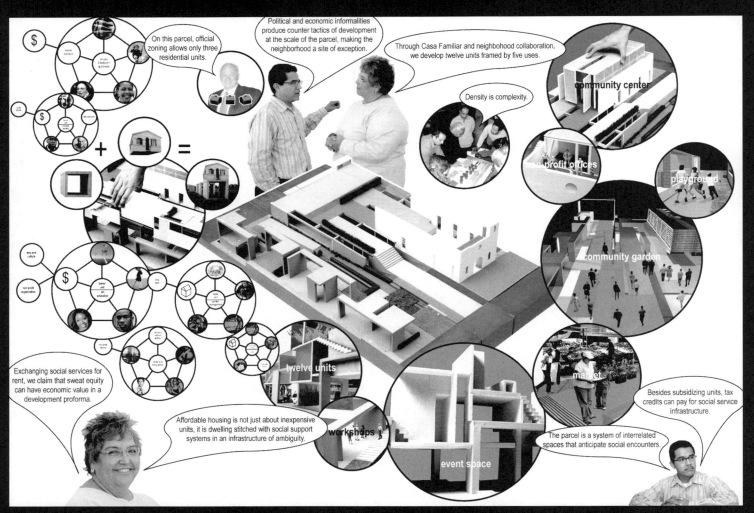

Parcel as system to frame complexity.

If, within this context, contemporary art, architecture, and urbanism do not engage the socio-political, economic, and cultural dimension of the territories they occupy, they are destined to continue being isolated as trivial formal events.

Epilogue: Home and Land Insecurity

The hardening of the Tijuana-San Diego border in the last decades from porous (light) to impermeable (solid) is precisely the opposite to the mutation of contemporary architectural and urban methodologies toward the city promoted by our institutions of representation, which have moved from "solidity" to "lightness." In this context, the border wall becomes an instrument of criticism, to question our current desire for an urbanism based on layered programmatic intensities and topological complexity, as well as contemporary architecture's quest for new formal expressions based on strategies of transformation and open-endedness. As much as these notions are liberating, it is questionable whether or not they are achievable under the discriminatory social policy pertaining to the "public" in the increasing neo-liberalist global city, a condition that is radicalized at the border. It is here where the spectral authority exerted from the center compromises once more the periphery's own independence, as Washington, D.C., flexes its political muscle to reaffirm the unconditional power of the nation-state at the expense of international socio-economic relations, demarcating its borders more emphatically than ever.

If, within this context, contemporary art, architecture, and urbanism do not engage the socio-political, economic, and cultural dimension of the territories they occupy, they are destined to continue being isolated as trivial formal events, perpetuating the idea of the city as a static repository of objects instead of revealing its potential as a dynamic field whose thickness is made of the complexity of its multiple forces and mutating histories and identities, its political ground.

In other words, as architects and artists are reclaiming the city as the privileged site for investigation and experimentation, searching for urban models that are more inclusive and heterogeneous, it is questionable whether or not these ideals can be achieved under the conditions that prevail at the beginning of the twenty-first century, as discriminatory political legislation against the public is augmented with intensified layers of "security" against invisible threats. In this sense, we are reminded that the policies being rolled out by the Department of Homeland Security might, like a Trojan horse, not be as benign as they seem. For in their blind desire to reinforce barriers, to lock out what is different and unpredictable, they of course run the risk of locking the door on the wrong side.

It is at critical thresholds, such as the San Diego-Tijuana border, where we witness how the foreclosing of shared horizons is provoking alternative urban and artistic practices to cross the property line and enter into the politics of public culture, denouncing the incremental privatization and erosion of social institution by the current urban policies emerging from Washington, D.C.

Sunil Bald is a partner in Studio SUMO, a New York-based architecture collaborative he co-founded with Yolande Daniels. Previously, he worked for Antoine Predock Architect. Recent SUMO projects include a temporary space for the Museum of African Art in Long Island City; MoCADA, a museum of contemporary art in Brooklyn's BAM cultural district; and the Josai University New School of Management in Sakado, Japan. Mr. Bald has received a Young Architects award from the Architectural League, a Graham Foundation fellowship, a NYFA fellowship, a Fulbright Fellowship, and was a finalist in MoMA's Young Architects program. On receiving his M. Arch from Columbia, he was awarded the AIA Medal. Over the last decade, Bald has taught design and theory at Cornell, Columbia, University of Michigan, Parsons, and Yale. He also has an enduring research interest in modernism, popular culture, and nation-making in Brazil, a subject about which he has published a series of articles.

Neeraj Bhatia, born in Canada, is an architect and urban designer. He is currently a Fulbright fellow carrying out post-professional graduate research at MIT. His research centers on the role of civic institutions—particularly the public library—in a liberal, pluralist society.

Edward R. Burian is an architect in San Antonio, Texas, whose practice, writing, and teaching focus on the issues of place, sensory experience, and materials. He edited and wrote, *Modernity and the Architecture of Mexico*, (University of Texas Press, 1997), which was translated into Spanish as *Modernidad y arquitectura en México* (Gustavo Gili, 1998). His forthcoming book, *The Architecture and Cities of Northern Mexico, 1821–2006*, explores the undervalued architectural culture of the region. His essays have appeared in *Landa García Landa Arquitectos, Monterrey, México* (Arquine and Editorial RM, 2006) and *Cruelty and Utopia: Cities and Landscapes of Latin America* (Princeton Architectural Press, 2005), as well as periodicals such as *Arquine*, *Artes de México*, *A+U*, and *Praxis*. He received his B.S. in architecture from the University of Southern California and M. Arch. degree from Yale, has taught at several schools of architecture in the American Southwest, and was a visiting professor at the ITESM in Monterrey, Mexico. Currently he is an associate professor at the University of Texas at San Antonio.

Cao Fei is a Guangzhou-born artist who currently divides her time between Guangzhou and Beijing. She graduated from the Affiliated Middle School of Guangzhou Academy of Fine Arts in 2001 and is a co-founder of Alternative Archive with Ou Ning. Most recently, Fei was included in the 2007 Venice Biennale and was a contributor to the Da Sha Lan project for *Beijing Case: Culture of the High Speed Urbanism*. She exhibits extensively around the world and is represented by Lombard-Freid Fine Arts in New York.

Teddy Cruz is a Guatemalan-born architect and founding principal of Estudio Teddy Cruz in San Diego. Over the past decade, Cruz has demonstrated a deep commitment to advancing architectural and urban planning projects that address the global political and social problems that proliferate on the international border between San Diego and Tijuana. His firm has been recognized in collaboration with community-based, non-profit organizations, such as Casa Familiar, for its work on housing and its relationship to an urban policy more inclusive of social and public programs for the city. Cruz founded the Border Institute (BI), dedicated to research on border urbanism, at Woodbury University, where he taught until 2005. Cruz was recently appointed to the newly-created, tenured research and teaching post of Artist in Public Culture/Urban Space in the Visual Arts Department at the University of California, San Diego.

Filip De Boeck is the program director of the Africa Research Center and chair of the Department of Social and Cultural Anthropology at the Katholieke Universiteit Leuven. Since 1987, he has conducted extensive field research in both rural and urban communities in the Democratic Republic of the Congo (ex-Zaire). Together with Alcinda Honwana, he edited *Makers and Breakers: Children and Youth in Postcolonial Africa*

(James Currey: forthcoming). His most recent publication is *Kinshasa: Tales of the Invisible City*, a joint book project with photographer Marie-Françoise Plissart (Ludion, 2004).

Alexander D'Hooghe is an assistant professor at MIT. Originally from Belgium, he is putting the finishing touches on his Ph.D. dissertation at the Berlage Institute, a postgraduate laboratory affiliated with Technische Universiteit Delft that focuses on architecture, urban planning, and landscape design. He holds a Master of Architecture in urban design from the Harvard Graduate School of Design and a master's degree in architectural engineering from Katholieke Universiteit Leuven. A founding member of the design firm ORG, D'Hooghe has also practiced as an urban designer and architect with the Chan Krieger firm, Boston, and with Professor Marcel Smets in Belgium. He has taught at the GSD both as an instructor and a visiting critic.

Tina DiCarlo is currently founding a London-based architecture think tank for media and strategy and working on two publications on contemporary architecture: *Watching CCTV [Two Exhibitions]* (forthcoming 2007) and *Beyond Form* (forthcoming 2008). As a former curator of architecture and design at the Museum of Modern Art, New York, she has organized numerous exhibitions, including: *OMA in Beijing: China Central Television Headquarters by Rem Koolhaas and Ole Scheeren, CCTV by OMA* (Beijing), *The Highline*, *Tall Buildings*, and *The Changing of the Avant-Garde: Visionary Works from the Howard Gilman Collection*. She is a regular contributor to *Log: Observations on Architecture, Landscape and the Contemporary City*, has published in *Artforum*, *Domus China*, *Urban China*, and *34*, and lectures frequently. DiCarlo holds a Master of Architecture degree from the Harvard Graduate School of Design and advanced degrees in philosophy and art history from the Courtauld Institute, London.

Keller Easterling is an architect, urbanist, and writer. Her newest book, *Enduring Innocence: Global Architecture and Its Political Masquerades* (MIT, 2005), researches familiar spatial products in difficult or hyperbolic political situations around the world. Her previous book, *Organization Space: Landscapes, Highways and Houses in America*, applies network theory to a discussion of American infrastructure and development formats. Easterling is also the co-author of *Call It Home*, a laser-disc history of suburbia, as well as *American Town Plans*. She is an associate professor at the Yale School of Architecture.

Sze Tsung Leong is a New York-based photographer and painter who has recently published his first monograph, *History Images* (Steidl, 2006), and is represented by Yossi Milo Gallery, New York. His work is included in the permanent collections of the Museum of Modern Art, New York, the San Francisco Museum of Modern Art, the High Museum of Art in Atlanta, the Brooklyn Museum of Art, the International Center of Photography, and the Santa Barbara Museum of Art, among others. In 2006, twenty-two pieces from his *History Images* series were shown as one of four monographic exhibitions at the High Museum of Art. His work has also been shown in exhibitions including *Landscape: Recent Acquisitions* at MoMA, the 2006 Havana Biennial, the 2004 Taipei Biennial, and *Painting as Paradox* at Artists Space. In 2005, he received a John Simon Guggenheim Memorial Foundation Fellowship.

Reinhold Martin is an associate professor of architecture and the director of the Ph.D. program in Architecture and the Master of Science in Advanced Architectural Design program at Columbia University. He is also a founding co-editor of the journal *Grey Room*, a partner in the firm of Martin Baxi Architects, and has published widely on the history and theory of modern and contemporary architecture. He is the author of *The Organizational Complex: Architecture, Media, and Corporate Space* (MIT Press, 2003), and the co-author, with Kadambari Baxi, of *Entropia* (Black Dog, 2001) and *Multi-National City: Architectural Itineraries* (Actar, 2007). His areas of research include postwar modern architecture and contemporary architectural theory, spatial theory and globalization, and speculative architectural design. He is currently working on a book that re-theorizes what used to be called postmodernism.

Brian McGrath is the founder and principal of Urban-Interface, an urban design and architectural practice that combines new research in urban ecology and digital communication technologies. McGrath received his Master of Architecture degree from Princeton University and his Bachelor of Architecture from Syracuse University. He has been in practice as a registered architect in New York since 1985 and in New Jersey since 2002. He was a Fulbright senior scholar in Thailand from 1998 to 1999 and teaches at Columbia and New School Universities in New York and Chulalongkorn University in Bangkok.

Alona Nitzan-Shiftan is a senior lecturer at the Faculty of Architecture and Town Planning, Technion-Israel Institute of Technology. She studies post-World War II architectural culture, particularly in Israel and the U.S., and focuses her research on cross-cultural contexts in light of recent thought in the fields of nationalism, Orientalism, and post-colonialism. She holds a Ph.D. and an S.M.Arch.S. from MIT, a B.Arch. *cum laude* from the Technion and was recently the Mary Davis Fellow and the Kress Postdoctoral Fellow at the Center for Advanced Study in the Visual Arts at the National Gallery, Washington, D.C. She was a Lady Davis Fellow at the Technion and received grants from the trusts of Arthur Goldreich (Bezalel), William Sandberg (Israel Museum), and the Aga Khan Program (MIT and Harvard). Her publications appeared in *Architectural History*, *Theory and Criticism*, *Harvard Design Magazine*, *Jama'a*, and *Thresholds* as well as in edited volumes such as *The End of Tradition*. She is currently working on *Israelizing Jerusalem: the Politics of Architecture and Beauty in a Contested City* and researching I.M. Pei's East Building, the subject of an exhibition she co-curated at the National Gallery.

Ou Ning was born in Guangdong province, China, and is a graphic designer, curator, and artist currently based in Guangzhou and Beijing. He graduated from Shenzhen University and is founder of U-thèque Organization, Sonic China Productions, and Alternative Archive. His recent works include the Da Sha Lan project for *Beijing Case: Culture of High Speed Urbanism* and the San Yuan Li project, for which he collaborated with the artist Cao Fei. In 2005, Ou Ning curated the landmark *Get It Louder* exhibition and is currently organizing *Get It Louder II* for 2007.

Vyjayanthi Rao is an urbanist and ethnographer whose work primarily concerns the relation between aesthetics, ethics, and globalization in the contemporary period. She has written and published on urban interventions including such phenomenon as land-value speculation through slum redevelopment, terror attacks on critical infrastructure sites, construction of new economy sites, preservation of heritage structures, and citizens' research initiatives using new media technologies. She is currently finishing a book manuscript tentatively titled *Infra-City: Space, Violence, and Speculation and the Global City* and has articles forthcoming in *Public Culture* and *Built Environment*. She teaches anthropology and international affairs at the New School in New York.

Nina Rappaport is an architectural critic, curator, and publications director at the Yale School of Architecture. She has taught the seminar "The Post-Industrial Factory" at City College and Yale and "The Vertical Urban Factory", a graduate studio at Parsons. As a Design Trust Fellow, she led the project *Long Island City: Connecting the Arts*, published by Episode in 2006. She is the author of "The Consumption of Production" in *Praxis*, (summer 2003) and "Post–Industry" for the catalogue *Industry!* at the Norsk Forum in Oslo in 2006.

Ole Scheeren is partner of the Office for Metropolitan Architecture and director of the Rotterdam and Beijing offices. As partner-in-charge of OMA's most ambitious project to date, he is leading the design and construction of the China Central Television Station (CCTV) and the Television Cultural Center (TVCC) in Beijing. Scheeren is responsible for OMA's work throughout Asia, including the Beijing Books Building, Crystal Media City, and the forthcoming Prada Epicenter in Shanghai, as well as a residential tower in Singapore. Since 1999 he has directed OMA's work for Prada and completed the Prada Epicenters in New York and Los Angeles. He has led numerous other projects, including the Los Angeles County Museum of Art, the Leeum Cultural Center in Seoul, and a competition for the master plan of Penang Island.

AbdouMaliq Simone is an urbanist whose work primarily concerns social complexion, the city-making practices of low-income majorities in the Global South, and the intersections among multiple forms of governance and spatial production. Simone is presently Professor of Sociology at Goldsmiths College, University of London. He has been a recipient of Rockefeller and Ford Foundation visiting fellowships at New York, Columbia, and Yale Universities. His key publications include *In Whose Image?: Political Islam and Urban Practices in Sudan* (University of Chicago, 1994) and *For the City Yet to Come: Changing Urban Life in Four African Cities* (Duke University Press, 2004).

Nader Tehrani received Bachelor of Fine Arts and Bachelor of Architecture degrees from the Rhode Island School of Design in 1985 and 1986, respectively. He continued his studies at the Harvard Graduate School of Design, where he received a Master of Architecture degree in urban design in 1991. Tehrani attended a post-graduate program in history and theory at the Architectural Association in London. A tenured associate professor of architecture at Massachusetts Institute of Technology, Tehrani has also taught at the Harvard Graduate School of Design, Rhode Island School of Design, and Georgia Institute of Technology, where he served as the Thomas W. Ventulett III Distinguished Chair in Architectural Design. Professionally, Tehrani is a principal at Office dA, where he has received numerous international awards, including nine Progressive Architecture awards, the Harleston Parker Award, an Academy Award from the American Academy of Arts and Letters, and, more recently, the Cooper-Hewitt National Design Award for Architecture.

Srdjan Jovanovic Weiss is an architect and founder of Normal Architecture Office (NAO) working on relations between New York and Serbia. Weiss received a Master of Architecture degree from the Graduate School of Design at Harvard University. He participated in the group thesis *Harvard Project on the City: Shopping,* mentored by Rem Koolhaas, and contributed to the book published in 2003 by Taschen. From 1996 to 2000 he worked with Richard Gluckman, Robert Wilson, and Jenny Holzer on various design and art projects. Between 1998 and 2003 his own artistic and design work appeared under the name Normal Group for Architecture. Weiss won the Gold Medal of Centro del Arte y Comunicacion of Buenos Aires and the Gold Medal of the Brazilian Architecture Biennial for design competitions for young architects between 1993 and 1994. He has won competition prizes for *BLUR,* the project for the extension of Mies van der Rohe's Barcelona Pavilion in 1998; *Hotel Normal,* for a hotel in the city of Belgrade under heavy political pressure in 1999; and *GGB-Belgrade City Gallery,* to commemorate the life of Zoran Djindjic, the late reform politician of Serbia, in 2003.

Yan Lei, born in the Hebei province of China, is a Beijing-based artist and painter. He graduated from Zhejiang Academy of Fine Arts and has exhibited in Hong Kong and throughout China. Most recently his *Super Lights* series was included in the Armory Show in New York and Art Basel in Swizterland.

Zhang Jinli is a resident of Beijing. From June 2005 to March 2006, he protested the demolition of his restaurant and residence at 117 Meishi Street, Beijing.

Image Credits

Cover
Photo: "A Mirage," from the series *Cosplayers*
(2004), © Cao Fei.

Abu Dhabi
pp. 4–5, 12–13
Photo: Ben Lowy, ben.lowy@benlowy.com
(2007).

pp. 6–7
Illustration: reproduced from *Dubai* by
Robin Moore; used by permission of Bantam,
a division of Random House, Inc.

pp. 10-11, 16
Photos: Keller Easterling.

Bangkok
pp. 17–19, 26, 28–29
Photos: Brian McGrath (2005).

p. 20
Top–illustration: Brian McGrath (2005),
collage from weather.com downloads;
middle & bottom–illustrations: Danai
Thaitakoo and Brian McGrath, Urban
Ecology Lab, Chulalongkorn University
Faculty of Architecture (2006);
nighttime satellite imagery acquired by
the Defense Meteorological Satellite
Program (DMSP) of the U.S. Air Force,
distributed by the U.S. Geological
Survey.

p. 21
Illustrations: Brian McGrath, assisted by David
Reidel and Seher Aziz.

p. 22–23
Illustrations: Danai Thaitakoo and Brian
McGrath, Urban Ecology Lab, Chulal
ongkorn University Faculty of Architecture
(2006).

p. 24
Illustration: Terdsak Tachakitkachorn (2006),
from 1932 Army Headquarters map.

p. 25
Top–Illustrations: Central Shopping
District model constructed by
Chulalongkorn University Faculty
of Architecture students: Chaiyot
Jitekviroj, Kobboon Chulajarit, Krittin
Vijittraitham, Nara Pongpanich, Pornsiri
Saiduang, Ratchawan Panyasong,
and Yuttapoom Paojinda, with the
assistance of Chulalongkorn faculty:
Mark Isarangkunna Ayuthaya, Terdsak
Tachakitkachorn,
and Kaweekrai Srihran; bottom–photo:
Brian McGrath (2005).

p. 27
Photo: Pornsiri Saiduang.

Beijing
pp. 30–31, 38–41
Photo: © Sze Tsung Leong, Courtesy Yossi
Milo Gallery.

pp. 32-33
Illustration: © Yan Lei.

pp. 36–37
Top–photos: © Ou Ning; bottom–photos:
left to right: © OMA; © Sze Tsung Leong,
Courtesy Yossi Milo Gallery; © Sze Tsung
Leong, Courtesy Yossi Milo Gallery; © Sze
Tsung Leong, Courtesy Yossi Milo Gallery;
© OMA; © Sze Tsung Leong, Courtesy
Yossi Milo Gallery.

pp. 42–43
Illustrations: © OMA.

pp. 44–45
Photo: © Cao Fei

Belgrade
pp. 48, 53, 54
Photo: Dubravka Sekuli.

p. 57
Photo: Bas Princen.

Brasília
pp. 58–59
Photo: Frederico Mendes (1981).

p. 60
Top–illustration: reproduced from Oscar
Niemeyer, "Forma e Funçao na Arquitetura,"
in *Módulo* 3 (June 1960); bottom–illustration:
reproduced from postcard, collection of author.

p. 61
Photo: Google Earth (2006).

p. 62
Illustration: reproduced from *Passos da Paixo*
(Alumbramento, 1989).

p. 63
Photo: reproduced from G. E. Kidder
Smith, *Looking at Architecture* (Harry N.
Abrams, 1990).

p. 64
Bottom–illustrations: reproduced from
Lucio Costa, "Plano Piloto," *Módulo* 18.

p. 65
Top-illustration: reproduced from Esther
da Costa Meyer, *The Work of Sant'Elia* (Yale
University Press, 1995); bottom–illustration:
reproduced from Lucio Costa, "Plano Piloto,"
Módulo 18.

p. 66
Top and middle–photos: author;
bottom–photo: © 2007 TerraMetrics.

p. 67
Photo: Public Archive of the Department
of Historic and Artistic Patrimony, Brasília
(Arquivo DePHA).

pp. 68–69
Photo: Marcel Gautherot.

Brussels
pp. 72, 74–77
Illustrations: Alexander D'Hooghe and
Neeraj Bhatia.

Dakar, Khartoum, and Kinshasa
pp. 78–79
Photo: © Marie-Françoise Plissart.

pp. 81, 84-85, 89
Photos: © Guy Tillim.

Jerusalem
p. 94
Top–Photo: Milner Moshe, courtesy of The
National Photo Collection, The State of Israel
(06.05.1995); bottom–photo: Kluger Zoltan,
courtesy of The National Photo Collection, The
State of Israel (03.30.1947).

p. 95
Top–illustration: Franz Krauss, issued by the
Tourist Development Association of Mandate
Palestine (1936); bottom–illustrations: Arieh
El-Hanani for Keren Hayesod booklet cover,
Jerusalem, courtesy of The Central Zionist
Archives (1932).

p. 96
Illustration: advertisement of Egged Buses
Cooperative for its Tel-Aviv Jerusalem line,
Nadal Advertising, courtesy of The Central
Zionist Archives (c. 1950s).

p. 98
Top–photo: Alona Nitzan-Shiftan (2006);
bottom–illustration: poster of the IDF for
the Independence Day, The Central Zionist
Archives (1956).

p. 99
Left–photo: Cohen Fritz, courtesy of The
National Photo Collection, The State of Israel
(22.04.1969); Right–photo: Ben Gershom
Amos, courtesy of The National Photo
Collection, The State of Israel (09.08.2000).

p. 100
Photos: Moshe Safdie, from Safdie in
Jerusalem, RIBA lecture.

p. 101
Top–photo: Isamu Noguchi, courtesy of the
Isamu Noguchi Foundation, December 1970;
bottom–photo: Alona Nitzan-Shiftan (c. 1970s).

p. 102
Top left–photo: Alona Nitzan-Shiftan
(2004); top right–photo: A. Yasky,
courtesy J. Sivan Architects + Architect Rachel
Feller – Associates; bottom right–photo: Moshe
Safdie, from Safdie in Jerusalem,
RIBA lecture.

p. 103
Photo: "The Spirit of Israel," reproduced
from Life magazine (1973).

p. 104
Photo: "Women cross boundaries",
reproduced from catalogue of *Comme Il Faut*
fashion line (2004).

Kuwait City
pp. 105–113
Photos and illustrations: Office dA (2007).

Manila
pp. 114-120
Photo: Laguna Park, Cavite Economic Zone.

Mexico City
p. 121
Photo: Fernando Cordero; courtesy of Landa
García Landa Arquitectos.

p. 122
Photos: reproduced from http://
imagenesaereasdemexico.com.

p. 123
Top-photo: reproduced from http://
imagenesaereasdemexico.com; bottom-photo:
GDU, Arq. Mario Schjetnan Garduño and Arq.
José Pérez Maldonado, reproduced from James
Grayson Trulove, *Mario Schjetnan* (Rockport,
2002), p.15.

p. 124
Illustration: reproduced from H. J. de Blij, ed.,
"Atlas of North America" (Oxford University
Press, 2005); map: Octopus Publishing Co.,
United Kingdom.

p. 126
Photos: Luis Gordoa; courtesy of Arq. Mauricio
Rocha Iturbide.

p. 127
Top–illustrations: Arq. Mauricio Rocha Iturbide;
bottom–illustrations: Landa García Landa
Arquitectos.

p. 128
Top–photo: Jorge Vértiz, courtesy of Landa
García Landa Arquitectos; bottom–photo:
Landa García Landa Arquitectos, reproduced

from *XIII Premio Obras* CEMEX (2004).

p. 129
Top left–illustration: Landa García Landa
Arquitectos; top right–illustration: GDU, Arq.
Mario Schjetnan Garduño and Arq. José Pérez
Maldonado; bottom–photo: Fernando Cordero,
courtesy of Landa García Landa Arquitectos.

p. 130
Top–photo: Edward R. Burian Collection of
Mexico and the American Southwest; bottom–
photo: Gabriel Figueroa, courtesy of GDU, Arq.
Mario Schjetnan Garduño and Arq. José Pérez
Maldonado.

p. 131
Top left–photo: Gabriel Figueroa, courtesy of
GDU, Arq. Mario Schjetnan Garduño and Arq.
José Pérez Maldonado; bottom left–photo: Arq.
Gustavo Lipkau; right–illustrations: Arq. Gustavo
Lipkau.

p. 132
Illustrations: Arq. Gustavo Lipkau.

p. 133
Photos: TEN Arquitectos, Arq. Enrique Norten.

p. 134
Photo: Diámetro Arquitectos.

New Delhi
pp. 136–140, 143–149
Photos: Reinhold Martin and Kadambari Baxi.

p. 141
Photo: Joseph Allen Stein, courtesy of David
Stein.

p. 146
Illustrations: advertisements reproduced from
Architecture + Design (2002).

Washington
pp. 150–151
Illustrations: Reproduced from the joint testimony
of Deborah J. Spero and Gregory Giddens
before the U.S. House of Representatives
Committee on Homeland Security (November
15, 2006).

p. 152
Left–photo: Gary Garcia, bokehshot@gmail.
com; middle-photo: Alex Webb, © Magnum
Photo; right–photo: Teddy Cruz.

pp. 153–160
Illustrations and photos: Teddy Cruz.